T0339976

# Institutional Translation and Interpreting

This collection brings together new insights around current translation and interpreting practices in national and supranational settings. The book illustrates the importance of further reflection on issues around quality and assessment, given the increased development of resources for translators and interpreters. The first part of the volume focuses on these issues as embodied in case studies from a range of national and regional contexts, including Finland, Switzerland, Italy, Spain and the United States. The second part takes a broader perspective to look at best practices and questions of quality through the lens of international bodies and organizations and the shifting roles of translation and interpreting practitioners in working to manage these issues. Taken together, this collection demonstrates the relevance of critically examining processes, competences and products in current institutional translation and interpreting settings at the national and supranational levels, paving the way for further research and quality assurance strategies in the field.

**Fernando Prieto Ramos** is Full Professor and Director of the Centre for Legal and Institutional Translation Studies (Transius) at the University of Geneva, Switzerland.

# Routledge Advances in Translation and Interpreting Studies

49 Translation and Hegel's Philosophy
A Transformative, Socio-Narrative Approach to A.V. Miller's
'Cold-War' Retranslations
*David Charlston*

50 Indigenous Cultural Translation
A Thick Description of Seediq Bale
*Darryl Sterk*

51 Translating Molière for the English-speaking Stage
The Role of Verse and Rhyme
*Cédric Ploix*

52 Mapping Spaces of Translation in Twentieth-Century Latin
American Print Culture
*María Constanza Guzmán Martínez*

53 A Century of Chinese Literature in Translation (1919–2019)
English Publication and Reception
*Edited by Leah Gerber and Lintao Qi*

54 Advances in Discourse Analysis of Translation and Interpreting
Linking Linguistic Approaches with Socio-cultural Interpretation
*Edited by Binhua Wang and Jeremy Munday*

55 Institutional Translation and Interpreting
Assessing Practices and Managing for Quality
*Edited by Fernando Prieto Ramos*

For more information about this series, please visit https://www.routledge.
com/Routledge-Advances-in-Translation-and-Interpreting-Studies/book-
series/RTS

# Institutional Translation and Interpreting

Assessing Practices and Managing
for Quality

Edited by
Fernando Prieto Ramos

Routledge
Taylor & Francis Group

NEW YORK AND LONDON

First published 2021
by Routledge
52 Vanderbilt Avenue, New York, NY 10017

and by Routledge
2 Park Square, Milton Park, Abingdon, Oxon, OX14 4RN

*Routledge is an imprint of the Taylor & Francis Group, an informa business*

© 2021 Taylor & Francis

*Library of Congress Cataloging-in-Publication Data*
A catalog record for this title has been requested

ISBN: 978-0-367-21023-6 (hbk)
ISBN: 978-0-429-26489-4 (ebk)

DOI: 10.4324/9780429264894

# Contents

*List of Contributors*     vii

Assessing Practices in Institutional Translation
and Interpreting     1
FERNANDO PRIETO RAMOS

PART I
Translation and Interpreting for National and
Regional Institutions     7

1   A Comparative Approach to Assessing Assessment:
Revising the Scoring Chart for the Authorized
Translator's Examination in Finland     9
LEENA SALMI AND MARJA KIVILEHTO

2   Lexical Readability as an Indicator of Quality in
Translation: Best Practices from Swiss Legislation     26
PAOLO CANAVESE

3   Assessing Translation Practices of Non-professional
Translators in a Multilingual Institutional Setting     44
FLAVIA DE CAMILLIS

4   Translation in the Shadows of Interpreting in US Court
Systems: Standards, Guidelines and Practice     62
JEFFREY KILLMAN

5   Developing an Evaluation Tool for Legal Interpreting
Quality Control: The INTER-Q Questionnaire     84
MARÍA JESÚS BLASCO MAYOR AND
MARTA SANCHO VIAMONTE

**PART II**
**Translation and Interpreting at International Institutions** 109

6 Every Second Counts: A Study of Translation Practices in
the European Commission's DGT 111
MARÍA FERNÁNDEZ-PARRA

7 Ensuring Consistency and Accuracy of Legal Terms in
Institutional Translation: The Role of Terminological
Resources in International Organizations 128
FERNANDO PRIETO RAMOS

8 Corrigenda of EU Legislative Acts as an Indicator of
Quality Assurance Failures: A Micro-diachronic Analysis
of Errors Rectified in the Polish Corrigenda 150
ŁUCJA BIEL AND IZABELA PYTEL

9 The Impact of Translation Competence on Institutional
Translation Management and Quality: The Evidence
from Action Research 174
FERNANDO PRIETO RAMOS AND
MARIAM SPERANDIO

10 Interpreting at the United Nations: The Effects of
Delivery Rate on Quality in Simultaneous Interpreting 190
LUCÍA RUIZ ROSENDO, MÓNICA VARELA GARCÍA, AND
ALMA BARGHOUT

Managing for Quality: Practical Lessons from
Research Insights 209
FERNANDO PRIETO RAMOS

Index 213

# Contributors

**Alma Barghout** is a senior interpreter at the United Nations Office at Geneva. She holds a BA in Translation and an MAS in Interpreter Training, and is a doctoral candidate at the University of Geneva's Faculty of Translation and Interpreting. Her main research lines focus on quality challenges in simultaneous interpreting and interpreting in the field.

**Łucja Biel** is an associate professor and head of the Corpus Research Centre at the Institute of Applied Linguistics, University of Warsaw, Poland. She is the Editor-in-Chief of the *Journal of Specialised Translation*. She has published widely on legal and EU translation, translator training and corpus linguistics.

**María Jesús Blasco Mayor** is an interpreter and translator who teaches interpreting at Jaume I University (Spain) since 1998. Her PhD research centered on the comprehension component of interpreter training. She has participated in several research projects and published at leading journals on her research interests, which include legal interpreting quality.

**Paolo Canavese** is a research and teaching assistant at the University of Geneva's Faculty of Translation and Interpreting and member of the Transius Centre. He conducts research in the field of legal and institutional translation studies, with a focus on barrier-free State-to-citizen communication and accessibility of law.

**Flavia De Camillis** works at the Institute for Applied Linguistics at Eurac Research since 2015, where she is a doctoral candidate with a dissertation on the assessment of translation practices in the multilingual administration of the Province of Bolzano (South Tyrol).

**María Fernández-Parra** is a senior lecturer in translation and interpreting and MA director at Swansea University, where she teaches and researches on translation and technology topics. She is also the secretary of Swansea University's Language Research Centre and treasurer of the Association of Programmes in Translation and Interpreting Studies of the UK and Ireland (APTIS).

**Jeffrey Killman** is an associate professor of Spanish translation at the University of North Carolina at Charlotte, where he teaches a range of topics, including legal translation, translation technologies and translation theory. His research centers on legal translation and translation technologies. He is also state-certified as a Spanish court interpreter.

**Marja Kivilehto** is a senior lecturer in Swedish translation at Tampere University. Her research interests include certified translation and translation in the Swedish-Finnish context. She teaches practical translation courses, and has also lectured on research methods for translation studies.

**Fernando Prieto Ramos** is a full professor and director of the Centre for Legal and Institutional Translation Studies (Transius) at the University of Geneva's Faculty of Translation and Interpreting. He regularly publishes on legal and institutional translation, and has also translated for various organizations, including several years of in-house service at the World Trade Organization.

**Izabela Pytel** is a graduate of the MA in Translation at the University of Warsaw's Institute of Applied Linguistics, as well as a translator trainer and an English/German/Polish translator.

**Lucía Ruiz Rosendo** is an assistant professor at the Faculty of Translation and Interpreting, University of Geneva. She is also a professional conference interpreter in the institutional market. Her research focuses on the impact of multiple factors on the quality of simultaneous interpreting and the interpreter's role in conflict-related situations.

**Leena Salmi** is a senior lecturer in French at the University of Turku. Her research interests include post-editing, translation quality assessment and certified translation. Her teaching focuses on practical translation, translation technology, post-editing and translation company simulation.

**Marta Sancho Viamonte** is a translator and interpreter who teaches at the Universities of Milan and Genoa. In 2018, she obtained her PhD with a dissertation on the evaluation of court interpreting quality. She is an active member of AssITIG and AITI accredited to interpret before the courts of Milan.

**Mariam Sperandio** is a graduate of the MA in Translation at the University of Geneva's Faculty of Translation and Interpreting. She has experience as a project manager and communication specialist in the areas of community engagement, public relations and human resources in high-profile international environments.

**Mónica Varela García** is chief interpreter at the International Labour Organization. Her previous career was at the United Nations, as a senior interpreter. She teaches interpreting at the MA in Conference Interpreting of the University of Geneva's Faculty of Translation and Interpreting since 2017. Her main research line is about the impact of speed on simultaneous interpreting quality.

# Assessing Practices in Institutional Translation and Interpreting

*Fernando Prieto Ramos*

What are the daily tasks of institutional translators in international translation services and what kind of tools do they use? What types of errors are more often overlooked in their work and when do they require formal correction after translations are published? How can issues of clarity, consistency and accuracy in particular be tackled? What is the impact of speech delivery speed on simultaneous interpreting performance? How do small organizations and local administrations without institutionalized language services deal with translation and interpreting needs? How can they improve the quality of multilingual communication in cost-effective ways? What are the risks of outsourcing and non-professional arrangements? What can be learnt from the latest developments in translator and interpreter certification schemes and quality guidelines? These are some of the most relevant questions addressed in the chapters of this book. The authors share the common aim of shedding light on institutional translation and interpreting settings in order to identify quality gaps, needs, best practices and actions for improvement. All contributions thus revolve around the central concern of quality, more specifically, by examining the multiple aspects of translation competence and institutional processes that can have a bearing on the final product. In other words, the overall approach adopted is a holistic one that recognizes that process, competence and product are inextricably intertwined (Prieto Ramos 2015, 23–27).

Focus is placed on public institutions and administrations at the regional, national and international levels, including legislative bodies, court settings and certified translation for official purposes more broadly. The national and regional contexts selected cover a wide range of illustrative translation policies in multilingual and monolingual administrations (see, e.g., Meylaerts 2011). The following table provides an overview of the specific settings, themes and main quality aspects examined by each chapter.

DOI: 10.4324/9780429264894

Overview of settings, themes and main quality aspects examined

| Institutional setting | Main theme | Main translation/interpreting quality aspects | | |
|---|---|---|---|---|
| | | Competence | Process | Product |
| *Part I. National and regional institutions* | | | | |
| 1 Finland (certified translation) | Assessment criteria in certification examination | X | X | X |
| 2 Switzerland (legislative bodies) | Lexical readability as quality indicator in legal translation | | | X |
| 3 South Tyrol (provincial administration)* | Non-professional translation profiles and practices* | X | X | |
| 4 United States (courts)* | Translation policies and qualification requirements* | X | X | |
| 5 Italy, Spain (courts)* | Questionnaire for quality control in court interpreting* | X | X | X |
| *Part II. International organizations* | | | | |
| 6 European Commission (EU) | DGT translators' practices and tools | X | X | |
| 7 EU, UN, WTO | Consistency and accuracy of legal terminology in translations | | X | X |
| 8 EU (law-making institutions) | Correction rates and nature of corrigenda of EU legislative acts | | | X |
| 9 International organizations (anonymized)* | Impact of translation competence on processes and product quality* | X | X | X |
| 10 UN | Effects of speed on simultaneous interpreting quality | X | X | X |

* Settings that include some form of non-professional translation or interpreting (by unqualified translators or interpreters).

All authors offer insights from their original research, drawing on a diversity of angles and methods, which include direct observations, corpus analysis, interviews and surveys. Far from stereotypes and debates about the divide between academic and practical perspectives, all contributions present applied research that is supported by the authors' professional experience or is the result of close cooperation between re-searchers and practitioners in the observed settings. This illustrates a trend of maturity in the collaboration, as well as converging interests, between academia and the translation industry, as new market and tech-nological developments call for innovative approaches and data-driven adaptations.

In the case of large international organizations, cooperation has reached unprecedented levels and is nurturing fruitful dialogue between stakehold-ers and a growing wealth of studies on institutional translation and in-terpreting, in particular in the EU institutions (see, e.g., Svoboda *et al.* 2017; Prieto Ramos 2018). Well-established language services in this kind of setting are ideally positioned to monitor and refine their practices as exemplars of institutional translation and interpreting. The same applies to national multilingual bodies with long traditions in the field such as Canadian or Swiss institutions.

However, fully-fledged language services are far from being the norm among national and international institutions that have translation and interpreting needs. In many situations, these needs are addressed in a diversity of alternative ways, ranging from outsourcing (to freelance translators or interpreters) to other informal arrangements involving non-professional in-house or external supports, for example, through crowdsourcing and volunteer translation (see, e.g., Antonini *et al.* 2017; Jiménez-Crespo 2017). In our experience, these informal solutions apply to a myriad of small institutional entities where ad hoc multilingual ar-rangements are shaped by limited funding and lack of relevant in-house expertise in the field.

While it is difficult to empirically map practices in such a diverse and fragmented landscape, it seems apparent that the combined translation and interpreting needs of this heterogeneous category are massive. At the international level alone, there are 41,772 active organizations, of which 5,630 are intergovernmental (including supranational institu-tions) and 36,142 are non-governmental, according to the latest edition of the *Yearbook of International Organizations* (Union of International Associations 2019, 27). Three chapters of this book shed light on the under-researched reality of institutions without "conventional" in-house translation services, as illustrated by a regional administration, the court systems of three different countries and two international organizations (see the table above).

**Part I** of the volume is devoted to national and regional institutional settings. In Chapter 1, Leena Salmi and Marja Kivilehto describe the ra-tionale behind revising the error-based scoring chart of the Finnish Au-thorized Translators' Examination, which is a requirement for certifying official translations (most often for judicial and administrative bodies – for an overview of practices in other countries, see Vigier *et al.* 2013). To that end, they analyzed feedback from assessors and two corpora of translations assessed according to the new chart and its previous version. The comparison of these data and with the holistic assessment approach of the Australian National Accreditation Authority for Translators and Interpreters (NAATI) signaled potential avenues for further development. Chapter 2, by Paolo Canavese, focuses on lexical readability as an indicator of linguistic clarity of Italian translations within Swiss trilingual legislation. The findings of lexical analyses show the benefits of promoting clear legal drafting as a good practice to make legislation more readable.

In Chapter 3, Flavia De Camillis presents the design and results of a survey conducted among civil servants who translate administrative documents in the bilingual province of South Tyrol, Italy. The study provides insights into the profiles and practices of these non-professional translators (following the features defined by Antonini *et al.* 2017, 7) as a first step to identify priority needs and actions for improvement. The last two contributions in Part I concentrate on judicial settings. In Chapter 4, Jeffrey Killman explores the diversity of approaches to translation in federal and state courts in the United States, and highlights the implications of varying qualification requirements, still underdeveloped compared to court interpreting. By contrast, as contended by María Jesús Blasco Mayor and Marta Sancho Viamonte in Chapter 5, there are no certification systems for court interpreters in EU countries such as Italy and Spain, despite Directive 2010/64/EU on the right to interpretation and translation in criminal proceedings. In order to fill this gap, the authors propose INTER-Q, a questionnaire for legal professionals to assess the directly observable aspects of legal interpreters' performance such as manners and knowledge of legal terms and procedures.

Part II, on translation and interpreting for international organizations, starts with a study by María Fernández-Parra (Chapter 6) on the day-to-day tasks of translators at the European Commission's Directorate-General for Translation (DGT). The data obtained from observation of a sample group of translators, and supported by retrospective interviews, provide empirical evidence of the nature and duration of their translation, revision and terminological activities, and of the tools they use in these processes. The results reveal swift interactions with technology to "make every second count" under tight time constraints, and corroborate the crucial relevance of revision and terminological resources in ensuring quality. Chapter 7, by the editor, also addresses the latter aspect. It centers on terminological consistency and accuracy as conditions for semantic univocity, and on the instrumental role of institutional resources in improving these quality indicators with regard to legal terminology, which usually requires research during the translation process. The diachronic scrutiny of English-Spanish translations of three illustrative terms in the main EU institutions, the United Nations (UN) and the World Trade Organization suggests significant correlations between legal asymmetry and translation accuracy levels, and between intertextual consistency and accuracy fluctuations. The study also discusses the low congruity of the renderings with the limited guidance of institutional terminological resources on legal system-specific terms.

In the following contribution (Chapter 8), Łucja Biel and Izabela Pytel explore similar issues through the lens of corrigenda of EU legislative acts. They investigate the number and nature of corrections in light of the maturity of the Polish Eurolect since Poland's accession to the EU. The findings highlight a growing trend of corrigenda in Polish, in line with previous research on corrigenda in French and Spanish (Prieto Ramos 2020), as well as the prominence of terminological and phraseological issues as the largest category of errors corrected. Terminological inconsistencies are also part of the error analyses conducted in two cases of action research reported in Chapter 9 (co-authored with Mariam Sperandio). Both cases entailed "taking action and creating knowledge" about the actions (Coghlan and Brannick 2001, xi) in two institutional settings that initially had no in-house service or staff devoted to managing translation. The interventions included professional project management and revision in the first setting (versus review in the initial approach) and professional translation (versus prior non-professional translation) in the replication study. The correlational examination of error score reduction against profile changes empirically shows the benefits of introducing translation expertise in each setting. Finally, in Chapter 10, Lucía Ruiz Rosendo, Mónica Varela García and Alma Barghout take us to the interpreting booths of the UN in order to assess the performance of ten staff interpreters in their simultaneous rendering of three speeches at different speeds. They measure the impact of high speed on the severity of information omissions, as opposed to less critical omissions at more moderate delivery rates.

All the findings presented in the volume have important implications for professional practices and quality assurance in particular. They hold many lessons for practitioners, trainers, researchers and institutional decision-makers which will be further elaborated in the concluding remarks.

## References

Antonini, Rachele, Letizia Cirillo, Linda Rossato, and Ira Torresi, eds. 2017. *Non-Professional Interpreting and Translation: State of the Art and Future of an Emerging Field of Research.* Amsterdam and Philadelphia: John Benjamins. doi:10.1075/btl.129.

Coghlan, David, and Teresa Brannick. 2001. *Doing Action Research in Your Own Organization.* London: Sage Publications.

Jiménez-Crespo, Miguel A. 2017. "How Much Would You Like to Pay? Reframing and Expanding the Notion of Translation Quality through Crowdsourcing and Volunteer Approaches." *Perspectives* 25(3): 478–491. doi:10.1080/0907 676X.2017.1285948.

Meylaerts, Reine. 2011. "Translational Justice in a Multilingual World: An Overview of Translational Regimes." *Meta: Translators' Journal* 56(4): 743–757. doi:10.7202/1011250ar.

Prieto Ramos, Fernando. 2015. "Quality Assurance in Legal Translation: Evaluating Process, Competence and Product in the Pursuit of Adequacy." *International Journal for the Semiotics of Law* 28(1): 11–30. doi:10.1007/ s11196-014-9390-9.

Prieto Ramos, Fernando, ed. 2018. *Institutional Translation for International Governance: Enhancing Quality in Multilingual Legal Communication.* London: Bloomsbury.

Prieto Ramos, Fernando. 2020. "Facing Translation Errors at International Organizations: What Corrigenda Reveal about Correction Processes and Their Implications for Translation Quality." *Comparative Legilinguistics* 41: 97– 133. doi:10.14746/cl.2020.41.5.

Svoboda, Tomáš, Łucja Biel, and Krzysztof Łoboda, eds. 2017. *Quality Aspects in Institutional Translation.* Berlin: Language Science Press. doi:10.5281/ zenodo.1048173.

Union of International Associations, ed. 2019. *Yearbook of International Organizations 2019–2020. Volume 5: Statistics, Visualizations and Patterns.* Leiden: Brill.

Vigier, Francisco, Perla Klein, and Nancy Festinger. 2013. "Certified Translators in Europe and the Americas: Accreditation Practices and Challenges." In *Legal Translation in Context: Professional Issues and Prospects*, edited by Anabel Borja Albi and Fernando Prieto Ramos, 27–51. Oxford, Bern, Berlin, Brussels, Frankfurt am Main, New York, Vienna: Peter Lang.

# Part I

# Translation and Interpreting for National and Regional Institutions

# 1 A Comparative Approach to Assessing Assessment

## Revising the Scoring Chart for the Authorized Translator's Examination in Finland

*Leena Salmi and Marja Kivilehto*

## 1.1 Introduction

There is a broad scope of translation quality assessment, and it can occur in various contexts: translator training, machine translation and technical communication, to give a few examples (e.g. Angelelli and Jacobson 2009; Gouadec 2010). Our focus in this chapter is on assessment related to translator certification: the assessment system in the Authorized Translator's Examination in Finland. This examination determines whether the examinees have the professional competence needed for producing so-called "official" or "certified" translations (i.e. legally valid for certain purposes and institutions), but the context can also be considered pedagogical to some extent, since the examinees who fail receive feedback that highlights their abilities and shortcomings (cf. Saldanha and O'Brien 2013, 96).

In our previous articles (Kivilehto and Salmi 2017; Salmi and Kivilehto 2018), we have discussed the assessment system of the Finnish Authorized Translator's Examination and compared it to assessment systems in other certification examinations. The system itself, in its present form since 2008, has been described by Salmi and Penttilä (2013), and is the topic of a recent publication (in Finnish) by the Finnish National Agency for Education (EDUFI) (see Hiirikoski 2017; Kemppanen 2017; Miettunen 2017). We have also examined how a sample of translations have been assessed in the examination. Our purpose has been to gain more information for developing the assessment system of the Finnish examination to make it more valid and reliable, as we have noticed some validity- and reliability-related problems in how the assessment has been applied to translations in the examination (Kivilehto and Salmi 2017).

The scoring chart for assessing translations in the examination was revised in 2017. Previously, the chart comprised two parts, and the translations were marked for both content (C-errors) and language quality (A-errors). The scoring chart currently has three parts, taking into account task accomplishment (T-errors), equivalence of content (C-errors),

DOI: 10.4324/9780429264894-1

and acceptability and readability (A-errors). The previous chart contained 14 error types (see the full chart in Kivilehto and Salmi 2017), while the new one contained only seven.

This chapter presents a comparison of the scoring charts before and after 2017. We describe our process of revising the scoring chart and analyze how it has been applied. The purpose of the comparison is to see if the assessment in the examinations should be further developed, and if so, in what way. In our earlier work, we have discussed similar systems in use elsewhere (e.g. Norway, Germany, Canada or the United States; see Kivilehto and Salmi 2017; Salmi and Kivilehto 2018), and this chapter describes that of the Australian National Accreditation Authority for Translators and Interpreters (NAATI), as a possible way of developing the assessment.

## 1.2 Translation Quality Assessment in Translator's Examinations

### 1.2.1 Assessment Practices

Translation quality assessment can be product-, process- and/or user-oriented. Product-oriented assessment is usually based on text analysis and comparing source and target texts (Saldanha and O'Brien 2013, 98–99). One of the best-known, text-based models is that of House (2015), who approaches assessment from the perspective of systemic-functional linguistics and calls her model functional-pragmatic. The principal assessment criterion in House's model is functional equivalence, which can only be reached in translation that is not source culture dependent, i.e. covert translation (House 2015, 60). Otherwise what we are dealing with are different kinds of versions (House 2015, 59). As for process-oriented assessment, it takes a holistic approach to assessment and emphasizes contextual factors such as translator competence and the context in which translations are produced. Examples of process-oriented assessment systems are standards such as the ISO 17100. User-oriented assessment, for its part, focuses on factors such as readability, acceptability and usability, and approaches assessment from an individual's point of view. This means that assessment is related to individual user attributes: reading skills and motivation for reading the translation (Saldanha and O'Brien 2013, 99–100). User-oriented assessment is taken one step further by Suojanen, Koskinen and Tuominen (2015), who introduce practical methods for user-centered translation.

When assessing translations, it is recommended to pay attention to the assessment setting, those doing the translation and the genre and purpose of the translation (House 2015). This applies to examination contexts as well. In the case of the Authorized Translator's Examination in Finland, the texts to be translated fall into the category of legal texts, and thus special attention must be paid to strategies of translating legal texts. According to Vanden Bulcke and Héroguel (2011, 241), four aspects should be taken into account when assessing translations of legal texts: legal texts as category, genre characteristics, text function and translation strategies. When it comes to certified translations, they often fall into the category of judicial texts (e.g. summons, pronouncements and judgments) and texts that are applications of law (e.g. official documents, contracts and wills). This implies that translations are to be authentic translations that describe the reality of the source text (ST) as closely as possible (Vanden Bulcke and Héroguel 2011, 234, 243). Undoubtedly, the translations must be comprehensible for end users, but as the end users are often experts of the field in question, they may be expected to have the prior knowledge needed for interpreting legal texts of different legal systems. Authenticity, for its part, amounts to foreignizing as a translation strategy. Translations should correspond to STs as closely as possible even with regard to macro- and microstructures, i.e. text structure, phraseology, terminology, syntax and style (Vanden Bulcke and Héroguel 2011, 214). This view is also shared in studies with Danish lawyers and legal translators as informants (Hjort-Pedersen 2016).

Assessment models can roughly be categorized as analytical or holistic (Lommel et al. 2015). *Analytic assessment* focuses "on the identification of precise issues within the object being assessed, such as (for a translation) identification of specific mistranslations, spelling errors," whereas *holistic assessment* emphasizes "overall characteristics of the object being assessed, such as (in the case of translated texts) reader impression, sentiment, clarity, accuracy, style, whether it enables a task to be completed, and so forth" (Lommel et al. 2015, Section 1.3.2). In assessing certified translation, it is justified to use an analytic rather than a holistic model, since precision is highly valued. Analytic assessment often results in error analysis rather than a comparison of the translation against "ideal" criteria that describe either what the translation should be like or the translation skills it should demonstrate (Angelelli 2009, 40–41; Turner, Lai, and Huang 2010). Error analysis has been regarded as a valid way of measuring translation quality, and this is why it is used in many certification examinations (cf. Hale et al. 2012, 58). An example of this is the certification examination managed by the American Translators Association (ATA 2017). Nevertheless, criterion-referenced assessment can be as valid as error-based assessment (Turner, Lai, and Huang 2010), and at least one certification system, that of the Australian NAATI, has adopted criterion-referenced assessment.

### 1.2.2 Assessment in NAATI Certification Examination

In this section, we discuss the assessment of the Australian certification examination of NAATI. The reason for choosing the NAATI assessment is the fact that it is criterion-referenced, and we see this as one possibility for developing the assessment of the Finnish Authorized Translator's Examination.

In Australia, the certification examination offered by NAATI takes place several times a year in different language combinations (NAATI 2020a) and has three levels of translator certifications: Certified Advanced Translator, Certified Translator and Recognized Practicing Translator (NAATI 2020b). The Certified Advanced Translator test consists of three tasks: two translations of texts of 400 words and one revision of a translation of 400 words. All STs are written by specialists for specialist readers. They can be research papers, legal briefs or trade agreements, to name a few examples. The test duration is eight hours (NAATI 2020c). The Certified Translator test consists of two translation tasks and one revision task, but the STs are non-specialized texts and shorter (about 250 words) than those in the Certified Advanced Translator test, and they deal with different topics and represent different domains. The domains range from government, legal, health, technology and science to business, society, culture, social services and immigration. The test duration is three and a half hours. In both tests, computers may be used and all kinds of reference materials are allowed. However, neither the use of the Internet nor contacting other people is permitted (NAATI 2020d). For Recognized Practicing Translators, there is no certification test.

The assessment methods of both the translation and revision tasks are criterion-referenced. Two criteria are applied, which means that two competencies are assessed: transfer competency and language competency. For translation tasks, transfer competency means competency in transferring the meaning of the ST, following the translation brief and applying textual norms and conventions, whereas for revision tasks, it means revision skills and competency in applying knowledge of translation standards. As regards language competency, it includes language skills enabling the transfer of meaning. The assessment criteria are considered at five levels, called Bands, of which 1 is the highest and 5 the lowest level. To pass the test, examinees need to achieve at least Band 2 (in some cases 3) for each criterion (NAATI 2020d, 2020e). Bands 2 and 3 for transfer competency and language competency in the translation test for Certified Translator are explained in Table 1.1 (cf. NAATI 2020e).

The overall criteria for NAATI translation examinations are wider than the two criteria described earlier. The NAATI criteria, or competencies, are nine in total, ranging from competencies in transfer, language, research and domain and document types to intercultural, thematic and technological competencies. The examinees are expected to satisfy some prerequisites before taking the certification examination. Prerequisite screening tests are organized in language competency (English proficiency), ethical competency and intercultural competency (NAATI 2020c, 2020e).

*Table 1.1* Transfer competency and language competency for Certified Translator in the NAATI translation test (NAATI 2020c)

| | Transfer competency | | | Language competency |
|---|---|---|---|---|
| | *Meaning transfer skill* | *Follow translation brief* | *Application of textual norms and conventions* | *Language proficiency enabling meaning transfer* |
| Pass requirements | At least Band 2 | At least Band 2 in one of the two criteria, and at least Band 3 in the other | | At least Band 2 |
| Band 2 | Translates the propositional content and intent of the message, with few instances of **minor** unjustified omissions, insertions and/or distortions. **Mostly** demonstrates ability to resolve most translation problems appropriately. | Follows the specifications provided in the translation brief. Produces a text which **mostly** takes into account the purpose of the target text, a specified audience and type of communication. | Demonstrates ability in the use of register, style and text structure appropriate to the genre and **mostly** consistent with the norms and conventions of the target language. | **Mostly** uses written language competently and idiomatically, in accordance with the norms of the target language. **Mostly** demonstrates competent use of lexicon, grammar and syntax, including orthography, punctuation and terminology. The target text contains only a few minor errors that **do not impact on understanding.** |
| Band 3 | Translates the propositional content and intent of the message, with several **minor** and/or any **major** unjustified omissions, insertions and/or distortions. Demonstrates **some** ability to resolve translation problems appropriately. | Demonstrates **some** ability to follow the specifications provided in the translation brief, but does not in several instances take into account the purpose of the target text, a specified audience or type of communication. | Demonstrates **some** ability in the use of register, style and text structure appropriate to the genre and consistent with the norms and conventions of the target language. | Demonstrates **some** ability to use written language idiomatically, in accordance with the norms of the target language. Demonstrates **some** ability to use lexicon, grammar and syntax, including orthography, punctuation and terminology. The target text contains several errors that **impact on understanding.** |

In recruiting assessors, NAATI looks for examiners who have a NAATI certification at an appropriate level and a tertiary qualification in translating, interpreting, language, linguistics or a related discipline. In addition, they have to have near-native competence in the languages they assess, extensive professional experience as a translator or interpreter, commitment to ethical practice and ability to work with others (NAATI 2020f). Each task is assessed by two assessors who work independently. If the assessors disagree with each other about the examinee's performance, i.e. whether s/he should pass or fail, additional assessors will be brought in (NAATI 2020g).

## 1.3 The Finnish Authorized Translator's Examination

### 1.3.1 Overview of the Examination

In Finland, the EDUFI[1] is the authority that grants the status of an authorized translator with the right to produce legally valid translations, after an applicant has passed the Authorized Translator's Examination or has obtained a Master's degree in translation that includes at least six ECTS credits in certified translation (L 1231/2007). The system is managed centrally for the sake of uniformity, impartiality and equality for the examinees. In the examination, several language combinations are possible, depending on the number of examinees who wish to be tested in a particular language pair and on the availability of qualified assessors. The possibility of becoming authorized on the basis of a university degree in translation, though, applies only to the language combinations available in translator training programs in Finland and only in translation into Finnish or Swedish, including between these two languages. In addition, the status can be granted on the basis of university studies in translation into the student's first language only.

No prerequisites are set concerning the educational background of those wishing to take part in the examination. The examination is offered once a year, usually in November. It tests the examinees' competency in the professional practice of authorized translator and their translation competency in two specialist fields (EDUFI 2019a). In sum, the examination consists of three parts:

1    a multiple-choice test on the professional practice of authorized translators (45 minutes);
2    one translation assignment in the field of law and administration (2 hours 45 minutes);
3    one translation assignment in a field chosen by the examinee (business and economics, medicine, technology or education; 2 hours 45 minutes).

Computers are allowed during the examination. Internet sources and other reference materials may be used during the translation tests. However, the use of translation memories, machine translation and email is not allowed, nor may examinees contact other people (EDUFI 2019a).

### 1.3.2 Assessment in the Examination

In the examination, both language and translation skills are examined using two translation assignments. The assignments are assessed by two assessors. One of them is an expert in the source language (SL) and the other in the target language (TL), though both should be somewhat familiar with both languages. The assessment is performed in accordance with the assessment criteria for language and translation skills (FNBE 2012, 8). The assessors perform the assessments individually, but not completely independently: they are expected to discuss their individual assessments and come to a shared conclusion. If they cannot agree, an additional assessor is usually brought in. To ensure a fair assessment, it is important that the assessment criteria are transparent and consistent, and that the examinees know how the assessment system has been applied to their translations (EDUFI 2019b). The examinees do not have the possibility to appeal to a higher body if they are not satisfied with the assessment, but they have the right to ask the Authorized Translators' Examination Board to reassess their translations (FNBE 2012, 9).

Regarding the qualifications of the assessors, they must have at least a Master's degree and a sound knowledge of translating pragmatic texts in the examination languages. In exceptional cases, a Bachelor's degree may be accepted instead of a Master's degree if the person is a native speaker of the TL. In addition to these criteria, assessors must have completed an assessor training acknowledged by the Finnish National Agency for Education. They are entered into the assessor register for five years; examiners may renew their assessor status, provided that they still satisfy the criteria and have been maintaining their assessment skills (A 1232/2007, Section 12; L 1231/2007, Section 14).

The assessment of translation assignments in the examination is based on an error analysis. The assessors verify how well the source and target texts correspond to each other and how acceptable the translations are as target texts. The first element is generally known as *accuracy* or *adequacy* (Toury 2012, 79), and it relates to what the Multi-Dimensional Quality Metrics (MQM) framework defines as the "extent to which the informational content conveyed by a target text matches that of the source text" (Lommel et al. 2015, Section 1.2). The second element, known in the MQM as *fluency*, refers to "properties of the target text such as grammar, spelling, and cohesion" (Koby et al. 2014, 415).

### 1.3.3 Revision of the Assessment System

From 2008 to 2017, the assessors applied a scoring chart containing the two categories of accuracy and fluency: accuracy errors were categorized as errors in the equivalence of content (C-errors) and fluency errors as errors in acceptability and readability (A-errors). Both categories included seven error types. Acting both as researchers and members of the Examination Board, we decided to conduct research on how the scoring chart was applied in practice (Kivilehto 2016, 2017; Kivilehto and Salmi 2017). It became clear that some of the error types were used often, while others were used only rarely (Kivilehto 2016; Kivilehto and Salmi 2017). That is why we decided to propose a new, simplified scoring chart.

As members of the Examination Board, we were able to start the revision work. In the course of it, we applied a user-oriented process, which included a survey and usability testing (see Suojanen et al. 2015). Seminars on the preparation and the assessment of the translations are organized three times a year for the examination assessors within the system (see Salmi and Kinnunen 2015, 235). We started the process in November 2016, in one of these seminars, by surveying the views of the assessors on the assessment criteria (reported in Salmi and Kivilehto 2018, 184–185). We also presented two proposals for simplified assessment criteria, one error-based and the other criterion-based, which were tested in the seminar by the participants. The assessors preferred the error-based criteria, and so, in the following seminar in January 2017, we presented two proposals for error-based criteria. In February–May 2017, the proposal favored by the assessors in the seminar was tested by four experienced assessors. In May 2017, we held a seminar on the scoring chart development with both assessors and translator trainers, where some further adjustments were made. Finally, in November, we had a new scoring chart that was applied in the examination of 2017.

The new scoring chart contains three error categories and seven error types. The errors are categorized as T-errors, C-errors and A-errors. T-errors related to errors in task accomplishment, C-errors related to equivalence of content, and A-errors related to acceptability and readability of text. The category of T-errors was introduced so that special attention could be paid to the characteristics of certified translations such as providing an appropriate heading for the translation and the use of translators' notes. Table 1.2 shows the error types in the new scoring chart.

To compare the previous chart (see Kivilehto and Salmi 2017, Appendix) with the new one, the previous seven A-errors have been combined into two types. As for C-errors, the earlier division into types was more primarily based on where the error occurred: on the level of sentence, grammatical structure or term (e.g. "C2 – A wrong term leading

*Table 1.2* The scoring chart in the Authorized Translator's Examination in Finland

| T-errors<br>*Task accomplishment* | C-errors<br>*Equivalence of content* | A-errors<br>*Acceptability and readability of text* |
| --- | --- | --- |
| T1<br>The translation has **no heading** that identifies it as a translation.<br>(5 error points) | C1<br>**Omission** (word, term, reference relation or a wider entity).<br>(2, 5 or 10 points) | A1<br>The **syntax, morphology, style, register or idiomaticity** of the translation does not follow the norms of the target language.<br>(2, 5 or 10 points) |
| T2<br>The **function** of the translation has been **disregarded**.<br>(2, 5 or 10 points) | C2<br>**Insertion** (word, term, reference relation or a wider entity).<br>(2, 5 or 10 points) | A2<br>**Spelling or orthography** does not follow the norms of the target language.<br>(2 points) |
|  | C3<br>A word, term or a wider **entity does not correspond** to the source text.<br>(2, 5 or 10 points) |  |

to the misinterpretation of the translation – 9 error points" or "C6 – Misinterpreted structure – 6 to 2 error points"). The chart also listed separately critical errors that would lead to failing the examination, for example, the C2 error mentioned earlier, or leaving out an entire sentence (C1). The new chart (Table 1.2) focuses more on what the error is like: an element is missing, an element has been inserted or an element does not otherwise correspond to the ST.

In the previous chart, error severity was combined with error type and each error category contained information on how many error points could be given. In the new chart, the severity of errors has three levels: minor (2 points), severe (5 points) and critical (10 points). To fail a translation, only one critical error is enough. The maximum score allowed ranges from 25 to 30, depending on the difficulty of the translation assignment. If an error recurs consistently throughout the text, it is penalized only once.

## 1.4 Assessment in Practice

In this section, we present an analysis of how the new scoring chart has been applied. The material analyzed contains all the assessed translations from one language setting, the candidates in the language pairs

English-Finnish and Finnish-English, in 2017 and 2018 when the new scoring chart was in application. The data analyzed here consist of translations by nine examinees in the English-Finnish language pair and by 19 in the Finnish-English language pair, altogether 28 examinees. Coincidentally, the number of examinees is the same as in our previous study with data from 2012 to 2014 (Kivilehto and Salmi 2017, 63). Since each examinee produces two translations, there are 56 translations, and as each translation is assessed by two assessors, the data include 112 assessments. Table 1.3 presents the number of translations analyzed.

Three different assessors were involved, all of whom have several years of experience in the examination, and who had also done the assessments analyzed in our previous study (Kivilehto and Salmi 2017). Table 1.4 shows the different error types per language pair, while Table 1.5 presents the results per examination year.

As can be seen in Table 1.4, the most common error type is C3 (a word, term or wider entity that does not correspond to the ST), with 1,112 occurrences. This is similar to our earlier study where the most common type was C7, "an individual word/term that is imprecise, unsuitable or irrelevant or an omission or an addition not essentially affecting the

*Table 1.3* Number of translations analyzed, by language pair

|  | 2017 | | | 2018 | | |
|---|---|---|---|---|---|---|
|  | *Examinees* | *Translations* | *Assessments* | *Examinees* | *Translations* | *Assessments* |
| English-Finnish | 6 | 12 | 24 | 3 | 6 | 12 |
| Finnish-English | 8 | 16 | 32 | 11 | 22 | 44 |
| Total | 14 | 28 | 56 | 14 | 28 | 56 |

*Table 1.4* Error types marked in the English-Finnish and Finnish-English translations

| Error type | ENG-FIN | | FIN-ENG | | All | |
|---|---|---|---|---|---|---|
|  | *Number* | *%* | *Number* | *%* | *Number* | *%* |
| C1 | 28 | 3.4 | 69 | 4.2 | 97 | 3.9 |
| C2 | 8 | 1.0 | 46 | 2.8 | 54 | 2.2 |
| C3 | 474 | 56.9 | 638 | 39.2 | 1,112 | 45.2 |
| A1 | 166 | 19.9 | 545 | 33.5 | 711 | 28.9 |
| A2 | 110 | 13.2 | 171 | 10.5 | 281 | 11.4 |
| T1 | 17 | 2.0 | 68 | 4.2 | 85 | 3.5 |
| T2 | 30 | 3.6 | 89 | 5.5 | 119 | 4.8 |
| Total | 833 | 100.0 | 1,626 | 100.0 | 2,459 | 100.0 |

meaning of the text" (Kivilehto and Salmi 2017, 63). In both categories, terminology errors explain the high frequency of the most commonly used error type. As we noted earlier, "producing legally valid translations requires accuracy and precision" and the examination texts are "LSP texts that usually contain specific terminology" (2017, 66). Terminology errors are also the explanation given by two experienced assessors (Hiirikoski 2017, 45–46; Miettunen 2017, 72): the translation may be grammatically correct, but the terminology used by the examinee is not the one used in the special field in question, or the examinee fails to recognize the terms used in the ST (see also Kivilehto 2017).

Again, as in our earlier study, the next most common error type is an acceptability error A1 (the syntax, morphology, style, register or idiomaticity of the translation does not follow the norms of the TL). In the previous scoring chart, this was error A5, "structural error not causing misinterpretation," which falls within the scope of the current error type A1.

The least often used error type is C2, insertions. Contrary to the earlier study, there are no error types that do not occur at all in this data. This was, in fact, one of the goals of the revision: to have a scoring chart with no error types that are never used. In the data from 2012 to 2014, an error type that did not occur at all was C3, described as "the translation function is disregarded, leading to an inadequate result" (Kivilehto and Salmi 2017, 64). In the present data, insertion (type C2) is the least frequent error type, with 54 occurrences altogether.

Table 1.4 also shows that more errors have been marked in the translations into English ($n = 1,626$) than into Finnish ($n = 833$). This is consistent with our earlier results from 2012 to 2014 (Kivilehto and Salmi 2017, 63). However, as Table 1.3 shows, there were more examinees translating into English (8 in 2017, 11 in 2018) than into Finnish (6 in 2017, 3 in 2018), resulting in 76 assessed translations into English and 36 into Finnish. This amounts to 21.4 errors on average in the translations into English and 23.1 errors into Finnish, so there seems to be no significant difference in the average number of errors.

As regards the distribution of error types per year (Table 1.5), although the number of examinees in both 2017 and 2018 was the same (14), more errors were marked in 2018. There was an increase in all error types except the most common one, C3. The quantitative analysis conducted for this study cannot give a straightforward explanation for this. However, as mentioned, the majority of examinees in 2018 translated from Finnish into English (11 out of 14, see Table 1.3). As Hiirikoski (2017) points out in his analysis of 107 translations into Finnish and 119 translations into English in 2008–2015, translating in this direction seemed to account for more errors than translating into Finnish. We do not have information on the examinees' linguistic background (mother tongue or other language skills) or their competence in translating that

*Table 1.5* Error types marked per year and language direction

| Error type | 2017 | | | | 2018 | | | |
|---|---|---|---|---|---|---|---|---|
| | Number | % | ENG-FIN | FIN-ENG | Number | % | ENG-FIN | FIN-ENG |
| C1 | 23 | 2.1 | 10 | 13 | 74 | 5.4 | 18 | 56 |
| C2 | 11 | 1.0 | 1 | 10 | 43 | 3.2 | 7 | 36 |
| C3 | 565 | 51.5 | 371 | 194 | 547 | 40.2 | 103 | 444 |
| A1 | 279 | 25.4 | 88 | 191 | 432 | 31.7 | 78 | 354 |
| A2 | 120 | 10.9 | 80 | 40 | 161 | 11.8 | 30 | 131 |
| T1 | 27 | 2.5 | 12 | 15 | 58 | 4.3 | 5 | 53 |
| T2 | 73 | 6.6 | 14 | 59 | 46 | 3.4 | 16 | 30 |
| Total | 1,098 | 100.0 | 576 | 522 | 1,361 | 100.0 | 257 | 1,104 |

might explain the differences, as the examinees are not asked to provide such information. We do not either have exact numbers of how many examinees have passed in each language pair, and statistics published by EDUFI (2019c) show that the overall passing rate is practically the same in both years, 16.9 (12 examinees) in 2017 and 16.7 (11 examinees) in 2018.

## 1.5  Discussion and Conclusions

The comparison of the results on the application of the previous and the new scoring charts shows that the error types most often used are similar: problems with terminology and with the target text syntax (in the earlier results) or its syntax, morphology, style, register or idiomaticity (in the latest results). What is different is that all error types were used with the new scoring chart, contrary to the data from 2012 to 2014. In addition, the assessors' comments on the new chart have been positive. Already during the test phase described in Section 1.3.3, two of the experienced assessors explicitly stated in their written comments that the new system is clear and easy to use, and makes it easier to select the error type. We have not made a comparison of the point scores given, because the scale in the earlier scoring chart was from 1 to 9 as opposed to 2, 5 or 10 points in the new one. However, according to the feedback gathered from the assessors three times a year, there is no reason to believe that the change in the scale has led to failing a translation that would have been accepted using the previous scale.

The aim of our studies in this area has been to increase knowledge of the assessment of translations in examination settings, as well as to contribute to developing the assessment of the Finnish Authorized Translator's Examination. As terminology clearly seems to stand out as a problematic area, separating it as a category of its own might be considered when developing the error-based scoring chart in the future. In fact, in the MQM typology (Lommel et al. 2015), "terminology" is a category of its own, separate from "accuracy" and "fluency."

Another idea for developing the examination might be to consider the introduction of two levels of competence, as is the case in the NAATI system described earlier. The statistics (EDUFI 2019c) show that the passing rates of the examination have varied between 8% and 29.9%. The acceptance threshold must be high, as the examination is used to "sort the wheat from the chaff." As Miettunen (2017, 74) puts it, the resulting translation must be "nearly errorless." The translations approved need to render the contents of the ST and reflect the legal system of the source culture, and they need to be accurate and precise. Yet, although all translators are not always able to produce a "nearly errorless" translation, they may be able to produce a translation that is suitable for some other purpose than serving as a legally valid document. Therefore, an authorization with two levels of competence might be an idea worth considering: one level for producing legally valid translations that need to reflect the legal system of the source culture, and the other level for translating "in general," where localizing the text for the target reader is possible. It might also be worth thinking about replacing one of the translation tests with a revision test in line with NAATI (see Section 1.2.2). In real situations where no *one* person has all the knowledge needed, cooperation between a Finnish native translator and an English native reviser (or vice versa) could be a solution. Revision is also a compulsory part of the translation process described in the ISO 17100 standard, and revising skills are equally relevant for the growing practice of post-editing of machine translation. Therefore, it might be a good idea to test revision skills in the examinations.

The assessment of translations in the NAATI examination is criterion-based, which shows that criterion-based assessment can function in certification settings. However, an error-based system also enables detailed feedback to the examinees about the issues that are problematic in their translations. Should a switch to criterion-based assessment be considered, it should be ensured that similar feedback can still be provided to the examinees.

A survey to practicing authorized translators was conducted in 2018 (see Oksanen and Santalahti 2020), and another one was carried out among those who took the exam in November 2019 (see Kivilehto 2020). The translations in the examination are assessed anonymously, and we do not have background information on the examinees (for example, whether they are translating into their first or second language), but we hope to explore their educational background and their reasons for taking the exam. The experienced assessors have the gut feeling that there are candidates who are bilingual or subject experts in a field, but do not have a background in language studies or translating, and who come to "try their luck" (Kemppanen 2017, 58–59; also Hiirikoski 2017, 43). Kemppanen (2017, 58) also points out that as translators with university training now have the possibility of getting the official accreditation in the language pair of their translation studies, the examinees are more likely not to be formally trained in translation and therefore may not have the necessary skills to pass the exam.

Our plans also include a qualitative analysis on the application of the new scoring chart (Kivilehto 2019), to shed light on the difference shown in Table 1.5. Assessment is always subjective, at least to some extent. However, when assessment criteria and error classification categories are clearly defined, this hopefully leads to more uniformity, impartiality and equality in assessment. The criteria should be comprehensible and easy to use, and we believe that this can best be achieved in cooperation with those who apply them – by taking a user-centered perspective.

## Note

1 Up to 2017, the EDUFI used the English abbreviation FNBE.

## References

A 1232/2007 = *Valtioneuvoston asetus auktorisoiduista kääntäjistä* [Government Decree on Authorised Translators]. Accessed June 30, 2019. http://www.finlex.fi/fi/laki/ajantasa/2007/20071232.

Angelelli, Claudia V. 2009. "Using a rubric to assess translation ability: Defining the construct." In *Testing and Assessment in Translation and Interpreting Studies: A Call for Dialogue between Research and Practice*, edited by Claudia V. Angelelli and Holly E. Jacobson, 13–47. Amsterdam: John Benjamins.

Angelelli, Claudia V., and Holly E. Jacobson, eds. 2009. *Testing and Assessment in Translation and Interpreting Studies: A Call for Dialogue between Research and Practice*. Amsterdam: John Benjamins.

ATA (American Translators Association). 2017. *ATA Certification Program Framework for Standardized Error Marking Version 2017*. Accessed June 30, 2019. https://www.atanet.org/certification/Framework_2017.pdf.

EDUFI (The Finnish National Agency for Education). 2019a. *Auktorisoidun kääntäjän tutkinto* [The Authorized Translator's Examination]. Accessed July 30, 2019. https://www.oph.fi/fi/palvelut/auktorisoidun-kaantajan-tutkinto.

EDUFI (The Finnish National Agency for Education). 2019b. *Arvioijan käsikirja 2018. Auktorisoidun kääntäjän tutkinto. Toimintaohjeet tutkintotehtävien arvioijalle* [Handbook for Assessors 2018. Authorized Translator's Examination. Instruction for Assessors of the Examination Assignments]. Helsinki: Opetushallitus.

EDUFI (The Finnish National Agency for Education). 2019c. Auktorisoidun kääntäjän tutkinnon tulokset 2008–2018 [Results of the Authorized Translator's Examinations 2008–2018]. Accessed September 29, 2019. PDF available via https://www.oph.fi/fi/palvelut/auktorisoidun-kaantajan-tutkinto.

FNBE (The Finnish National Board of Education). 2012. *Qualification Requirements for Authorized Translators' Examinations 2012.* Regulations and Guidelines 22/011/2012. Accessed June 30, 2019. https://www.oph.fi/download/191792_qualificationrequirements.pdf.

Gouadec, Daniel. 2010. "Quality in translation." In *Handbook of Translation Studies*, edited by Yves Gambier, and Luc van Doorslaer, 270–275. Amsterdam: John Benjamins.

Hale, Sandra B., Ignacio Garcia, Jim Hlavac, Mira Kim, Miranda Lai, Barry Turner, and Helen Slatyer. 2012. *Improvements to NAATI Testing. Development of a Conceptual Overview for a New Model for NAATI Standards, Testing and Assessment. The National Accreditation Authority for Translators and Interpreters (NAATI).* Accessed March 13, 2020. https://www.naati.com.au/media/1062/intfinalreport.pdf.

Hiirikoski, Juhani. 2017. "Lain ja hallinnon käännöstehtävät englannin kielessä" [Translation tasks in the special field law and administration, with reference to translating from and into English.] In *Auktorisoidun kääntäjän tutkinnon historiaa ja nykypäivää* [The Authorized Translator's Examination: Past and Present], edited by Tarja Leblay, 37–48. Opetushallitus, Raportit ja selvitykset 2017:16. Accessed March 13, 2020. https://www.oph.fi/fi/tilastot-ja-julkaisut/julkaisut/auktorisoidun-kaantajan-tutkinnon-historiaa-ja-nykypaivaa.

Hjort-Pedersen, Mette. 2016. "Free vs. faithful – Towards identifying the relationship between academic and professional criteria for legal translation." *English Language Overseas Perspectives and Enquiries* 13(2): 225–239. doi:10.4312/elope.13.2.225-239.

House, Juliane. 2015. *Translation Quality Assessment. Past and Present.* Abingdon: Routledge.

Kemppanen, Hannu. 2017. "Auktorisoidun kääntäjän tutkinnon tehtävien laadinta ja arviointi: venäjän kielen näkökulma." [Preparing and assessing translations for the Authorized Translator's Examination: The Russian language perspective.] In *Auktorisoidun kääntäjän tutkinnon historiaa ja nykypäivää* [The Authorized Translator's Examination: Past and Present], edited by Tarja Leblay, 49–60. Opetushallitus, Raportit ja selvitykset 2017:16. Accessed September 29, 2019. https://www.oph.fi/fi/tilastot-ja-julkaisut/julkaisut/auktorisoidun-kaantajan-tutkinnon-historiaa-ja-nykypaivaa.

Kivilehto, Marja. 2016. "*Käännösfunktion huomiotta jättäminen, joka johtaa epätäsmälliseen lopputulokseen.* Auktorisoidun kääntäjän tutkinnon käännöstehtävien arvioinnista." [*The translation function is disregarded, leading to an inadequate result.* On assessing translation assignments in the authorised translator's examination]. In *Text and Textuality. VAKKI Publications* 7, edited by Pia Hirvonen, Daniel Rellstab, and Nestori Siponkoski, 391–401. Vaasa: University of Vaasa. Accessed October 4, 2019. http://www.vakki.net/publications/no7_eng.html.

Kivilehto, Marja. 2017. "Miten auktorisoidun kääntäjän tutkinnon käännöstehtävät vastaavat tutkinnon tavoitteita erikoisalojen kääntämisen näkökulmasta?" [How do the translation assignments in the authorised translator's examination meet the requirements of the examination from the point of view of specialised translation?]. In *MikaEL. Electronic Journal of the KäTu Symposium on Translation and Interpreting Studies*, edited by Ritva Hartama-Heinonen, Marja Kivilehto, Liisa Laukkanen, and Minna Ruokonen, Vol. 10,

136–149. Accessed October 4, 2019. https://www.sktl.fi/liitto/seminaarit/mikael-verkkojulkaisu/.

Kivilehto, Marja. 2019. "Mellan uppgifts-och examenskontext. Var befinner sig examinanden?" [Between the assignment and examination contexts. Where is the examinee?]. Presentation at the Conference of *Svenskans beskrivning 37* in Turku, May 10, 2019.

Kivilehto, Marja. 2020. "'Vahvistan, että tämä käännös on …'. Autenttisuuden dilemma(ko?) auktorisoidun kääntäjän tutkinnossa" ['I confirm that this translation is …'. Dilemma (?) of authenticity in Authorized Translator's Examination]. Presentation at *Symposium 2020 – Workplace Communication III. XXXX International VAKKI Symposium*. February 6–7, 2020 in Vaasa, Finland.

Kivilehto, Marja, and Leena Salmi. 2017. "Assessing Assessment: The Authorized Translator's Examination in Finland." *Linguistica Antverpensia, New Series: Themes in Translation Studies* 16: 57–70.

Koby, Geoffrey S., Paul Fields, Daryl Hague, Arle Lommel, and Alan Melby. 2014. "Defining translation quality." *Revista Tradumatica* 12, 413–420.

L 1231/2007 = *Laki auktorisoiduista kääntäjistä* [Act on authorised translators]. Accessed June 30, 2019. http://www.finlex.fi/fi/laki/ajantasa/2007/20071231.

Lommel, Arle, Aljoscha Burchardt, Attila Görög, Hans Uszkoreit, and Alan Melby, eds. 2015. "Multidimensional quality metrics (MQM) issue types." Accessed September 28, 2019. http://www.qt21.eu/mqm-definition/definition-2015-12-30.html.

Miettunen, Markku. 2017. "Englanti: kokemuksia talouselämän erikoisalasta." [English: Experiences on assessing translations in the special field of economics]. In *Auktorisoidun kääntäjän tutkinnon historiaa ja nykypäivää* [The Authorized Translator's Examination: Past and Present], edited by Tarja Leblay, 67–74. Opetushallitus, Raportit ja selvitykset 2017:16. Accessed September 29, 2019. https://www.oph.fi/fi/tilastot-ja-julkaisut/julkaisut/auktorisoidun-kaantajan-tutkinnon-historiaa-ja-nykypaivaa.

NAATI (National Accreditation Authority for Translators and Interpreters). 2020a. *Certified Translator*. Accessed July 1, 2019. https://www.naati.com.au/certification/certification-testing/certified-translator/.

NAATI (National Accreditation Authority for Translators and Interpreters). 2020b. *Descriptors for Translator Certifications*. Accessed 3 June 30, 2019. https://www.naati.com.au/media/1586/descriptors-for-translator-certifications-version-1-june-2017pdf.pdf.

NAATI (National Accreditation Authority for Translators and Interpreters). 2020c. *Certification Scheme Design Summary*. Accessed June 30, 2019. https://www.naati.com.au/media/2397/certification-scheme-design-summary_may2019.pdf.

NAATI (National Accreditation Authority for Translators and Interpreters). 2020d. *Certified Translator Test. Candidate Information*. Accessed June 30, 2019. https://www.naati.com.au/media/2232/ct_candidate_information.pdf.

NAATI (National Accreditation Authority for Translators and Interpreters). 2020e. *Certified Translator Test Assessment Rubrics*. Accessed June 30, 2019. https://www.naati.com.au/media/2231/ct_assessment_rubrics.pdf.

NAATI (National Accreditation Authority for Translators and Interpreters). 2020f. *Expression of Interest. NAATI Examiner Panels.* Accessed June 30, 2019. https://www.naati.com.au/media/1983/examiner-eoi-info-handout-18pdf.pdf.

NAATI (National Accreditation Authority for Translators and Interpreters). 2020g. *How Are Certification Tests Marked?* Accessed June 30, 2019. https://www.naati.com.au/certification/certification-testing/.

Oksanen, Henrik, and Miia Santalahti. 2020. "Auktorisoidun kääntämisen tila 2019. Kyselytutkimus auktorisoitujen käännösten tekstilajeista ja auktorisoidun kääntäjän ohjeiden käytöstä." [The status of authorized translating in 2019. Survey on text genres of legally valid translations and on using the instructions for authorized translators.] In *MikaEL, Electronic Journal of the KäTu Symposium on Translation and Interpreting Studies*, edited by Ritva Hartama-Heinonen, Laura Ivaska, Marja Kivilehto, and Minna Kujamäki, Vol. 13, 25–42. Accessed May 17, 2020. https://www.sktl.fi/liitto/seminaarit/mikael-verkkojulkaisu/.

Saldanha, Gabriela, and Sharon O'Brien. 2013. *Research Methodologies in Translation Studies.* London & New York: Routledge.

Salmi, Leena, and Tuija Kinnunen. 2015. "Training translators for accreditation in Finland." *The Interpreter and Translator Trainer,* 9 (2): 229–242.

Salmi, Leena, and Marja Kivilehto. 2018. "Translation quality assessment: Proposals for developing the authorised translator's examination in Finland." In *Legal Translation and Court Interpreting: Ethical Values, Quality, Competence Training*, edited by Annikki Liimatainen, Arja Nurmi, Marja Kivilehto, Leena Salmi, Anu Viljanmaa, and Melissa Wallace, 179–198. Berlin: Frank & Timme.

Salmi, Leena, and Ari Penttilä. 2013. "The system of authorizing translators in Finland." In *Assessment Issues in Language Translation and Interpreting*, edited by Dina Tsagari and Roeland van Deemter, 115–130. Frankfurt am Main: Peter Lang.

Suojanen, Tytti, Kaisa Koskinen, and Tiina Tuominen. 2015. *User-Centered Translation.* New York: Routledge.

Toury, Gideon. 2012. *Descriptive Translation Studies – and Beyond.* Revised 2nd edition. Amsterdam/Philadelphia: John Benjamins.

Turner, Barry, Miranda Lai, and Neng Huang. 2010. "Error Deduction and Descriptors – A Comparison of Two Methods of Translation Test Assessment." *Translation & Interpreting. The International Journal for Translation & Interpreting Research* 2(1): 11–23.

Vanden Bulcke, Patricia, and Armand Héroguel. 2011. "Quality issues in the field of legal translation." In *Perspectives on Translation Quality*, edited by Ilse Depraetere, 211–248. Berlin & Boston: De Gruyter Mouton.

# 2    Lexical Readability as an Indicator of Quality in Translation

## Best Practices from Swiss Legislation

*Paolo Canavese*

## 2.1  Background

Currently, the importance of striving for quality in institutional communication is indisputable. In recent decades, we have seen growing interest in making legal and administrative language more accessible, especially thanks to the emergence of plain language initiatives around the world (Adler 2012; DGT 2013). They kick-started prolific reflections within academia and different national and supranational institutions and propagated the idea that comprehensible law is not only possible, but can also be considered a civil right (as the title of the volume edited by Eichhoff-Cyrus and Antos [2008] suggests).

The question of accessibility to the law is even more important in multilingual contexts, where, more often than not, a further layer is added between production and reception of a legal text: translation. Undoubtedly, translation makes the legislative process longer, more expensive and represents a potential source of mistakes and divergences between language versions. At the same time, however, the hypothesis that translation can serve as a catalyst for clear legislation is widespread in the literature. It claims that the "cognitive elaboration in another language" (Mori 2018, 238) required by translation can help identify shortcomings in the linguistic formulation of a norm and improve both the source and the target texts. Therefore, it is no coincidence that quality has attained a central position in legal translation studies (Prieto Ramos 2015, 12) and has attracted the attention of many multilingual institutional settings such as Switzerland (Egger and Ferrari 2016, 505–507).

This chapter aims to show that Swiss multilingual legislation can be taken as an example of clear legal drafting. With this in mind, Section 2.1.1 provides a brief overview of Swiss institutional multilingualism, explaining to what extent clarity is deep-rooted in Swiss legal culture and how recent developments might have contributed to further improve the quality of federal legislative acts. The idea of this chapter being to back up this theoretical stance with empirical data, Section 2.1.2 describes

DOI: 10.4324/9780429264894-2

how, within the scope of this study, lexical readability was selected as an indicator of the broader concept of "quality." Moving from the background illustrated in Section 2.1, Section 2.2 defines the methodology adopted in this study. The results are presented and discussed in detail in Section 2.3 and some concluding remarks are offered in Section 2.4. This chapter is part of a broader corpus-based study that takes into account a much wider range of readability and comprehensibility aspects of Swiss legislation.

### 2.1.1 Swiss Multilingual Legislation and Clarity

Switzerland is a quadrilingual country, where German, French and Italian are both national and official languages, whereas Romansh is a national language only.[1] Legislation is published simultaneously and is equally binding in the three official languages,[2] whereas Romansh versions only exist for a limited number of important legislative acts and have a mere informative function. Once published, legislative acts are equally authentic and it is not possible to distinguish between the source and the target text, or even to refer to them as such. However, as it is also the case of other multilingual institutional contexts, such as the EU institutions (Felici 2010), translation is an essential step to ensure multilingual law-making. Due to the position of Italian as a minority language, Swiss federal legislation is almost always drafted in German, to a lesser extent in French or co-drafted in these two languages and then translated into Italian (Zwicky and Kübler 2018, 17–21).

Analyzing and contrasting how drafting (and translation) quality is pursued in multilingual institutional settings are key to exchanging best practices. From this perspective, the Swiss context can offer interesting insights. In fact, Switzerland has a long tradition of clear legal drafting, as shown by the principle of "popular law" which inspired the founding father of the Swiss Civil Code, Eugen Huber, at the beginning of the 20th century. Huber (1914, 12) believed that the law must be accessible not only to the professionals who are called to interpret and implement it but also to all who are subject to it, as far as the subject matter allows for it. This principle has never faded since and still guides the drafting work of the Federal Administration and Federal Assembly today.[3]

In recent decades, various steps have been taken toward an even clearer legislation, which have not only helped to consolidate Huber's principle but also to improve the quality of legal and institutional texts in the "third language." Italian was fully equalized, at least *de jure*, to the other two official languages in 1974.[4] Since the 1970s, however, the way in which federal authorities produce, or translate, legislation and other institutional texts in Italian has changed significantly. This study and, more broadly, the research project it belongs to aim to empirically track the effects of this progressive change on the linguistic side of Swiss federal legislation. For this purpose, a corpus covering the period 1974–2018 was compiled (see Section 2.2) and divided into three sub-periods. These sub-periods show the main developmental phases marking clarity awareness and the importance of Italian as an official language. The evolution from a period to the next is gradual and the transition is blurred. As such, the three periods mainly respond to a practical need and should not be taken as watertight compartments.

Period 1 (1974–1992) corresponds to the beginning of full institutional trilingualism. During those years, the volume of legislative acts was small and few translators dealt with their translation into Italian (Egger 2011, 41). Institutional texts in Italian used an artificial language, far from common use, and were extremely influenced by the German source text (Berruto 1984). Borrowing Fantuzzi's metaphor (1995, 444), they were born *in vitro*. From the 1990s, the first measures toward a broader reflection around quality-related questions started to appear. In 1990, the first issue of *LeGes*, a journal specialized in the quality of Swiss legislation, was published. In the same period, the translation sector underwent deep reorganization efforts. This is the main feature of period 2 (1993–2006), which was characterized by a better definition of structures, processes and competences aimed at making translation more efficient (Pini 2017, 115–116). These efforts enabled the recruitment of more Italian-language translators.

At the beginning of the 21st century, the interest in assuring quality in legislation became particularly evident. Guidelines on legal drafting started to be produced and seminars on legistics, legal translation and terminology[5] to be organized. Moreover, the Italian Division of the Central Language Services at the Federal Chancellery became a member of the Network for the Excellence of Institutional Italian (REI). All these changes led to period 3 (2007–2018), when the status of Italian was further consolidated and the concern for quality gained a central position. The success of these measures was confirmed by Berruto (2012), who, some 30 years after his first observations, reported big steps forward in the quality of Swiss institutional Italian. In particular, one could set the beginning of period 3 in 2007, when the concern for quality was first enshrined in the law:

> Art. 7 Comprehensibility
> [1] The federal authorities shall endeavour to ensure that their language is appropriate, clear and comprehensible and shall ensure that gender-appropriate wording is used.
> [2] The Federal Council shall take the measures required; in particular, it shall arrange for the basic and advanced training of employees and the provision of the required aids.

The legal provision of clarity and comprehensibility expressed in art. 7 of the Languages Act of 2007 (CC *441.1*), and reiterated in art. 2 para. 2

of the Languages Ordinance of 2010 (CC *441.11*), testifies to what extent clarity is a precondition in Swiss institutional communication.

Using these contextual elements, this study sets out to provide empirical evidence to confirm that Swiss legislation in Italian is, in reality, clear. It also intends to shed light on how the historical developments outlined earlier might have contributed to improving its quality. To date, little empirical research has been conducted in this field. Uhlmann (2014, 177–178) calls for more studies in the field of (computational) linguistics aiming to assess the level of linguistic clarity of Swiss legislation. Berruto (2012, 14), an attentive observer of the dynamics of Swiss Italian, also stresses the diachronic dimension and the need for more corpus-based quantitative studies on the quality of Swiss institutional Italian. The analyses presented in this chapter provide some answers to these *desiderata*.

### 2.1.2 *Operationalizing the Concept of Quality*

Quality is a very broad concept with multiple facets. Only by combining reflections on context, competence and product may we draw a comprehensive overview of the level of quality of a legal (translated) text, as encapsulated in the holistic approach proposed by Prieto Ramos (2015). Any analysis of the product, as is the case of the study described in this chapter, cannot be isolated from the other quality-related aspects. Previous research has concentrated, for example, on equivalence, consistency, textual fit and clarity (Biel 2017), legal terminology consistency and adequacy (Prieto Ramos and Guzmán 2018) or compliance to existing guidelines, an essential tool in institutional translation to ensure quality and efficiency (Svoboda 2017, 76–79).

In this study, Swiss legislative acts are investigated in the light of their linguistic accessibility. Accessibility is not meant in the sense of *Leichte Sprache* (Bredel and Maaß 2016), i.e. an easy-to-read variety of language that can be understood by people with cognitive and learning disabilities or with low language proficiency. The focus is rather on *Einfache Sprache* (ibid., 526–533), plain (legal) language (Adler 2012) and *bürgernahe Rechts- und Verwaltungssprache* (Eichhoff-Cyrus and Antos 2008, part 3). These three, largely overlapping concepts refer to another type of complexity reduction, i.e. avoiding unnecessary complexity without having to compromise the content level. This can also be referred to as "clarity." In the legal field, clarity is a double-sided definition, as explained by Flückiger and Grodecki (2017, 33):

> On qualifiera [...] de clarté linguistique la propriété d'un texte de loi d'être formulé de manière compréhensible pour ses destinataires et de clarté normative celle d'un texte de loi d'être formulé de sorte à y lire – et comprendre – directement et facilement la norme à suivre dans un cas concret.[6]

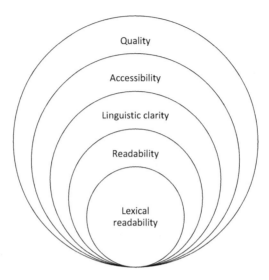

*Figure 2.1* Lexical readability as an indicator of quality.

Only the side of linguistic clarity is examined in this study.

The concept of quality has been operationalized, within the scope of this chapter, by some specific aspects of lexical readability, as exemplified in Figure 2.1. Linguistic clarity can be defined as the combination of two elements: readability and comprehensibility (Piemontese 1996, 79–122). Readability is a quantitative measure that focuses on different levels of language. It includes analyses on the shallow level of a text, i.e. sentence and word length, and can be assessed *via* different formulae, as the Gunning Fog Index or, specifically for the Italian language, the Gulpease Index. Readability can be also investigated on the lexical and syntactic level, taking into account aspects like the use of a basic vocabulary, syntactic dependencies or the use of subordination. Comprehensibility, in contrast, deals more with qualitative aspects such as the logical structure of a text, its production and reception and, consequently, varies according to those participating in a communicative act. Thus, the willingness of the addressees to understand the text, as well as their previous knowledge of the subject matter, and of the producer to make themselves understood are central elements of comprehensibility.

## 2.2 Methodology

To check whether and how the lexical profile of Swiss federal legislation has been simplified over recent decades, a corpus study was undertaken through the analysis of LEX.CH.IT, a corpus of Swiss legislation in Italian covering the third language regime.[7] It comprises all federal legislative acts passed between 1974 and 2018, for a total of 366 texts and over 1.1 million tokens. It is divided into three subcorpora that correspond to the three periods described in Section 2.1.1.

A review of the main guidelines on clear legal drafting and of previous studies on legal Italian inspired the methodological framework of this study. These works primarily recommend that legislative texts should use current and modern vocabulary (Federal Office of Justice 2007, 381) and avoid archaic and complex words and expressions that do not fulfill any denotative purpose (Borghi 2011, 323; Serianni 2012, 91–93) to be accessible. A two-step, mostly quantitative analysis looked at whether and to what extent Swiss legislation follows these preconditions.

The use of modern vocabulary was investigated by running a comparison of LEX.CH.IT with two lexicons: the *Vocabolario di base della lingua italiana* (Basic Italian Vocabulary, "BIV," De Mauro 1980; 2016) and the *Lessico di frequenza dell'italiano parlato nella Svizzera italiana* (Frequency Lexicon of Spoken Swiss Italian, "LIPSI," Pandolfi 2009). The BIV consists of a list of approximately 7,000 words commonly used by Italian native speakers and accessible to the general public. Since the publication of its first version in 1980, it has been used in a large number of readability studies and is included in most available tools for automatic readability assessment.[8] The LIPSI comprises approximately 13,000 lemmas and is the only lexicon developed with a focus on the Swiss variety of Italian. More specifically, it captures spontaneous spoken and broadcasting language. To run the comparison, LEX.CH.IT was automatically lemmatized with the help of the POS-tagger TagAnt (Anthony 2015) and the output was used as a basis to create a wordlist of lemmas. The automatic comparison of this wordlist with the BIV and the LIPSI made it possible to create a list of difficult words used in Swiss legislation, calculate their percentage and carry out further qualitative analyses.

Regarding the use of archaic and complex words and expressions, a bottom-up approach was adopted. The guidelines and previous studies mentioned earlier often comprise examples of archaic and complex words to be used with care. They were collected in a list of approximately 180 items[9] and sorted out in different categories. This study took into account a specific category of functional words, i.e. "archaic connectives." The concordance function of AntConc (Anthony 2018) was used to count their occurrences across three subcorpora and to check the contexts in which they were used. The log likelihood ratio significance test (Rayson and Garside 2000) was used to define relevant diachronic trends.[10]

## 2.3 Results and Discussion

### 2.3.1 Use of Current and Modern Vocabulary

Investigating to what extent Swiss legislative acts make use of current and modern vocabulary helps to get a first image of their lexical profile. The results of the automatic comparison of LEX.CH.IT with the BIV and the LIPSI are displayed in Table 2.1.

*Table 2.1* Percentage of BIV and LIPSI words in LEX.CH.IT

| Readability indicator | P1 | P2 | P3 |
| --- | --- | --- | --- |
| BIV % | 49.23 | 46.40 | 48.94 |
| LIPSI % | 63.49 | 62.16 | 63.63 |
| BIV+LIPSI % | 67.22 | 65.72 | 67.01 |

Almost five lemmas out of ten belong to the BIV and more than six to the LIPSI. Overall, these figures indicate a high level of lexical readability. Besides, the lack of diachronic development suggests that this has always been a feature of Swiss legislation.[11] A comparison with other readability studies available in the literature fully confirms these assumptions. For instance, Venturi (2013, 150) analyzed a corpus of Italian legislation and found out that only around 20% of its vocabulary belongs to the BIV. Preliminary findings from another unpublished study (Canavese and Felici 2019), in which LEX.CH.IT was compared with the corpora of the Eurolect Observatory Project (Mori 2018), point to the same outcome. They suggest that Swiss legislation has a higher percentage of basic vocabulary compared to EU directives, to their transposition measures in the Italian legislation and to Italian domestic legislation without any link to EU law (i.e. corpus A, B and C of the Eurolect Observatory Project). In fact, only 30–35% of the vocabulary of these three corpora belongs to the BIV. Of course, comparing corpora that have been assembled and analyzed by different researchers for different purposes requires caution. Regarding the aims of this chapter, it is important to highlight the existence of a wide gap between the figures related to Swiss legislation and to other varieties of legal Italian. This gap supports the hypothesis that Swiss law is lexically accessible.

An excerpt of the Federal Act on Geoinformation is reported here to exemplify the type of non-common words that appear in Swiss legislation according to the two lexicons. Non-BIV words are marked in bold and non-LIPSI ones in italics. Observing this example, as well as the analysis of the 100 most frequent non-BIV and non-LIPSI lemmas, contributed to expanding the interpretation of the quantitative data reported earlier.

(1) Art. 2 Campo d'applicazione

[1] La presente legge si applica ai *geodati* di base di diritto federale.

[2] Si applica ad altri *geodati* della **Confederazione**, sempre che la *rimanente* **legislazione** federale non disponga altrimenti.

[3] Le prescrizioni in materia di *geodati* si applicano per *analogia* anche ai dati *geologici* della **Confederazione**.

[4] I capitoli 3, 4 e 5 sono *poziori* alle prescrizioni *derogatorie* di altre leggi federali.[12]

First, it must be noted that the BIV was not developed with a focus on Switzerland. This is illustrated, for instance, by the fact that the word *Confederazione* is not contained in it. Many other words related to the administrative, cultural and geographical peculiarities of Switzerland, such as *Cantone*, *franco* and *Berna*, are missing in the BIV, although they are likely to be perfectly understood and actively used by any italophone living in Switzerland. In light of this diatopic difference between the language variety of the corpus under analysis and the lexicon used, the high percentage of BIV words found in LEX.CH.IT is still more meaningful. A similar consideration can be put forward concerning the non-overlapping diamesic and diastratic dimensions captured by LEX.CH.IT and the LIPSI. The former is a corpus of written texts produced by highly qualified civil servants, while the latter is based on a corpus of oral texts produced by a heterogeneous sample of speakers. This difference in language variety makes the high scores obtained in the first step of this study even more surprising.

Among the non-basic words, some specialized lexis is worth noting. A number of legal words and expressions are found such as *legislazione*, *per analogia*, *poziore* and *prescrizioni derogatorie* ("legislation," "by analogy," "preferential," "derogating provisions"). It is not always straightforward to draw a line between terms, pseudo-terms, phraseology and superfluous archaisms. More interdisciplinary research involving linguists, legal drafters and legal experts could help determine whether and how these lexical items can actually be simplified. At the same time, terminology is a key element of any language for specific purposes and it is not always possible, or even desirable, to simplify it. In the legal field, this could undermine the accuracy of a legislative act and result in a reduction of normative clarity. It was expected that both the BIV and the LIPSI would treat legal terms as difficult lexical items. Indeed, these two lexicons were modeled around the general language and the effect of this diaphasic difference is not surprising.

Besides legal terminology, some terms have also been found that belong to other specialized fields regulated by the law such as economics and finance, technology, social security, medicine, pharmacy and migration. In example (1), the term *geodato* illustrates this, even if article 3 of the same act provides an explanation for it:

> (2) geodati: dati **georeferenziati** che descrivono, con un determinato riferimento temporale, l'estensione e le caratteristiche di determinati spazi e opere, **segnatamente** la posizione, la natura, l'**utilizzazione** e i rapporti giuridici[13]

The strategy of defining key terms is often proposed to explain difficult or obscure terms in a specialized text, although in legislative acts definitions have the drawback of making the interpretation of the norm less flexible (Sabatini 1990, 702). Whether, however, in this specific case, the explanation reported in (2) really enables the general public to grasp the meaning of *geodata* is another question that goes beyond the domain of readability and touches upon comprehensibility. For this type of terms, the same considerations formulated in relation to legal terminology hold true.

A last category to be discussed concerns complex and archaic words which, unlike legal and technical terms, could be more easily simplified such as *segnatamente* and *utilizzazione* ("notably," "usage") in example (2). These two words, like many others, are contained in the LIPSI, but not in the BIV. This might be due to the fact that the former was not developed with a view on text simplification in contrast to the latter.[14] In any case, some complex words may still be accessible thanks to some inference by the reader. *Utilizzazione*, for instance, shares the same root as the simpler variant *utilizzo*. On the other hand, the connective *sempre che* ("provided that") is considered easy to grasp, as both the adverb *sempre* ("always") and the conjunction *che* ("that") that constitute it are basic words. However, its alternative univerbated spelling *sempreché* is absent from both lexicons. This connective, which will be discussed in greater detail in Section 2.3.2, might therefore not be very accessible, although it is not seized by any of the two lexicons. This is the main downside of working with single words instead of phrasemes.

Another methodological limitation lies in the fact that the percentage values were calculated relying on an automatic comparison of the corpus with the two lexicons. As a consequence, it was not possible to capture the semantic value of each word. This is crucial in the case of legal language, which fully draws from common language to create its terminology. A same word can be easy to understand if it is used in a meaning and completely inaccessible if used in another, rare one.

Despite these limitations, which can also be seen as an inherent characteristic of quantitative research, the results presented in this section are a useful starting point to describe the lexical profile of Swiss legislation.

Two thirds of the vocabulary of LEX.CH.IT belong at least to one of the two lexicons, which suggests that Swiss legislation has always had a good level of quality in terms of lexical readability.

### 2.3.2 Use of Archaic Connectives

While the quantitative data discussed earlier point to a stable level of readability, investigating some specific complex lexical elements provides a more fine-grained image of how the level of readability changed throughout the period in question. The focus here is put on what Mortara Garavelli (2001, 155) defines as "bureaucratic fossils," i.e. complex and often archaic words and expressions that are overused in legal and administrative texts. They are preferred over their simpler variants because they serve to elevate the register, even if they do not fulfill any denotative purpose. There is a wide range of such elements that were classified by Serianni (2005, 127–159) under the umbrella term *tecnicismi collaterali* ("pseudo-technicisms"). They occur in many languages for specific purposes (LSPs), including legal language.[15] These phenomena range from micro-syntactic choices, such as the omission of indefinite articles and verbs with an unusual argument structure, to the use of complex prepositions and prepositional phrases and the preference for higher-register synonyms.

The last category is examined here with a particular focus on archaic connectives. The decision to concentrate on this subset of functional words was determined by the fact that, compared to other types of content words, connectives are more easily replaceable with more accessible synonyms. Observing how their frequency progressed over the three periods should provide a clue on whether making legislation linguistically more accessible is an actual concern. The results of this analysis are displayed in Table 2.2. The connectives analyzed are listed in column 1. Column 2 contains potential equivalent items that fulfill the same grammatical and syntactical function and convey the same meaning. Columns 3, 4 and 5 report the occurrences of each connective in the three periods, expressed in normalized frequencies per million words. The arrows in column 6 show if the use of an archaic connective decreased ($\downarrow$) in a statistically significant way, indicating a trend toward simplification, increased ($\uparrow$), indicating a trend toward complexification, or remained stable ($\rightarrow$). The direction of the arrow was determined based on the log likelihood ratio test, whose results are reported in columns 7 and 8.[16]

Overall, the archaic connectives analyzed show a decreasing frequency trend. *Allorché*, *onde* and *pertanto* disappeared in P3, *giusta*, *ove* and *ovvero* experienced a drastic drop and the use of *sempreché* and *qualora* decreased considerably. The only connective that does not show any statistically significant development is *allorquando*, whose

*Table 2.2* Distribution of archaic connectives across the subcorpora

| Connectives | Equivalents | Occurrences (nf pmw) | | | Trend | LL | |
|---|---|---|---|---|---|---|---|
| | | P1 | P2 | P3 | | P1 > P3 | P2 > P3 |
| *allorché* ("when")[a] | *quando* | 31 | 15 | 0 | ↓ | +14.51 | +7.66 |
| *allorquando* ("when") | *quando* | 6 | 11 | 3 | → | +0.41 | +1.79 |
| *giusta* ("under") | *secondo* | 982 | 380 | 17 | ↓ | +406.63 | +153.22 |
| *nonché* ("as well as") | *e, anche, inoltre* | 643 | 1,391 | 1,213 | ↑ | −58.90 | +4.78 |
| *onde* ("so as to") | *per* | 22 | 2 | 0 | ↓ | +10.15 | +1.09 |
| *ove* ("shoud it...") | *se (+ind.)* | 289 | 96 | 26 | ↓ | +85.94 | +16.12 |
| *ovvero* ("or") | *oppure/cioè,* | 193 | 19 | 3 | ↓ | +80.99 | +5.07 |
| *pertanto* ("therefore") | *perciò, quindi* | 19 | 17 | 0 | ↓ | +8.70 | +8.75 |
| *sempreché* ("provided that") | *se (+ind.)* | 205 | 212 | 67 | ↓ | +24.48 | +30.62 |
| *qualora* ("in the event that") | *se (+ ind.)* | 432 | 550 | 242 | ↓ | +18.04 | +47.76 |

a   The English translation is used to inform on the meaning of these connectives. However, it was not possible to find equivalents that also have the same usage label that all these connectives have in common, i.e. "archaic."

occurrences are very low in any case. *Nonché* is the only element that almost doubled its occurrences from P1 to P3. A study on a bilingual parallel corpus could illustrate whether this development is due to language contact: the presence of *nonché* in the Italian version of Swiss legislation might be determined by the use of *sowie* in the source text in German.

*Giusta* is probably the best example to illustrate the lexical simplification that intervened over the timespan examined. It is an archaic preposition that shares the same graphic form as the adjective *giusto* (right, correct) in feminine gender. This case of homography could lead to miscomprehension of a norm, like in example (3):

(3) Art. 41 Persone senza tirocinio e privatisti
   [1] Il maggiorenne, che non ha imparato la professione **giusta** la presente legge, è ammesso all'esame finale di tirocinio, se ha esercitato la professione almeno per un tempo pari a una volta e mezzo la durata prescritta del tirocinio.[17]

At a first reading, one could think that *giusta* qualifies the noun *professione* ("the right profession") and not grasp the syntactic relation between the nominal group *la presente legge* ("this act") that follows and the rest of the sentence.

Another case of potential ambiguity is represented by *ovvero*. In fact, it has a disjunctive function ("or") in the legal language and normally introduces an explanation in the common language ("that is").

(4) Art. 59 Competenze speciali della polizia
   [1] La polizia impedisce il proseguimento della rotta se accerta che il battello circola senza essere stato ammesso alla navigazione oppure che il suo stato o il suo carico mette in pericolo il traffico **ovvero** viola gravemente le prescrizioni sulla protezione dell'ambiente.[18]

The readers could misinterpret the sense of the norm and understand that the conditions or the cargo of a vessel are considered dangerous to traffic when they seriously violate environmental protection requirements. Of course, this would be an illogical interpretation and, at a second reading and with some inferential effort, they could reconstruct the sense of the norm: serious violations of environmental requirements are one of the three cases listed in this article in which the police shall stop the vessel.

Opting for a simple variant does not only resolve potentially ambiguous or unclear formulations, as in the two examples above, but might also contribute to simplifying syntax. The conditional conjunctions *ove*, *sempreché* and *qualora* are not only lexically more difficult than the conjunction *se* ("if") but also require the subjunctive instead of the indicative mood. In example (5), replacing *ove trattisi* with *se si tratta* (avoiding the enclitic form as well) makes the syntactic structure of the sentence much more accessible.

(5) Art. 89 Commissione di sorveglianza
   [2] Assiste il Consiglio federale in tutte le questioni finanziarie dell'assicurazione contro la disoccupazione, in particolare **ove trattisi** di modificare i tassi di contribuzione, nel qual caso ha essa stessa diritto di proposta, o di determinare le spese amministrative computabili delle casse.[19]

The aim of this section was not to propose to directly replace these archaic connectives with their easier variants,[20] but rather to show their diachronic development. The phase-out of most of these complex lexical elements is encouraging and indicates a clear intent to make legislation linguistically more accessible, even if the starting point was already good in terms of lexical readability, as suggested by the results discussed in the first step.

## 2.4 Conclusions

This chapter has attempted to show from both a theoretical and an empirical perspective that Switzerland can be considered as a model of clear legal drafting. Compared to other countries that are endeavoring to achieve clear legislation, such as Germany,[21] Switzerland can count on a much longer tradition in this field. The principle of "popular law," upon which the Swiss Civil Code of 1907 is founded, for example, was not a precondition for the German equivalent drafted at the same time (Flückiger 2016, 85). The fact that the Swiss Civil Code also served as a model for other countries (Jagmetti 2014, 35) and is considered as a source of inspiration for modern formal legal drafting (Flückiger and Delley 2006, 136–138) are two cases in point. Huber's ideal has survived until present day and has been revitalized and built on through recent measures. From the 1970s, quality awareness started to spread and various initiatives appeared toward a more efficient multilingual law-making process and better legal drafting and translation. They resulted in the legal provision of clarity and comprehensibility, that was integrated into the law in 2007, and served to enhance the quality of Swiss legal and institutional Italian.

The corpus study presented earlier has captured this twofold nature of drafting quality in Swiss legislation through linguistic data of lexical readability. Our quantitative and qualitative analyses show how the lexical profile of Swiss legislative acts has changed over the last 50 years. The first step of the analysis showed that, overall, Swiss legislation makes use of current vocabulary. This confirms the hypothesis that clarity has always been a central consideration of legal text quality in Switzerland. The second step presented a selection of ten archaic connectives. Their occurrences decreased throughout the three periods considered, thus testifying an intent to make legislation linguistically more accessible. This also shows that best practices in legal drafting and translation go hand in hand with a more accessible legislation and allow for smoother communication between the State and all linguistic communities. Of course, these conclusions are to be confirmed by analyzing additional aspects of readability and comprehensibility, such as further lexical features (other types of archaic and complex words or the use of foreign words), aspects related to syntactic complexity and information structure. While much interesting work lies ahead, this study has put together some first pieces of a much wider and more complex puzzle, which is the multifaceted field of quality in Swiss trilingual legislation.

## Notes

1 See art. 4 and 70 of the Swiss Constitution of 18 April 1999, status as of 1 January 2020, CC *101*.
2 See art. 14 of the Publications Act, status as of 26 November 2018, CC *170.512*.

3 Huber's recommendations, like "three paragraphs per article, one sentence per paragraph, one idea per sentence at most" and, more generally, the principle of "popular law" itself, became a rule of thumb and are integrated in the existing guidelines for legal drafting, as the *Guide de législation* (Federal Office of Justice 2007, 359).

4 Italian was first recognized as a Swiss national language in the 1848 Constitution and, since then, its status has constantly improved. For a historical overview, see Pini (2017).

5 See https://www.bk.admin.ch/bk/fr/home/documentation/seminaires-et-cours. html (last accessed 3 January 2020).

6 "Linguistic clarity is the property of a legal text to be formulated in such a way as to be comprehensible to its addressees, whereas normative clarity is the property of a legislative act to be formulated in such a way as to read – and understand – directly and easily the norm to be followed in a specific case" (our translation).

7 Canavese (2019) offers an in-depth description of LEX.CH.IT, an overview of the project this chapter is drawn from, and indicates potential future applications of this corpus.

8 Two examples are the online tool Corrige (http://www.corrige.it/) and READ-IT, an NLP tool developed at the ILC in Pisa (described in Dell'Orletta, Montemagni and Venturi 2011).

9 An alternative method could have consisted in detecting these items manually, resorting to the frequency list of LEX.CH.IT and analyzing, for instance, the 1,000 most frequent words. This method, however, has a major drawback, i.e. it is not always easy to state intuitively what is a complex or archaic word and what is not.

10 Setting a significance level of $\alpha = 0.1$. This means that if the result of the test is over 6.63, there is a probability of 1% that the observed differences are due to chance ($p < 0.01$).

11 The three subcorpora have slightly different sizes. To make sure that this does not influence the results presented here, the same analysis was carried out based on a sample of 300,000 randomly selected tokens and on the 3,000 most frequent lemma types for each subcorpus. Regardless of the methodology adopted, the percentage of BIV and LIPSI words is stable throughout the three periods.

12 "Art. 2 Scope / [1] This Act is valid for official geodata under federal legislation. / [2] It is valid for other federal geodata provided its use is not regulated by other federal legislation. / [3] The regulations for geodata apply by analogy to federal geological data. / [4] The Third, Fourth and Fifth Chapters hereof shall take priority over divergent provisions of other federal acts" (official, non-binding translation in English, reference in LEX.CH.IT: 20071005_LGI).

13 "*geodata* means geospatial data that is related in time to the dimensions and characteristics of certain spaces and objects and in particular their position, nature, use and legal relationships" (see previous note).

14 For instance, the comprehensibility tests carried out to develop the BIV were not part of the LIPSI project.

15 Cortelazzo (2008) tested Serianni's classification on legal language and confirmed its validity. Further empirical studies have been conducted, for instance, by Rovere (2005).

16 In case of a statistically significant development from P1 to P3, an upward or downward arrow was attributed. A rightward arrow indicates, on the contrary, a non-statistically significant development from P1 to P3.

17 "Art. 41 Persons not having completed an apprenticeship and self-learners / [1] An adult who has not learned the profession pursuant to the Act is admitted

to the final examination of the apprenticeship if he or she has practiced the profession for a period of one and a half times the duration of the apprenticeship" (Vocational and Professional Education and Training Act of 19 April 1978, reference in LEX.CH.IT: 19780419_LPF, our translation).

18 "Art. 59 Special police competences / [1] The police shall prevent the continuation of the course if they ascertain that the vessel is sailing without having been admitted to navigation or that its condition or cargo is endangering traffic or seriously violating environmental protection requirements" (Federal Act on Inland Navigation, reference in LEX.CH.IT: 19751003_navigazione_interna, our translation).

19 "Article 89 Supervisory Board / [2] It assists the Federal Council in all financial matters relating to unemployment insurance, in particular when it comes to changing contribution rates, in which case it has the right to make proposals itself, or to determine the eligible administrative costs of the funds" (Federal Act on Compulsory Unemployment Insurance and Insolvency Benefits, reference in LEX.CH.IT: 19820625_LAD, our translation).

20 Visconti (2009), for instance, argues that some conditional connectives which seem to be equivalents can have a different degree of coercive strength (*nella misura in cui* vs. *a condizione che*) or indicate a different degree of probability (*nell'ipotesi che* vs. *nel caso in cui*).

21 In 2019, for instance, the German National Regulatory Control Council (Nationaler Normenkontrollrat) commissioned a report (*Erst der Inhalt, dann die Paragrafen*) on current law-making processes in Germany. It contains a state of the art and some recommendations (see https://www.normenkontrollrat.bund.de/nkr-de/service/publikationen/gutachten/nkr-gutachten-2019-erst-der-inhalt-dann-die-paragrafen--1680554, accessed 8 January 2020).

# References

Adler, Mark. 2012. "The Plain Language Movement." In *Oxford Handbooks in Linguistics Series*, edited by Lawrence M. Solan and Peter M. Tiersma, 67–83. Oxford/New York: Oxford University Press. doi:10.1093/oxfordhb/9780199572120.013.0006.

Anthony, Laurence. 2015. *TagAnt* (version 1.2.0). Windows. Tokyo: Waseda University. https://www.laurenceanthony.net/software.

Anthony, Laurence. 2018. *AntConc* (version 3.5.7). Windows. Tokyo: Waseda University. https://www.laurenceanthony.net/software.

Berruto, Gaetano. 1984. "Appunti sull'italiano elvetico." *Studi linguistici italiani* 10: 76–108.

Berruto, Gaetano. 2012. "L'italiano degli svizzeri." Paper presented at Nuit des Langues, Berne, November 8. https://m4.ti.ch/fileadmin/DECS/DCSU/AC/OLSI/documenti/BERRUTO-2012-Italiano-degli-svizzeri-Berna-conferenza.pdf.

Biel, Łucja. 2017. "Quality in Institutional EU Translation. Parameters, Policies and Practices." In *Quality Aspects in Institutional Translation*, edited by Tomáš Svoboda, Łucja Biel and Krzysztof Łoboda, 31–57. Berlin: Language Science Press. doi:10.5281/zenodo.1048183.

Borghi, Marco. 2011. "Riflessioni sull'uso dell'italiano nella legislazione svizzera." In *Mehrsprachige Gesetzgebung in der Schweiz. Juristisch-linguistische Untersuchungen von mehrsprachigen Rechtstexten des Bundes und der Kantone*, edited by Rainer J. Schweizer and Marco Borghi, 319–334. Zurich: Dike.

Bredel, Ursula, and Christiane Maaß. 2016. *Leichte Sprache. Theoretische Grundlagen Orientierung für die Praxis*. Berlin: Duden.

Canavese, Paolo. 2019. "LEX.CH.IT: A Corpus for Micro-Diachronic Linguistic Investigations of Swiss Normative Acts in Italian." *Comparative Legilinguistics* 40: 44–65. doi:10.14746/cl.2019.40.3.

Canavese, Paolo, and Annarita Felici. 2019. "Plain Legal Language through Translation: a Comparison of EU, Swiss and Italian Legislative Texts." Paper presented at the 1st International Conference of the Austrian Association for Legal Linguistics. Vienna, November 8–10.

Cortelazzo, Michele A. 2008. "Fenomenologia dei tecnicismi collaterali. Il settore giuridico." In *Prospettive nello studio del lessico italiano: atti del IX Congresso SILFI*, edited by Emanuela Cresti, 137–140. Florence: FUP.

De Mauro, Tullio. 1980. *Guida all'uso delle parole*. 1st ed. Rome: Editori Riuniti.

De Mauro, Tullio. 2016. "Il Nuovo vocabolario di base della lingua italiana." *Internazionale*, December 23. https://www.internazionale.it/opinione/tullio-de-mauro/2016/12/23/il-nuovo-vocabolario-di-base-della-lingua-italiana.

Dell'Orletta, Felice, Simonetta Montemagni, and Giulia Venturi. 2011. "READ-IT: Assessing Readability of Italian Texts with a View to Text Simplification." In *Proceedings of the 2nd Workshop on Speech and Language Processing for Assistive Technologies*, edited by Norman Alm, 73–83. Association for Computational Linguistics. https://www.aclweb.org/anthology/W11-2308/.

DGT. 2013. *Document Quality Control in Public Administrations and International Organisations*. Luxembourg: Publications Office of the European Union.

Egger, Jean-Luc. 2011. "Le regole per la redazione dei testi ufficiali in italiano." In *Il linguaggio e la qualità delle leggi*, edited by Raffaele Libertini, 41–50. Padua: CLEUP.

Egger, Jean-Luc, and Angela Ferrari. 2016. "L'italiano federale svizzero: elementi per una ricognizione." *Studi italiani di linguistica teorica e applicata* 45(3): 499–523.

Eichhoff-Cyrus, Karin M., and Gerd Antos, eds. 2008. *Verständlichkeit als Bürgerrecht? Die Rechts- und Verwaltungssprache in der öffentlichen Diskussion*. Mannheim: Duden.

Fantuzzi, Marco. 1995. "Una lingua 'di frontiera'. Riflessioni su italiano di Svizzera e traduzioni." *Cenobio* 4: 435–452.

Federal Office of Justice. 2007. *Guide de législation: Guide pour l'élaboration de la législation fédérale*. Bern: FOJ.

Felici, Annarita. 2010. "Translating EU Law: Legal Issues and Multiple Dynamics." *Perspectives: Studies in Translatology* 18(2): 95–108. doi:10.1080/09076761003668289.

Flückiger, Alexandre. 2016. "La démocratie directe: un facteur de qualité de la loi en Suisse?" In *La qualité de la loi – Expériences française et européenne*, edited by Pierre Albertini, 81–107. Paris: Mare & Martin.

Flückiger, Alexandre, and Jean-Daniel Delley. 2006. "L'élaboration rationnelle du droit privé: de la codification à la légistique." In *Le législateur et le droit privé, Mélanges en l'honneur de Gilles Petitpierre*, edited by Christine Chappuis, Bénédict Foëx and Luc Thevenoz, 123–143. Geneva: Schulthess.

Flückiger, Alexandre, and Stéphane Grodecki. 2017. "La clarté: un nouveau principe constitutionnel?" *Revue de droit suisse* 136(1): 31–62.

Huber, Eugen. 1914. *Erläuterungen zum Vorentwurf des Eidgenössischen Justiz- und Polizeidepartements. Zweite, durch Verweisungen auf das Zivilgesetzbuch und etliche Beilagen ergänzte Ausgabe.* Berne. https://eugenhuber.weblaw.ch/(Texte>Erläuterungen).

Jagmetti, Riccardo. 2014. "Herasuforderung und Antwort." In *Vom Wert einer guten Gesetzgebung*, edited by Alain Griffel, 25–38. Berne: Stämpfli Verlag.

Mori, Laura. 2018. "Observing Eurolects: The Case of Italian." In *Observing Eurolects. Corpus Analysis of Linguistic Variation*, edited by Laura Mori, 192–242. Amsterdam: Benjamins Publishing House.

Mortara Garavelli, Bice. 2001. *Le parole e la giustizia. Divagazioni grammaticali e retoriche su testi giuridici italiani.* Turin: Einaudi.

Pandolfi, Elena Maria. 2009. *LIPSI: Lessico di frequenza dell'italiano parlato nella Svizzera italiana.* Bellinzona: Osservatorio Linguistico della Svizzera Italiana.

Piemontese, Maria Emanuela. 1996. *Capire e farsi capire. Teorie e tecniche della scrittura controllata.* Naples: Tecnodid.

Pini, Verio. 2017. *Anche in italiano! 100 anni di lingua italiana nella cultura politica svizzera.* Bellinzona: Casagrande.

Prieto Ramos, Fernando. 2015. "Quality Assurance in Legal Translation: Evaluating Process, Competence and Product in the Pursuit of Adequacy." *International Journal for the Semiotics of Law* 28: 11–30. doi:10.1007/s11196-014-9390-9.

Prieto Ramos, Fernando, and Diego Guzmán. 2018. "Legal Terminology Consistency and Adequacy as Quality Indicators in Institutional Translation: A Mixed-Method Comparative Study." In *Institutional Translation for International Governance: Enhancing Quality in Multilingual Legal Communication*, edited by Fernando Prieto Ramos, 81–101. London: Bloomsbury. doi:10.5040/9781474292320.0015.

Rayson, Paul, and Roger Garside. 2000. "Comparing Corpora using Frequency Profiling." In *Proceedings of the Workshop on Comparing Corpora Held in Conjunction with the 38th Annual Meeting of the Association for Computational Linguistics*, edited by Adam Kilgarriff and Tony Berber Sardinha, 1–6. Association for Computational Linguistics. http://ucrel.lancs.ac.uk/people/paul/publications/rg_acl2000.pdf.

Rovere, Giovanni. 2005. *Capitoli di linguistica giuridica: ricerche su corpora elettronici.* Alessandria: Dell'Orso.

Sabatini, Francesco. 1990. "Analisi del linguaggio giuridico. Il testo normativo in una tipologia generale dei testi." In *Corso di studi superiori legislativi 1988–1989*, edited by Mario D'Antonio, 675–724. Padua: CEDAM.

Serianni, Luca. 2005. *Un treno di sintomi. I medici e le parole: percorsi linguistici nel passato e nel presente.* Milan: Garzanti.

Serianni, Luca. 2012. *Italiani scritti.* 3rd ed. Bologna: Il Mulino.

Svoboda, Tomáš. 2017. "Translation Manuals and Style Guides as Quality Assurance indicators: The Case of The European Commission's Directorate-General for Translation." In *Quality Aspects in Institutional Translation*, edited by Tomáš Svoboda, Łucja Biel and Krzysztof Łoboda, 75–107. Berlin: Language Science Press. doi:10.5281/zenodo.1048190.

Uhlmann, Felix. 2014. "Qualität der Gesetzgebung: Wünsche an die Empirie." In *Vom Wert einer guten Gesetzgebung*, edited by Alain Griffel, 171–181. Berne: Stämpfli.

Venturi, Giulia. 2013. "Investigating Legal Language Peculiarities across Different Types of Italian Legal Texts: An NLP-based Approach." In *Bridging the Gap(s) between Language and the Law: Proceedings of the 3rd European Conference of the International Association of Forensic Linguistics*, edited by Rui Sousa-Silva, Rita Faria, Núria Gavaldà and Belinda Maia, 139–156. Porto: Faculdade de Letras da Universidade do Porto.

Visconti, Jacqueline. 2009. "A Modular Approach to Legal Drafting and Translation." In *Formal Linguistics and Law*, edited by Günther Grewendorf and Monika Rathert, 401–426. Berlin/New York: Mouton de Gruyter.

Zwicky, Roman, and Daniel Kübler. 2018. *Topkader und Mehrsprachigkeit in der Bundesverwaltung Vol. 13, Studienberichte des Zentrums für Demokratie Aarau*. Aarau: ZDA.

# 3 Assessing Translation Practices of Non-professional Translators in a Multilingual Institutional Setting

*Flavia De Camillis*

## 3.1 Introduction

The study presented in this chapter links two areas of Translation Studies: institutional translation and non-professional interpreting and translation (NPIT). It focuses on a public institution in the multilingual province of Bolzano (South Tyrol), located in northern Italy on the border with Austria, and more specifically on the role of its employees. In this area, Italian and German are co-official languages (DPR 670/1972, Art. 99) and Ladin is a recognized minority language. Accordingly, public bodies are multilingual (e.g. they communicate with their citizens in at least both official languages). The object of our study is the central provincial administration, which employs civil servants with mandatory competencies in Italian and German, and a very limited number of in-house translators. Given that the translation policies of the provincial administration have never been formalized and that its departments do not have dedicated translation services nor in-house translators, only two translation management scenarios are possible: translations are either outsourced or drafted by internal staff.

Based on the hypothesis that employees might be doing the job of translators, we first conducted a pilot study with semi-structured interviews to selected employees. In order to assess the institutional translation process, based on the results of the interviews, we designed a web-based survey addressed to the entire provincial staff. In so doing, we prepared the survey assuming that respondents were non-professional translators, as the interviews had suggested. Against this background, we performed an intense adaptation process of the questions of the survey, considering the target participants. On the one hand, this implied reducing the investigated contents, as we left out questions related to several specific aspects of translation practice (such as translation strategy, volume or quality). On the other hand, we obtained considerably more answers (as expected), and thus an overview over the whole institution.

In this contribution, we will first explain what we mean by "non-professional translation," following Antonini's definition (Antonini *et al.* 2017). Later, we will present the main results of the semi-structured

DOI: 10.4324/9780429264894-3

interviews conducted in the first stage of the study, as well as the design phase of the survey. We will then focus on how the survey was adapted and on its most relevant results related to non-professional translation, before drawing some conclusions.

## 3.2  Non-professional Translation in an Institutional Setting

One of the first authors to give attention to NPIT in Translation Studies was Brian Harris, who referred to "natural translation" as the competence of bilinguals to translate in both directions between two languages in everyday circumstances without special training for it (Harris 1976, 96). The association between bilingualism and non-professional translation is not casual. Many non-experts believe that the ability to translate comes from the knowledge of two languages, even if research on translation competence has vastly proved that language competence is only one piece of the puzzle (see e.g. Risku 1998; Presas 2000; Neubert 2000; Pym 2003; Hurtado 2017; EMT 2017). Among translators described in studies on non-professional translation settings, some only qualify as such owing to their proficiency in a second language (L2). This is evident in migratory contexts, where families living in a new country rely on their children's language skills to interact in public life (a situation known as "child language brokering"), since children learn a new language more quickly than adults (Angelelli 2010, 95).

NPIT recently developed into two main strands: translation and interpreting. As far as translation is concerned, several studies have focused on community translation, where the term "community" can refer to phenomena such as fansubbing and fandubbing (Díaz Cintas & Muñoz Sánchez 2006) or to translation between official and non-official languages (Córdoba Serrano 2016). The interpreting strand has concentrated on child language brokering, interpreting in health and other public contexts, as well as in war conflicts and human emergencies (for an overview, see Pérez-González and Susam-Saraeva 2012; Antonini *et al.* 2017). Even though these studies involve various dynamics and contexts, all of them share a common denominator: the presence of a "circumstantial," "occasional," "informal," "ad hoc" or "non-professional" translator or interpreter. Antonini's definition of "non-professional translator" takes into consideration a number of aspects that we will refer to in this contribution. First, a "non-professional translator" is different from an "unprofessional translator," a term that has a negative connotation based on the quality assessment of a given performance or behavior. "Non-professional," of course, does not mean that these people are incompetent or that their work is necessarily of very low quality. It rather means that they are *unqualified* (i.e. that they have received no specific education or training to translate or interpret). They have not been *recruited* nor are *paid* for the job; they do not comply with a specific *set of rules*, and do not gain *social prestige* for translating (Antonini 2017, 7).

NPIT in institutional settings has been addressed in several studies focused, for example, on ad hoc language brokers in healthcare institutions (Angelelli 2004; Baraldi and Gavioli 2017). However, multilingual institutions never really caught the attention of NPIT research, probably because their communication strategies more often involve professional translators and interpreters to ensure multidirectional translations (see e.g. Pym 2008; Meylaerts 2011, 746). In areas historically populated by minorities, a common translation regime is institutional monolingualism at the local level and multilingualism at the superior (federal, national) level. This model applies to Belgium (Meylaerts 2017) and Switzerland (Borghi *et al.* 2008), whereas the inverted model applies to South Tyrol.

We chose to study the translation practices of the provincial administration of South Tyrol because its translation policies differ from other similar linguistic realities. In fact, except for the Office for Language Issues, which exclusively deals with the translation of legal documents, no other official translation services are devoted to translating administrative documents within the provincial departments. Translation practices and quality cause concerns and complaints both in the institution and in the local public life. Moreover, as Antonini puts it, "the phenomenon is there, has existed for a long time and is unlikely to disappear soon" (2017, 9). A deeper understanding of institutional translation practices can have far-reaching consequences both for citizens' rights and identity (Meylaerts 2018, 230) and for employees' satisfaction. It may equally be relevant for other multilingual realities.

## 3.3  Setting: The Provincial Administration of South Tyrol

Meylaerts' fourth translation regime – institutional monolingualism at local level combined with institutional multilingualism at higher level (2011, 752) – was revised by the same author some years later, as she added a change of perspective (2018). Multilingualism at the local level and monolingualism at the higher level describe the South Tyrolean context. The national official language of Italy is Italian, but in South Tyrol German is co-official, as much as French is co-official in the Aosta Valley and Slovene is officially recognized in Friuli Venezia Giulia. Thus, Italy is monolingual at the national level, but some regions are multilingual. This certainly has consequences for the local translation regimes. The central (national) government does not translate national legislation into German, French or Slovene. Rather, local administrations use their resources to translate national legislation into the languages of their minority communities. For example, in South Tyrol the provincial Office for Language Issues occasionally translates the most important national laws and legal codes[1] into German.

As already mentioned, Italian and German are co-official languages and Ladin is a recognized minority language under Presidential Decree (DPR) No. 752/1976. The local public administration reflects South Tyrolean multilingualism both internally and externally. Internally, employees must master the official languages to the level required for their profile (from A2 to C1 level), as well as Ladin, if they belong to the Ladin language group (DPR 752/1976, Art. 3). Externally, each institution must publish the great majority of its documents in Italian and German (DPR 574/1988, Art. 4). Thus, communication works in two languages both inside and outside the administration. This double communication effort implies a significant translation volume. However, apart from legal texts translated and revised by the abovementioned Office for Language Issues, an unquantified amount of documents (e.g. reports, newsletters, instructions and official forms) is regularly published in Italian and German by the provincial offices. Our study constitutes the first attempt to formally assess who deals with these translations.

Following up on language policies, for the *official* translators of the institution we find a description of the translator profile in the Collective agreement of 8 March 2006. A translator of the provincial administration mainly translates administrative, legal and technical texts, corrects them when translated by others and gives advice on language issues. S/he holds at least a three-year degree in translation or a related qualification and has a C1 level in both Italian and German. However, the same Collective agreement mentions "translation activities" also as a general duty for all employees, without specifying any educational requirements nor language proficiency levels. On paper, it seems thus that language proficiency (the only requirement for all civil servants) is considered a sufficient condition to entrust employees with translation tasks.

Bilingualism plays an important role in South Tyrolean public life. The language proficiency certificate, for example, is called "certificato di bilinguismo" (bilingualism certificate), even when it only certifies an A2 proficiency level. *Bilingualism* in South Tyrol is thus a synonym for language competence in two languages, not necessarily for a high level of proficiency. However, in contexts where two cultural groups coexist, it is often the case that *natural bilinguals* (i.e. people raised with two languages and two cultures) "are assumed to be equally proficient in their two languages, although this tacit assumption has not been confirmed by empirical research" (Whyatt 2017, 51). It is therefore likely that South Tyrolean public institutions assume all civil servants to be *natural bilinguals*, regardless of their actual competence level. This could justify the decision to add translation work under the general duties of all employees.

Against this background, the TradAm project started in 2017 as a four-year project of Eurac Research, the University of Bologna and the Province of Bolzano. The project aims to describe the current translation practices in the provincial administration, by applying qualitative and quantitative social research methods. It combines in-depth interviews with a survey addressed to the entire administration staff – around 3,000 individuals. Moreover, bilingual administrative texts will be the object of a readability analysis. In the following sections, we will present the first two stages of the project, focusing on the aspects related to non-professional translation.

## 3.4  The Interviews

The first stage of the study consisted of semi-structured interviews with 20 civil servants and four key informants. Interviewees were selected from a list of employees who regularly perform translation tasks, provided by their respective directors. From that list, we selected 20 participants, prioritizing the more experienced employees and aiming at a balanced number of males (9) and females (11), as well as German (10) and Italian (10) native speakers. The interviews focused on translation practices. We asked the interviewees about: (1) the type and amount of texts they translate; (2) their translation strategies, resources, guidelines and training; and (3) their personal opinions on the overall institutional translation quality and procedures.

The results point to a rather pell-mell institutional translation practice. None of the interviewees works as an in-house translator. For all of them translation is thus part of their "general duties." Half of them hold a high school diploma, the other half a university degree and very few of them specialized in language-related topics. None of them had received any specific training courses on translation during their career. Most of them described their translation activity as irregular and very often unpredictable: some translate regularly, even on a daily or weekly basis, but the majority does it rarely or occasionally. Just one of them was able to report the number of texts translated over the previous year, but not the total amount of words. Apart from keeping track of their translated texts in a folder, none of them was able to report the overall translation volume in words or characters.

Furthermore, they did not mention any guidelines or set of rules applied during translation. Every office seems to manage its translation needs on its own. For example, there are offices where some staff serve as a reference on translation matters, mostly due to their high language proficiency. There are also offices where every employee "plays his/her part," translating or proofreading when required. In other cases, each employee translates his/her own texts. Revision is not performed regularly nor considered a mandatory step in the translation process. Some employees ask for a revision from time to time, especially when translating into their second language, in case of doubts or unclear terminology.

Finally, some interviewees mentioned a past collaboration with at least one professional translator in their respective offices. The help of professionals did not achieve the expected results, as they lacked expert domain knowledge and slowed down work.

> [I]l traduttore spesso non conosce la materia. [...] [A]vere un tradut-tore qua era sempre un problema, perché era da solo, non aveva mai [...] possibilità di confrontarsi con altri, era sempre insicuro, eccetera. Eh, abbiam deci-, alla fine siamo stat-, arrivati nelle con-dizioni di arrangiarci con quello che avevamo.[2]
>
> (int. 012)

Employees' domain expertise is probably a key factor in maintaining the current institutional translation regime, i.e. one of the main reasons why they are asked to translate instead resorting to professional translators.

The interviews sketched the picture of a multilingual institution where non-professional translators manage translation needs as they can. Going back to Antonini's definition of the non-professional translator, the inter-viewees appear *unqualified* for the translation job, as they do not hold a specific degree nor attended training courses in translation. The adminis-tration *did not recruit* them, nor *pays* them to work as translators. They do not conform to a *set of rules* or internal translation guidelines. Finally, even if some of them enjoy translating, they gain *no social prestige* doing it.

> Mir macht das Übersetzen sehr viel Spaß.[3]
>
> (int. 18)

> [M]antenere la bellezza della lingua se si ha la capacità di utilizzarla, se allora... diventa anche un gusto e non è solo una fatica, diventa una bella fatica.[4]
>
> (int. 23)

In the working environment, translation is generally considered a "dead-end" for career growth, a burden or a concern:

> [E]s ist für mich hier jetzt [...] nicht interessant mir noch mehr Übersetzungen herzuholen, weil das hier eine Sackgasse wäre für die berufliche Entwicklung.[5]
>
> (int. 08)

> Diciamo che quello delle traduzioni è sempre stato un problema all'interno della ripartizione. [...] [S]e glielo fai fare sporadica-mente [...] lo sopportano, e invece, eh... se devi fare sempre e solo quello o devi far tutto tu... [...] è pesante, è percepito come pesante, sì.[6]
>
> (int. 12)

The low social prestige of translation is a very important aspect to consider. It is both cause and consequence of the role it plays within the institution. The lack of in-house translators, as well as the fact that there is usually little time to do the translations and no formal schedule for this purpose, leads to the impression that the translation work does not enjoy full recognition as a formal step of the administrative process. It rather seems a policy of "someone will deal with it." Inadequate time and qualifications to complete translation assignments also contribute to feeling either non-competent or burdened with the task, if not both. In most cases, translation is perceived as a humble activity in the administrative procedure.

Our results depict the image of a multilingual institution where employees work as non-professional translators to ensure its multilingual functioning. If the interview results were confirmed on a larger scale, we would be able to conclude that the provincial administration has non-professional translators working in all its departments. With the aim of enriching the results of the interviews, we thus decided to submit a survey to the entire administration staff.

## 3.5  Survey Design and Results

Starting from our interview results, we designed the survey based on the assumption that *non-professional translation* is the translation strategy adopted by the provincial administration. In order to verify this hypothesis and identify the "typical" translation process in the same setting, we had to face the challenge of asking questions about translation to non-professional translators. This not only affected *how* we could word questions but also *what* we could ask, in terms of what non-professional translators are capable to report about their translation activity. For this reason, we had to choose between a detailed and very specific analysis of translation practices potentially leading to low responsiveness, and a more general analysis with a higher probability of yielding responses. Aiming to obtain a comprehensive picture of the current translation practices in the provincial administration, we opted for the second survey type, i.e. a set of questions more adapted to the profiles of our target participants.

If we look at surveys addressed to professionals, we realize a banal yet essential truth: researchers and respondents share concepts. Obviously, when concepts are not shared, definitions can help respondents understand what researchers are looking for. Given that our target audience consisted of non-experts in translation, we had to simplify and define even the most common concepts in translation. At the same time, we had to exclude questions on very specific aspects. Let us consider a couple of examples. In 2015, the International Association of Professional Translators and Interpreters conducted a survey on translation into a non-native language (IAPTI 2015). Among others, the survey included the following questions: "Q15. What volume of your work comes from translation from your native language into a non-native language (L1->L2)?" This question requires a respondent to be aware of how to measure translation volume. Although simple, for non-professional translators it is often difficult to answer this question. We could not ask our target audience about their translation volume, as the interviews had informed us that they never took note of it. A second example comes from a survey of the Italian Association of Translators and Interpreters (AITI 2013): "Q 21. Lavori con sistemi CAT?"[7] This question obviously requires the respondent to know what a CAT tool is. Again, the interviews had shown that civil servants not only do not employ CAT tools, but in most cases have never even heard of them.

Among the surveys previously conducted on institutional translation, we first considered the one carried out by Koskinen (2008) on social and relational aspects of Finnish translators working in the European Commission. However, the focus on cultural aspects was not finally relevant to our purposes. The second survey of reference was Vecchione's (2014a, 2014b), who completed a study on translators working in Italian ministries. In her work, we found several interesting topics that we included in our survey: reasons to outsource a translation (Q3), translation difficulties (Q6) and translators' approach to repetitive or already translated texts (Q9). Initially, we also included a question on translation strategies like Vecchione (Q10), but eventually decided to leave it out, as we considered it too difficult for non-professional translators.

As a result of this tailoring process, the final survey had 37 questions (compared to an initial draft including more than 60): 36 of them close-ended and one open-ended. It was structured into six sections:

1   General information: socio-demographic questions (e.g. on gender, age, career, contract and education).
2   Language proficiency: questions on the "bilingualism certificate," self-evaluation of proficiency levels in the three local languages, as well as use of other languages at work.
3   Translation process: this was the core of the survey, and started with a branching question on the completion of translation tasks in the previous 12 months. Respondents who answered positively we considered "translators" and they continued to all the other questions related to the translation process. Respondents who gave a negative answer completed a much shorter survey. In this section, we also inquired about translation competence, target language, translated text typologies and domains, frequency of self-translation, proofreading, revision, translation difficulties and approach to texts previously translated.

4   Translation management: translation requests, average time spent on one translation, average time spent on translation in general and on revision, and outsourcing.
5   Translation resources and tools, including translation guidelines, terminology and training on translation and associated topics.
6   Personal opinion on the overall translation management in the institution.

Between 3 and 24 October 2018, we invited 2,963 civil servants to fill out the survey via email. We received 1,276 completed submissions, which represent a response rate of 43%. In the following sections, we will concentrate on the profile of respondents, and on several groups of questions that exemplify the adaptation of the survey, as explained earlier, and highlight some of the most relevant results with regard to non-professional translation.

### 3.5.1  Staff Profile

Survey results helped us determine whether respondents could be considered non-professional translators according to Antonini's (2017, 7) definition. As explained in Section 3.3, the provincial administration does not employ in-house translators in its departments; it rather entrusts staff members with translation tasks. Translating employees are thus not recruited as translators, but they of course receive a salary, even if not specifically for their translation activity.

As for their education, almost half of the respondents we considered translators in practice hold a university degree (48%), while 49% hold a high school diploma and only 3% hold a middle school diploma. Among graduate respondents, most of them studied law (23%) and only 6.5% obtained a degree in language studies or related domains. Concerning workplace training, we asked if they had ever attended courses on translation, drafting or terminology. It resulted that only 2% of respondents had attended a course on translation, 4.3% had received training on terminology and 27% on drafting. Moreover, we asked the employees whether they referred to guidelines when drafting or translating documents: 85% of them answered negatively. Finally, we have no data on social prestige, as this topic was not included in the survey.

### 3.5.2  Translation Volume

As already explained, a significant limitation encountered was the impossibility to assess *how much* is translated within the provincial administration, as civil servants do not usually take note of it and are not familiar with the relevant measuring systems. As an alternative, we decided to assess the *time* spent translating, both on single translations and on all translation tasks in one year.

> 24) In media quanto tempo impiega per fare una traduzione? *(Se le traduzioni hanno lunghezza e complessità molto variabili, provi a fare una stima)* a) meno di due ore b) mezza giornata lavorativa (4 ore) c) una giornata lavorativa (8 ore) d) due-tre giornate lavorative e) più di una settimana.[8]
>
> 25) Negli ultimi 12 mesi quale percentuale del Suo lavoro è stata dedicata all'attività di traduzione? a) meno del 25% b) 25–49% c) 50–75% d) più del 75%.[9]

As shown in Figure 3.1, we gained valuable information on the time spent translating. Over 80% of respondents spend under a quarter of their working time translating, and around 14% no more than half of it. Again, for the majority (over 85%), the average is just a few hours on one translation.

These results give us two essential clues on translation volume: civil servants translate mostly short, possibly simple or repetitive texts, as they need an average of a couple of hours to accomplish the task. The overall time they report spending on a translation seems to confirm that translating is *one of many* administrative activities they perform. Translation concerns many employees, as 67% of respondents stated having translated texts in the previous 12 months, but for a few hours each time. If we consider that so many staff members spend up to a quarter of their working time translating, it follows that the current translation practices are deeply embedded in the institutional system and account for a significant proportion of public administration tasks. If considered

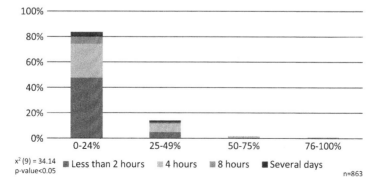

*Figure 3.1* Total average time spent translating one text.

in isolation, it may be seen as a small-scale activity, but, as a whole, it is absolutely widespread in the institutional system.

### 3.5.3 Translation Difficulties

As already mentioned in Section 3.5, we started with a question taken from Vecchione's (2014b) model survey. She proposed the following categories of translation difficulties: terminological-lexical, syntactical and textual, and other. We added "grammar," as grammar errors are not rare in texts published by the provincial administration. However, we considered a more explanatory wording necessary for a target audience that is not familiar with linguistic terminology. For this reason, we formulated the question as follows:

> 21) Con quale frequenza incontra le seguenti difficoltà quando traduce? (Sempre o molto spesso / Spesso / A volte / Raramente o mai): a) capire il significato del testo originale b) sapere o trovare i termini giusti c) costruire le frasi in modo corretto d) evitare errori grammaticali.[10]

As we can see in Table 3.1, the main challenge civil servants face when translating is related to terminology, as almost 40% of them often or very often have a hard time finding the correct terms. On the contrary, text comprehension does not cause many problems, as more than 90% of respondents reported rare or occasional difficulties with understanding source texts. Approximately one fourth of respondents often or very often struggle with building sentences, and grammar problems are frequent or very frequent for more than 20% of them.

The median value of this data set reveals that civil servants generally do not report great difficulties while translating. As shown in Figure 3.2, on average they face the aforementioned difficulties only sometimes (53%) or rarely (34%).

We should not forget that these data are based on self-evaluation. As such, they are a valid source of information concerning self-reported translation difficulties, but they cannot be used to assess translation quality or competence objectively.

*Table 3.1* Translation difficulties

| n = 863 | Never or rarely (%) | Sometimes (%) | Often (%) | Very often or always (%) |
|---|---|---|---|---|
| Text comprehension | 54.9 | 36.3 | 7.2 | 1.6 |
| Terminology | 9.0 | 51.4 | 31.5 | 8.0 |
| Building sentences | 25.8 | 48.6 | 20.3 | 5.3 |
| Grammar | 34.4 | 44.4 | 16.1 | 5.1 |

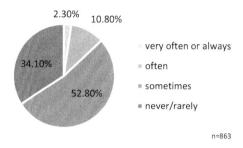

*Figure 3.2* Median value of translation difficulties' frequency.

### 3.5.4 Revision

According to ISO standard 17100:2015, revision is performed by the reviser (a person other than the translator), who examines the target language content against the source language content for any errors and other issues, and its suitability for purpose (ISO standard 17100:2015, section 5.3.3). Based on the exploratory interviews, revision appeared as an optional step of the institutional translation process. Our aim was therefore to assess how many employees also act as revisers, and how often they carry out this task. To do so, we considered the task from two perspectives: the request and the implementation of a revision. We then asked two questions: the first only to employees who translate, the second also to those who do not:

> 20) Con quale frequenza chiede a un'altra collaboratrice o a un altro collaboratore di rileggere le Sue traduzioni? a) sempre o molto spesso b) spesso c) a volte d) raramente o mai.[11]
> 26) Negli ultimi 12 mesi con quale frequenza Le è stato chiesto di rileggere traduzioni svolte da qualcun altro? a) una o più volte alla settimana b) una o più volte al mese c) una o più volte all'anno d) mai.[12]

We intentionally left out the term "revision," as it would not have had a technical meaning for our target audience. We simplified the concept using the verb *rileggere* in the Italian version and *durchlesen* in the German translation ("read"), which we considered more straightforward, also based on feedback from our pre-test.

The survey results confirm that revision is not a systematic practice. As pictured in Figure 3.3, the majority of translators ask colleagues to revise their translations often (31.3%) or sometimes (31.4%); only 25% do it very frequently, and 12% do it rarely or never. As far as the actual revision task is concerned (Figure 3.4), the proportions are similar. A third of the respondents never revise translations of other staff, more than 60% of respondents carry out revision from time to time (monthly or yearly) and only 10% do it very frequently (weekly).

Results also suggest a relation between translation and revision activity. As shown in Figure 3.5, translators are very frequently also revisers, while non-translators rarely revise translations. We can thus conclude that our "occasional translators" are also "occasional revisers." They seem to act as a communication node in their respective offices.

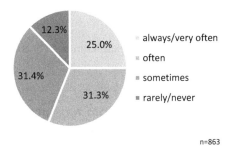

*Figure 3.3* Frequency of internal revision requests.

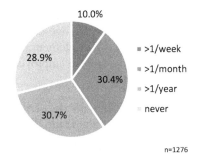

*Figure 3.4* Frequency of revision task.

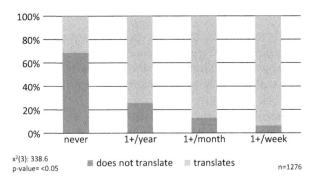

*Figure 3.5* Frequency of revision task per translation profile of staff.

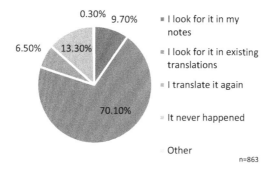

*Figure 3.6* Approach to previously translated texts.

### 3.5.5 Translation Technology

The semi-structured interviews showed that civil servants are generally not familiar with the concept of translation memories or CAT tools. For this reason, in the survey, we ruled out a direct question on the use of CAT tools. We preferred to assess the potential need for CAT tools, e.g. how employees deal with (parts of) texts previously translated, as the retrieval of similar translated texts is the main purpose of translation memories. To do so, we referred again to Vecchione (2014b, 4).

> 22) Di solito cosa fa se si accorge che una parte del testo che sta traducendo è stata già tradotta in passato? a) la traduce di nuovo b) la cerco nei testi vecchi c) la cerco tra i miei appunti d) non mi è mai successo e) altro.[13]

Figure 3.6 shows that the great majority (almost 80%) of translating civil servants consult existing translations or notes to retrieve previously translated text. Translation memories would then certainly be useful for them, as they would spare the time they otherwise need to find the correct file or the correct text segment. Also, administrative texts usually contain references to previously published documents. Using CAT tools could thus enhance the conformity and consistency of references.

However, while time saving would be a potential advantage of using CAT tools in the process, a more in-depth analysis of the overall needs, staff competencies and available technological options, including new machine translation software, would be required for any future action on translation technology.

### 3.6 Final Remarks

Based on the interviews and the survey results, we can affirm that translation management of non-legal texts in the provincial administration of South Tyrol relies on civil servants, who match the characteristics described by Antonini *et al.* (2017, 7) for non-professional translators. The Collective agreement of 8 March 2006 mentions translation as a general duty for all civil servants, and in-house translators are not officially part of the provincial organigram. Survey respondents who stated having translated texts in the previous 12 months were therefore normally *not recruited* as translators. They are mostly *not qualified* for the job; only 6.5% hold a degree in language-related disciplines, and 2% received training on translation. They do not regularly rely on a *set of rules* or codes for this activity; more specifically, 85% of them do not observe any guidelines on text drafting or translation. As for social prestige, at the semi-structured interviews of the pilot study, several interviewees described translation tasks as a burden that slows down the administrative process.

These findings suggest that translation policy in South Tyrol is the result of language policy, but "also the result of other policies that interact with language policy in different ways and at different levels" (González Núñez 2013, 486) such as institutional and education policies. Non-professional translation in a multilingual institutional setting may seem an unusual translation policy, as more often multilingual international institutions choose to hire in-house professional translators rather than relying on the language competencies of internal staff. However, this is probably not the case for smaller institutions with reduced financial resources. The earlier description could thus be a useful reference for the analysis of similar institutional settings of non-professional translation, especially among language minority communities.

Our study has contributed to a deeper understanding of internal translation practices, which may lead to a better control over translation activities. The awareness gained from the survey could lead, for example, to the setup of an institutional task force aimed at addressing the most evident shortcomings in translation management. One practical measure could focus on better scheduling translation assignments. The task force might also embark on the drafting of translation guidelines as well as on the organization of internal training courses on translation. More substantial measures might include designating one translation expert per office, or introducing specialized ad hoc translation tools.

These are just a few examples of how the institution could actively respond to insights from the survey results. Implementing corrective measures would not only support civil servants in their daily translation practice. It would also contribute to defining official translation policies with explicit information on who is in charge of translating for the institution, the process they should follow, the tools they may use and, in general, how the provincial administration should take care of its translations. The impact of such a translation policy on translation quality remains to be supported by evidence.

Finally, our case study sheds light on a setting of non-professional translation that could be of particular interest to other scholars working on NPIT. Although we did suspect that civil servants act as translators in many local institutional settings, there had not been many reported case studies to prove it until recently. Even less literature is available on how to gain useful information about translation processes and management from this particular type of translators, with few exceptions (Aguilar Solano 2015; Lomeña Galiano 2020). The questions posed in the survey represent a first attempt to get in touch with this group and better understand their practices and needs. These insights are precious not only for potential improvements in the institutions examined but also for translation experts to gain knowledge of how translation happens on the ground (Meylaerts 2018, 234). With our study, we hope to contribute to filling this gap.

## Notes

1 See the webpage of the Office for Language Issues: https://bit.ly/328IY7m.
2 [A] translator does not usually master the domain [...]. Having a translator in here was mostly a problem, because s/he was alone, s/he never had [...] the chance to discuss doubts with the colleagues, s/he always felt insecure and so on. So, we decided to sort it out on our own (our translation).
3 I have lots of fun translating (our translation).
4 To preserve the beauty of language, if you are able to use it, if then... it becomes a pleasure and it is not just a struggle; it becomes a nice struggle (our translation).
5 For me, it is not [...] convenient to ask for even more translations, because it would be a dead-end for my career.
6 Let's say that translations have always been a problem in the division. [...] If you have them do it occasionally, they bear with it. Otherwise, if one has to translate all the time or if you have to translate everything alone... it's a burden, it is perceived as a burden, yes (our translation).
7 Do you work with CAT tools? (our translation).
8 On average, how long does it take you to do a translation? (*If translations are of varying lengths and complexity, try to make an estimate*). (a) Less than two hours, (b) Half a workday (four hours), (c) A workday (eight hours), (d) Two to three workdays, (e) More than a week (our translation).
9 In the last 12 months, what percentage of your work did you spend translating? (a) Less than 25%, (b) 25–49%, (c) 50–75%, (d) More than 75% (our translation).
10 How often do you experience the following difficulties when translating? (Always or very often – Often – Sometimes – Rarely or never): (a) Understanding the meaning of the original text, (b) Knowing or finding the correct terms, (c) Building correct sentences, (d) Avoiding grammar errors (our translation).
11 How often do you ask a colleague to read your translation? (a) Always or very often, (b) Often, (c) Sometimes, (d) Rarely or never (our translation).
12 In the past 12 months, how often have you been asked to read translations made by someone else? (a) Once or many times per week, (b) Once or many times per month, (c) Once or many times per year, (d) Never (our translation).

13 What do you usually do when you notice that part of the text you are translating has already been translated in the past? (a) I translate it again, (b) I look for the translation in previous texts, (c) I look for the translation in my notes, (d) It never happened to me, (e) Other (our translation).

## References

Aguilar Solano, María. 2015. "Non-professional volunteer interpreting as an institutionalized practice in healthcare: A study on interpreters' personal narratives." *Translation & Interpreting* VII, no. 3: 132–148. doi:10.12807/ti.107203.2015.a10.

AITI – Associazione italiana traduttori e interpreti. 2013. "Indagine sul mercato dei traduttori e degli interpreti 2013." http://www.spaziotraduzione.org/sondaggio/traduzione.html.

Angelelli, Claudia Viviana. 2004. *Medical Interpreting and Cross-Cultural Communication.* Cambridge: Cambridge University Press.

Angelelli, Claudia Viviana. 2010. "A professional ideology in the making. Bilingual youngsters interpreting for their communities and the notion of (no) choice." *Translation and Interpreting Studies* 5, no. 1: 94–108. doi:10.1075/tis.5.1.06ang.

Antonini, Rachele, *et al.* (Eds.). 2017. *Non-professional Interpreting and Translation.* Amsterdam/Philadelphia: John Benjamins.

Baraldi, Claudio and Gavioli, Laura. 2017. "Intercultural mediation and "(non) professional" interpreting in Italian healthcare institutions." In *Non-professional Interpreting and Translation*, edited by Rachele Antonini *et al.*, 84–106. Amsterdam/Philadelphia: John Benjamins.

Borghi, Marco *et al.* (2008). "Schlussbericht. Juristisch-linguistische Untersuchungen von Rechtstexten der schweizerischen offiziellen Mehrsprachigkeit." http://www.snf.ch/SiteCollectionDocuments/nfp/nfp56/nfp56_schlussbericht_schweizer.pdf.

Córdoba Serrano, María Sierra. 2016. "Translation Policies and Community Translation: the U.S., a case study." *New Voices in Translation Studies* 14: 122–163.

Díaz Cintas, Jorge and Muñoz Sánchez, Pablo. 2006. "Fansubs: audiovisual translation in an amateur environment." *JoSTrans: The Journal of Specialised Translation* 6: 37–52.

EMT. 2017. *European Master's in Translation. Competence Framework 2017.* https://ec.europa.eu/info/sites/info/files/emt_competence_fwk_2017_en_web.pdf.

González Núñez, Gabriel. 2013. "Translating for linguistic minorities in Northern Ireland: A look at translation policy in the judiciary, healthcare, and local government." *Current Issues in Language Planning* XIV, no. 3: 474–489. doi:10.1080/14664208.2013.827036.

Harris, Brian. 1976. "The importance of natural translation." *Working Papers in Bilingualism* 12: 96–114.

Hurtado Albir, Amparo (Ed.). 2017. *Researching Translation Competence by PACTE Group.* Amsterdam/Philadelphia: John Benjamins.

Koskinen, Kaisa. 2008. *Translating Institutions. An Ethnography Study of EU Translation.* Manchester & Kinderhook: St. Jerome Publishing.

Lomeña Galiano, María. 2020. "Finding hidden populations in the field of translating and interpreting: A methodological model for improving access to non-professional translators and interpreters working in public service settings." *FITISPos-International Journal*, VII, no. 1: 72–91.

Meylaerts, Reine. 2011. "Translational justice in a multilingual world: An overview of translational regimes." *Meta* LVI, no. 4: 743–757. doi:10.7202/1011250ar.

Meylaerts, Reine. 2017. "Studying language and translation policies in Belgium: What can we learn from a complexity theory approach?" *Parallèles* XXIX, no. 1: 45–59.

Meylaerts, Reine. 2018. "The politics of translation in multilingual states." In *The Routledge Handbook of Translation and Politics*, edited by Fruela Fernández and Jonathan Evans, 221–237. New York: Routledge.

Neubert, Albrecht. 2000. "Competence in language, in languages, and in translation." In *Developing Translation Competence*, edited by Christina Schäffner and Beverly Adab, 3–18. Amsterdam/Philadelphia: John Benjamins.

Pérez-González, Luis and Susam-Saraeva, Şebnem. 2012. "Nonprofessionals translating and interpreting." *The Translator* 18, no. 2: 149–165. doi:10.1080/13556509.2012.10799506.

Presas, Marisa. 2000. "Bilingual competence and translation competence." In *Developing Translation Competence*, edited by Christina Schäffner and Beverly Adab, 19–31. Amsterdam/Philadelphia: John Benjamins.

Pym, Anthony. 2003. "Redefining translation competence in an electronic age. In defence of a minimalist approach." *Meta* 48, no. 4: 481–497.

Pym, Anthony. 2008. "Translation vs. Language Learning in International Institutions. Explaining the Diversity Paradox." *Cultus Journal: The Journal of Intercultural Mediation and Communication* V, no. 1: 70–83.

Risku, Hanna. 1998. *Translatorische Kompetenz. Kognitive Grundlagen des Übersetzens als Expertentätigkeit*. Tübingen: Stauffenburg.

Vecchione, Flavia. 2014a. "Tradurre per le istituzioni. Panoramica dei traduttori che operano nelle principali istituzioni governative italiane e della loro attività." *mediAzioni* 16: 1–33.

Vecchione, Flavia. 2014b. "Allegato. Questionario traduttori istituzionali." *mediAzioni* 16: 1–5.

Whyatt, Bogusława. 2017. "We are all translators: Investigating the human ability to translate from a developmental perspective". In *Non-Professional Interpreting and Translation : State of the Art and Future of an Emerging Field of Research*, edited by Rachele Antonini et al., 45–64. Amsterdam/Philadelphia: John Benjamins.

# 4 Translation in the Shadows of Interpreting in US Court Systems

## Standards, Guidelines and Practice

*Jeffrey Killman*

## 4.1 Introduction

The primary focus of language access for limited English proficiency (LEP) parties in the context of US courts has traditionally revolved around the provision of interpreting services while translation services have taken a backseat.[1] The focus on interpreting relates to the adversarial system used in common law countries like the United States (Ortega Herráez, Giambruno and Hertog 2013, 112), where the courtroom is a traditional place where justice may be obtained and disputes resolved through the application of legal rules and principles (Spohn, Hemmens and McCann 2019). Nevertheless, more attention has been given to court-related translation as different courts in the US have managed to reliably provide interpreting services and implement interpreter certification programs and as additional developments in language access policies, standards and guidelines have been made at the state level and by national and federal entities such as the National Center for State Courts (NCSC) and the Department of Justice (DOJ).

Moreover, increases in the number of LEP individuals have also stimulated initiatives in US courts to develop plans and practices for providing translation services (Mellinger 2017). In fact, the total population of LEP individuals in the US has increased by 83% (13,982,500–25,627,417) from 1990 to 2018, and the percentage of such individuals in the country has increased from 6.1% to 8.3% (MPI 2015; USCB 2018).[2] Approaches to deal with translation demands vary according to jurisdiction, whether at the federal, state or even county level, and may range from courts passing the burden of translation on to the LEP individuals themselves to courts handling all or a selection of their translation needs with the assistance of staff translators, independent contractors or even professional translation companies.

In terms of qualifications for court translators, there is also a significant degree of variability according to different courts, policies and guidelines. Unlike interpreter certification in the US context, which was

DOI: 10.4324/9780429264894-4

established in the judiciary sector first thanks to the Court Interpreters Act of 1978 (Mikkelson 2013, 68), acceptable means to qualify court translators are in the phase of gaining some traction, but very much lack uniformity and in some cases are more specific to court-related translation than in others. Moreover, additional consideration could be given to whether one type of certification or a combination of certification types might be more suitable for the translation of court-related texts or the transcription/translation of recordings serving as evidence.

This chapter discusses relevant translation policies, standards and guidelines that have come about at the national and federal level in the US, as well as their interface in the federal court system and in various state courts with historical and emerging language access needs in different geographical regions. Translation policies and developments in specific jurisdictions are discussed, as well as the various criteria they use to qualify practitioners. The chapter concludes with a synthesis of the data explored and a discussion of some pros and cons of certain practices, translator qualifications or combinations thereof.

## 4.2 National Court-Related Translation Policies, Standards and Guidelines

This chapter proposes that texts that are translated in US court systems primarily fall into one of two categories: (1) inbound texts: written materials and audio recordings submitted to the court as evidence, and (2) outbound texts: official forms and information resources provided by the court. Inbound texts are rendered to the language of the court, i.e. English, and in the case of documents, run the gamut from birth or death certificates to work verification letters or text messages. In the case of audio recordings, inbound texts include phone conversations or body camera recordings needing to be transcribed and translated. In either of these cases, the courts may determine how texts are translated and by whom, according to different criteria used. In the case of outbound translation, while language access plans and regulations might require materials to be translated out of English, courts have leeway for deciding which materials are translated and to which languages.

### 4.2.1 Federal Context

In the documentation and guidelines of the US federal court system, little or no mention is made to translation in comparison to interpretation or sight translation. For example, the only mention of translation in the *Federal Court Interpreter Orientation Manual and Glossary* is its glossary definition of transcription/translation of recordings (AOUSC 2014, 61). The *Standards for Performance and Professional*

*Responsibility for Contract Court Interpreters in the Federal Courts* features "translating" and "legal translating" in a few instances, though they are used as synonyms of "interpreting" or "sight translation."

The *Guide to [Federal] Judiciary Policy, Vol. 5: Court Interpreting*[3] does, however, include information on both inbound and outbound document translation and transcription/translation. For instance, § 550.20 refers to the "Translation of Documents Filed with the Court," pointing out there is an occasional need for inbound translation. Addressing the issue of finding qualified translators, § 550.20.10 recalls that "[t]he Court Interpreters Act [of 1978] does not address written translation requirements, and the Federal Court Interpreter Certification Examination (FCICE) tests high-level interpreting skills in both English and Spanish but does not test for translation skills." To find "qualified translators," this same section points us to "the American Translators Association or any other organization that tests translation ability [...] such as: the Language Services Unit of the State Department, or the Language Services Section of the Federal Bureau of Investigation." While the American Translators Association (ATA) certification, from quite possibly the largest translators association in the world, is perceived as having a particularly strong market value (Pym et al. 2012, 66), translation tests offered by the State Department and FBI are not as widely recognized or thought of by non-specialists in diplomacy or federal law enforcement. The federal guide, in § 550.20.40, stipulates that "[t]ranslations and transcriptions are not within the scope of the Court Interpreters Act, and payment for such services may not be funded from the general authorization for contract interpreting." This guide also highlights the limits of the FCICE in terms of its application to translation, as well as the limits of funding for translation work at the federal level, which relies on local funds as it is not covered by funding linked to the Court Interpreters Act of 1978. Nevertheless, federal court interpreters "report that they are often asked to translate sentencing letters addressed to the judge [...] from family members, friends, employers or other individuals willing to serve as character references for a defendant" (Ortega Herráez, Giambruno and Hertog 2013, 114).

In terms of outbound translation, § 550.30 of the guide provides that "[t]he recipient of an official court document is responsible for translation to another language if necessary for that party's understanding of the official document." Nevertheless, as § 550.30 also points out, "[a] number of [federal] courts have responded to changing demographics and now make available (either on the courts' websites or at the courthouses) unofficial forms and other information for individuals with limited English proficiency." While the federal judiciary might prefer to offload translation of official court documents to the potential users or requesters themselves, individual federal courthouses may find it beneficial to prepare translations of unofficial forms or other materials in cases where an ongoing need can be established. For example, the US District

Court for the Southern District of Texas, whose jurisdiction covers a significant portion of Texas's border with Mexico, includes select unofficial forms in Spanish in its online repository, e.g. its Waiver of Rights and Consent to Plea/Sentencing by Video Conference and its Waiver of Detention Hearing in different district court divisions such as Houston or Brownsville. Of course, the availability of such types of waiver in Spanish may contribute to the efficiency of a district court by helping it avoid certain types of appearance or hearing, which are time-consuming if unnecessary.

### 4.2.2 *State Context*

In the context of state courts, there are states that have historically had translation needs resulting from more sustained demographic trends, while there are others that have more recently had to keep pace with evolving demographics. Therefore, the past couple of decades have seen increased efforts on the part of state courts and the United States Department of Justice to improve LEP individuals' access to state courts (DOJ 2010; Jang 2014). The DOJ – at its 2014 event celebrating the 50th anniversary of Title VI of the Civil Rights Act of 1964 "Providing Language Access in the Courts: Working Together to Ensure Justice" – unveiled its *Language Access Planning and Technical Assistance Tool for Courts* (DOJ 2014). The DOJ tool is intended to help state courts identify language access needs and prioritize them according to availability of resources and the amount of time that would be needed to implement them. The primary goal is for a court system to devise a "Language Access Plan" that "identifies, prioritizes, coordinates and sets timeframes and responsibility for actions that are helpful to ensure that comprehensive, timely, effective, and free language assistance services are provided in court proceedings and operations" (ibid., 3). While the tool is indeed more comprehensive in assessing language access during proceedings and court interpreting services in general, it does substantially cover outbound translation[4] of court-provided materials, translator credentialing and translation quality.

The tool asks whether courts translate materials at no charge to LEP individuals, which is in stark contrast to the federal court system. It also asks whether translated materials include vital documents ("applications, court forms, consent or complaint forms, notices of rights, and letters or notices that require a response" [ibid., 2]), a court's website and if courts have a way of ensuring translation quality and documenting successful delivery of translations. Courts are also asked about whether they electronically store translations for future use, whether they share them with other courts (perhaps to pool resources) and whether courts use glossaries (in-house or otherwise), automatic translation services or software programs. The tool also has courts consider whether they have a credentialing system for translators, a means for ensuring that competent translators are provided and whether courts work with any specific organizations (NCSC, National Association of Judiciary Interpreters and Translators [NAJIT], ATA, American Bar Association [ABA]), other court systems or other entities to ensure translators' quality is assessed. On the basis of all these considerations, considerably more pressure is being exerted on state courts than on federal courts to provide a wider and more comprehensive array of translation services.

The *Guide to Translation of Legal Materials* (NCSC 2011) reminds state courts that the federal funding they receive requires them to provide not only interpreting services but also translation services. Focusing on the translation of official forms or information provided by state courts (i.e. outbound translation), the NCSC guide like, the previously discussed DOJ tool (DOJ 2014), helps identify court-produced materials that should be translated and credentials translators should have. Translators, ideally, would hold ATA certification according to this guide, but state systems may also assess the relevance of translators' general education and legal translation experience. The guide also points out the importance of language direction and how translators should ideally be native speakers of the languages to which they may be hired to translate. Language direction may be overlooked in court systems, in that court interpreters translate in both directions and awareness of the value of native or native-like written language skills may be overlooked.

Finally, the NCSC guide suggests translation best practices. It recommends maintaining a translation glossary to preserve consistency across translations of different texts and when more than one translator works on a single text, as well as providing the translator access to appropriate contextual information, relevant materials, such as previously translated texts, and a contact person to provide clarifications, guidance or additional information. Collaboration is proposed between the translator of an informal document, such as a handout, and its author or a subject matter expert, for the purposes of pre-editing the document according to a particular readership's needs. Though not as cost-effective or convenient as hiring a single translator for the job, the NCSC guide also recommends another translator edit the translation, before his or her edited version is also sent for further revisions or proofreading by yet another translator. To handle discrepancies, procedures are recommended for the different stakeholders to resolve differences openly and productively with an eye to product quality. In terms of style and formatting, recommendations are made for bilingual (target text below or after source text) or monolingual ("mirror image") formatting of translated forms, where bilingual formatting is deemed preferable for court forms and monolingual formatting more suited to instructions or informational brochures.

Though these DOJ and NCSC materials do not cover inbound translation, that does not mean that there are not needs that are similar to those in federal courts. North Carolina, for example, has intricate guidelines for translating "evidentiary materials for use in court proceedings" in the *Standards for Language Access Services in North Carolina State Courts* (NCAOC 2017, 111–114). Section 18.3 requires the party submitting documents or audio sources in a foreign language to obtain translations and transcription in all court proceedings, except in cases where the translations are rendered on behalf of district attorneys or indigent defendants and respondents who have a constitutional or statutory right to counsel (NCAOC 2017, 111). While the North Carolina Judicial Branch takes on financial responsibility in these cases, the courts in Kentucky (KSC 2017, 25–26) and Maryland (MJ 2019, 26), for example, stipulate that the parties submitting the materials in a court proceeding are always financially responsible. The Judicial Branch of Arizona in Maricopa County has also followed suit, as until recently it had borne the costs of the translation services it provided to Maricopa County agencies such as the Attorney General, County Attorney, Public Defender, Legal Defender, Legal Advocate or Court Appointed Counsel (ASCMC 2016). While the policy in New Mexico (NM) is to not bear transcription/translation costs (NMSC 2016, 2), practices have traditionally varied according to different NM courts as to whether they accept documents submitted in Spanish and translate them internally (NMJ 2013, 145), and in 2018 all NM courts started accepting and translating pleadings submitted in languages other than English in domestic violence cases (NMJ 2018, 14). Whether or not courts take on the costs or perform the services themselves, the ABA reminds courts of their "institutional interest in having adequate language services to capture evidence accurately and determine cases fairly on the merits" (2012, 33). This may even mean referring parties to qualified translators, if courts cannot provide such services on their own.

## 4.3 Translation Developments and Practices in State Courts

Given the more wide-ranging, detailed guidelines and standards for translation in the context of state courts, this section focuses on specific state court translation developments and practices that relate to these guidelines and standards in various ways. The examples discussed are illustrative of the current variability of such practices and developments. The variability in the single federal court system is considerably reduced in comparison, and state courts are in actuality the front line where "[t]he vast majority of cases – over 98 percent – are handled" (ABA 2008, 7). Examples include state courts with historical or emerging language needs and with divergent or parallel translation developments and practices from the West, Northeast and South of the United States.

Arizona, California, New Mexico and New York are examples of states with historical LEP needs where courts have made substantial commitments to language access in the area of translation. Courts in each of these states either include specific translation committees devoted to improving and increasing translation efforts or in the case of the Judicial Branch of Arizona in Maricopa County, a special department with "translation" is included in its designation: "Court Interpretation and Translation Services" (CITS). Maricopa County (with a population of almost 4.5 million [USCB 2019]) is Arizona's most populous county and the fourth most populous in the US with an LEP population of 8.9% (USCB 2018). CITS was created in the mid-1980s and currently has four staff "judicial translators,"[5] whose core tasks have primarily included transcription/translation (e.g. recorded law enforcement interviews in Spanish with suspects following their arrest) and will now focus more on translating court-generated documents and forms (ASC 2017). As mentioned in the preceding section, the court in this county recently decided to no longer bear the costs for its inbound translation services for other Maricopa agencies. In Arizona each court is in charge of developing its own language access plan (ASC 2011), and Maricopa has determined that "assisting these agencies in developing their cases against or defenses for the very litigants whose cases this Court will decide [...] may bring the Court's impartiality into question and create an appearance of impropriety" (ASCMC 2016, 1). Centering its efforts on outbound translation instead, CITS prioritizes the translation of vital documents such as complaints, release or waiver forms, claim or application forms or letters of findings (ibid., 11). For example, the wide collection of forms and instructions in this district court's Self-Service Center are available in English-Spanish bilingual format in a variety of areas: civil, criminal, deferral of court fees, domestic violence, family court, juvenile, probate, property tax and service of process (ibid., 10). Despite its more recent focus on the translation of vital documents, it should be pointed out that Maricopa's *Guidelines for the Transcription and Translation of Spanish Audio and Video Recordings* (MCJBA 2020a) are highly detailed, with extensive coverage of language-use and translation formatting and instructions supported by numerous examples and templates. Maricopa also asserts that the court "take reasonable steps to ensure that all staff or contracted individuals who serve as translators are briefed by Judicial Branch staff on the context and intended audience for the translated text" (ASCMC 2016, 12).

California is the most populous US state (39.5 million [USCB 2019]), where the percentage of speakers of a language other than English (44.6% [USCB 2018]) and that of LEP individuals (17.4% [ibid.]) are also the highest in the country. California has always stood out in recognizing language and interpreting needs, which led to the passage of Assembly Bill 2400 in 1978 (Dueñas González, Vásquez and Mikkelson 2012, 226). The most recent language access plan of the California Courts (JCC 2015) proposed the formation of a translation committee to create a translation protocol, which provides detailed translation policies and procedures (JCC 2016). Goal 4 of the language access plan (JCC 2015, 51–55) emphasizes the importance of high-quality translations being available to LEP individuals. The California Courts Online Self-Help Center had already been providing hundreds of pages of Spanish translated information, and the Judicial Council has translated vital domestic violence forms to Spanish, Chinese, Korean and Vietnamese, as well as almost all of the essential family law forms and information to Spanish. Nevertheless, inconsistency has been noted in the amount and quality of translations available on local courts' websites, in that most local courts did not provide any translations and when translations were provided, errors in certain cases were such that the information was legally inaccurate and hence not viable. Inconsistencies in translated court forms in different state jurisdictions have also been noted by Mellinger (2017). Another reason to revisit translation services was because legal services providers and other stakeholders had been requesting translations of more information and forms to complete translation collections in a particular area of law (e.g. family law) and to cover highly technical areas such as conservatorships and guardianships.

California's translation protocol points out that the Translation Advisory Committee has the continual responsibility of identifying written resources that should be considered for translation using various criteria to gauge frequency of use and importance (JCC 2016, 4–5), whereas "[p]lain language documents addressing high-volume case types and processes will be prioritized" (ibid., 3). This committee also recommends bilingual form formatting where possible, translating excerpts from very long documents or producing shorter texts with the critical information needing to be translated (ibid., 6). In addition to editing by a "second independent professional translator" (ibid., 21) and legal review of translated content by a "bilingual attorney, or similarly qualified subject matter expert, to ensure that all legal concepts have been accurately communicated and no meaning has been lost in the translation" (ibid.), the protocol places importance on safeguarding terminological consistency within and across translations and on the creation and maintenance of bilingual glossaries in order to do so (ibid., 11–12, 14–15). In addition to its wide array of translated forms, information and web pages, California's glossaries are substantial, with its robust Self-Help Glossary at the state level (JCC 2020b) and the Superior Court of Sacramento's 12 bilingual glossaries, including languages such as Arabic, Hindi, Mien, Romanian, Russian or Vietnamese (SSCC 2020). To ensure consistency and quality, the protocol states that the translator or translation vendor should be provided with any existing relevant glossaries, as well as relevant specifications and a contact person to whom to direct any inquiries about a translation commission (JCC 2016, 15).

In the State of New York (population of almost 19.5 million residents [USCB 2019]), 30.7% speak a language other than English and 13.2% have LEP (USCB 2018). It goes without saying that New York has always been an immigrant destination, and its Unified Court System (UCS) has historically had significant language services needs. The UCS's language access plan calls for a committee on translation to "establish standards for written translation" and describes a project to test the feasibility of providing translations of orders of protection in bilingual format (NYSUCS 2017, 28–29). Bilingual orders in various languages (Arabic, Chinese, Russian and Spanish) have been made available in family and domestic violence courts across the state in criminal and matrimonial cases (NYSUCS 2018a). Formatting challenges mentioned by the UCS include how to best "intersperse" the English and non-English text (ibid., 2). The following is an example of a bilingual protective order interspersing English and Spanish:

> IT IS HEREBY ORDERED that the above-named defendant (POR LA PRESENTE SE ORDENA que el(la) acusado(a) mencionado(a) anteriormente) Joseph E Jones (DOB: 12/13/1965) observe the following conditions of behavior (cumpla las condiciones de conducta que se detallan a continuación):
>
> (ibid., 12)

Interspersing, however, may make reading more difficult instead of facilitating it due to the ruptures in syntax and additional parenthesis. It seems preferable, for instance, to place the translation of the entire source sentence directly under it, i.e. in "parallel bilingual format" (NCSC 2011, 10–11). Doing so may also help avoid the omission of a translation of "(DOB: 12/13/1965)," which may have been avoided due to the additional complexity that would have been caused by a translation in parenthesis of this phrase in parenthesis.

While New York has focused on outbound translation of orders in domestic violence cases, New Mexico has centered its efforts on preparing bilingual Spanish domestic violence and domestic relations forms that can be filled out and submitted by self-represented litigants in Spanish (NMJ 2017, 12). The NM court receiving these domestic violence forms, in turn, has, as pointed out in the previous section, the responsibility of translating them, and the possibility of accepting the domestic relations forms is currently being explored (NMJ 2019, 11). This practice has increased the need for translation services to the point that the courts could no longer keep pace and awarded a contract to a translation company whose turnaround may be as quick as an hour or less (NMJ 2018, 14). This same vendor also took on outbound Spanish translations of "webpages, forms, manuals and other materials intended for the public" (ibid.). The following year, it was reported that the vendor translated all the 441,000+ words that were translated for the New Mexico Judiciary in 2019 (NMJ 2019, 11).[6] These translation developments build on the momentum of a substantial language access project grant setting in motion the New Mexico Judicial Translation Project Team to focus on statewide translation of forms and acceptance of documents in other languages (NMJ 2013, 17). This Translation Project is noteworthy, especially since New Mexico's population (2,096,829 [USCB 2019]) is significantly smaller than that of the other states and county discussed in this section. It attends to its 9.6% of individuals with LEP (USCB 2018) by providing translated resources such as those already discussed and others, e.g. website mirror pages in Spanish, pamphlets and guides about legal topics such as civil procedures, domestic violence and appeals, bilingual Spanish magistrate court intake forms and juror questionnaire and qualification forms in Spanish and Navajo (NMJ 2017).[7]

North Carolina is an interesting case in the South. Its LEP population has increased significantly since 1990. For example, from 1990 to 2010 its increase was the sharpest in the South and second sharpest in the US, with growth of 395% (MPI 2011, 4–5). Moreover, the latter period of such growth coincided with some of the DOJ's main enforcement efforts (Dueñas González, Vásquez and Mikkelson 2012, 257). As pointed out in the preceding section, North Carolina's inbound translation policies detail various circumstances in which either the parties submitting documents or audio sources or the state receiving them cover the costs for their translation to English (NCAOC 2017, 111–113). Regarding the translation of its forms to other languages, North Carolina pledges to continue providing bilingual versions of such forms as resources become available (ibid., 114). On the North Carolina Judicial Branch website, there are currently as many as 277 Spanish bilingual forms and 282 Vietnamese bilingual forms (the two non-English languages with forms available), with more or less equally significant coverage in areas such as civil and criminal law (32–33% and 31%, respectively), juvenile law (11–12%), special proceedings (7%), estate (7%) and small claims (6%). North Carolina's commitment to translation is also highlighted by the translation-specific position it created for a translator to "translate official court transcripts for use by the Appellate Defenders Office" (Ortega Herráez, Giambruno and Hertog 2013, 113).

## 4.4 Translator Qualifications

Of the state and county districts discussed so far, North Carolina also stands out in the level of description, variability and prioritization of qualifications it provides for document translators and transcribers/translators. It stipulates that the translation and transcription/translation work it funds should be performed by qualified practitioners, which includes individuals who have passed the now defunct National Judiciary

Interpreter and Translator Certification Examination (NJITCE), the ATA exam, the FCICE or the North Carolina Court Interpreter Certification Examination with a score of 80% or higher in all three sections of the oral exam component (sight translation, consecutive interpretation and simultaneous interpretation) (NCAOC 2017, 113–114). If translators with these qualifications are not available in a specific language combination, then translation work should be completed by individuals with "credentials from organizations that test translation ability, such as the Language Services Unit of the State Department, the Language Services Section of the Federal Bureau of Investigation, or the United Nations" (ibid., 114). In cases of last resort, where languages for which these credentials are not available, an academic credential in translation with the specific language in question may be accepted (ibid.). The inclusion of ATA certification or certification from the State Department or FBI aligns with the previously discussed recommendations in the federal *Guide to Judiciary Policy, Vol. 5: Court Interpreting.* While this same guide points out that the FCICE does not test translation skills specifically, in North Carolina this exam and its state interpreter exam at a specific threshold may qualify one to translate or transcribe/translate.

In the case of Tennessee, another Southern state with a sharp LEP population increase ranking fifth in the US (MPI 2011, 4–5), its credentialed interpreters are identified as able to translate written communication if necessary, the rationale being that they have taken the state oral interpreting exam "at least once and have translated written documents as part of their testing" (TAOC 2018b, 9). While it is true that credentialed court interpreters may have had to repeatedly take the oral component in order to pass the NCSC interpreter exam that Tennessee and many other states (e.g. Arizona, California, North Carolina, New Mexico) use, the written component of this exam does not cover translation or the other language (NCSC 2012; TAOC 2018a, 4). Perhaps sight translation – which is included in the oral component of the NCSC exam (NCSC 2017), state-specific exams such as New York's (NYSUCS 2018b, 3), the FCICE and the NJITCE – is being conflated with written translation. In the case of North Carolina, candidates must also pass a translation test with ten moderately difficult items in English they translate by hand and without access to resources. An example of such an item is "The victim's family identified his corpse in the morgue on the night of the drive-by shooting. The witnesses will receive subpoenas to appear in court for the first hearing" (NCAOC 2020).

Though New York does not spell out any specific translator qualification requirements, the position descriptions for court interpreters in its *Court Interpreter Manual and Code of Ethics* reveal that interpreters' "typical duties" include the translation of various official, technical, medical and legal documents, in addition to audio recordings in English or the other language (NYSUCS 2018b, 37–43), which is in line with New York position postings observations by Ortega Herráez, Giambruno and Hertog (2013, 113). The written exam component of New York's Spanish court interpreter exam includes multiple-choice translation sections to and from Spanish, in a way similar to the written FCICE. However, the sample tests (NYSUCS 2020b; USC 2019) available for both of these written exams differ in format and quality. The FCICE includes a little over three times as much translation content; half of the items are underlined portions of sentences for which you must choose the closest of four translation options in meaning. The other half of items are paragraph-length passages with underlined portions, for which, again, you must choose the best of four translations, but while considering both the sentence and whole-paragraph context of the underlined segment. In the case of New York, all the translation items are sentences (statements), for which you choose the entire-sentence translation option (A, B, C, D) that is closest. The following are item examples accompanied by their correct answer:

1   The speaker cleared his throat before starting his speech.

   A   El orador carraspeó antes de comenzar a [sic] su discurso.

2   He was told to begin after he had studied the matter thoroughly.

   B   Se le dijo que comenzara después [sic] que hubiera estudiado el asunto a fondo.

3   She was being pressured to make her decision.

   D   Ella fue presionaba [sic] para que tomara su decisión.

10  Tocaron a la puerta pero no conteste [sic] por temor a que me arrestaran.

   A   They knocked at [sic] the door but [sic] did not answer for fear that they would arrest me.

While whole sentence items capture more context than sentence-portion items, test takers may indeed be distracted by issues such as prepositional errors (1, 2, 10A), pronoun (10A–first-person singular)/accent (10) omissions and past-participle/typo mistakes (3D).

And while the written FCICE includes yet more context with its multiple-choice paragraph-length passages, the NJITCE, which was in use from 2001 to 2012, included a written non-multiple-choice translation component with full texts, one in English and one in Spanish, to qualify individuals to translate as well (Dueñas González, Vásquez and Mikkelson 2012, 1194–1195; Feuerle 2013, 87; González-Hibner 2015; NAJIT 2011; Palma 2015). Candidates had 40 minutes to complete the translation of each passage, "medical/penal, legal (financial/civil)," with dictionaries they could bring with them to the test (NAJIT 2011). It is important to note, however, that these whole-passage translations form part of a single test that also includes a battery of 121 multiple-choice items testing, in Spanish and English, candidates' knowledge of antonyms, synonyms, analogies, grammar and syntax, reading comprehension and ability to select correct translations of idioms and proverbs, in addition to testing their knowledge of the NAJIT code of ethics and professional responsibilities in English (ibid.). Dueñas González, Vásquez and Mikkelson (2012, 1194) note that testing these different areas in a single exam "presents challenges for accurate assessment of candidates' proficiency levels in each of these areas because [a] high score in one area can mask deficiencies in another, unless tests are scored separately."

Previously referred to by North Carolina, the federal *Guide to Judiciary Policy*, the *Guide to Translation of Legal Materials* (NCSC 2011) and the *Language Access Planning and Technical Assistance Tool for Courts* (DOJ 2014), ATA certification has become a recognized qualification in US court systems. The Judiciary of Maryland, which outsources all of its outbound translation needs to a translation company, states that "[t]ranslations are generated by individuals certified by the American Translators Association and are reviewed by a second certified translator" (MJ 2019, 26). In the case of inbound foreign language translation, Maryland recommends that parties and their attorneys hire ATA-certified translators (MJ 2020). In California, ATA certification is the first recommendation for translators in addition to "court or legal specialization" (JCC 2016, 9). NAJIT (2019, 2) also points out ATA certification as a viable qualification, but reminds us it is general in nature. The ATA exam, "a three-hour, open-book, proctored exam," requires candidates to translate two passages: a general text and either a scientific, technological or medical text or a legal, business or financial text (Koby and Champe 2013, 161–163). ATA exams also, as previously mentioned, can be to or from English, which California and the NCSC (2011) deem a key factor to consider.

When ATA-certified translators are not available in the California system, translators must be deemed qualified based on their experience, education and references (JCC 2016, 9). In the case of Maricopa County, however, neither translator nor interpreter certifications are mentioned. Both "interpreters and translators are qualified via a testing process to ensure their competence to provide interpretation/translation services in their respective foreign languages" (ASCMC 2016, 9). The Maricopa County qualifications review form for translation and transcription/translation contractors asks them to "provide proof of English and the foreign language proficiency skills" through a language services company Maricopa uses (MCJBA 2020b).

As mentioned earlier, translation tests offered by the State Department and FBI, or for that matter the UN as cited by North Carolina as well, tend to be viewed as specific to these entities and part of their employment or contractor application processes. Moreover, their availability might be on an as-needed basis. In the case of the FBI, most applicants take "listening and reading tests in the foreign language, a translation test from the foreign language into English and speaking tests in both English and the foreign language" (FBI 2020). Few details are provided about the various test items and the translation component in particular, other than that it is based on the Interagency Language Roundtable translation criteria (Brau 2014). The State Department open-book, in-person Language Services Translation Test, which is taken in a single language direction like the ATA exam, lasts four hours and consists of three texts: one dealing with a general international relations topic, another with either legal, administrative, economic or business content or a mixture thereof and the third text which covers a scientific or technological subject of current interest in foreign affairs (USDS 2019, 1). UN translation examination varies according to the position and has in recent cases been carried out from any computer online. For example, the written component of a 2017 competitive UN examination for English translators/précis writers included the translation of a general text from any of the UN official languages to English and the translation of a specialized text (either economic or legal, depending on the candidate's preference) to English from a different UN official language (i.e. not the same UN language as in the first translation) (UN 2017, 3). These translations could be completed from any computer with an internet connection and with the aid of any non-human resources of the candidate's choosing (ibid.). In the event the candidate successfully completed these two translations, as well as a précis-writing task and a text revision in English, he or she would be invited to complete a remote proctored translation to English without any resources, in addition to an interview (UN 2017, 4).

A wide variety of translation qualifications possibilities and variations exist within and across different US jurisdictions. In certain cases, translator-specific examinations, most often the ATA exam, are qualifications priorities or possibilities. In others, court interpreter certifications are deemed appropriate, whether or not they include a translation component, which may be more substantial in some cases than others. The NJITCE is in a category of its own, as it is for both interpreters and translators in the judicial context, but given that it is discontinued and its limited recognition by state courts during its administration, it is unlikely to be incorporated as a qualification at this time. Finally, there is the possibility that no established translator or interpreter certifications are referred to, and in-house training is emphasized or language skills testing is contracted with a third-party provider instead. Where certification, testing or training is not a possibility, experience, education and references may qualify practitioners depending on the jurisdiction.

## 4.5 Discussion and Conclusions

Given the limited or sporadic nature of budgeting for court-related translation, the fact that policies and legislation have a strong court interpreting focus, and the often project-based focus of outbound translation in particular, it is difficult for courts in the US to establish uniform or highly developed translation practices. These factors also impinge on the creation of stably defined notions of a court translator figure, let alone continuous positions or testing specifically focused on court-related translation. Unlike interpreters in many districts, translators are not needed by the courts on a daily basis and often do their work in places where they are not as visible to court stakeholders. The fruits of their labor may generate more long- than short-term benefits for LEP individuals or merely constitute an incremental, albeit important, step toward their equal access to justice before the law in a proceeding, whereas a court interpreter's services fulfill the immediate language needs of an LEP individual at a specific event or proceeding when he or she is scheduled to interact with or appear before the justice system. Nevertheless, recent federal pressure on courts and better defined guidelines and standards have, in a number of cases, raised awareness of the importance and utility of high-quality court-related translation services and, in some cases, of the qualifications of the practitioners themselves to ensure they are in a position to produce such quality. This awareness has led to the establishment of policies, standards and guidelines to improve the utility and quality of court-related translation.

State courts, in a number of cases, have focused considerably more on how written translation can increase language access to LEP individuals, leading to large-scale translation projects of court forms and information resources, experimentation with creating bilingual forms to be filled out and submitted in the foreign language and development of quality-control practices such as source and target text revision, providing translators access to a contact person, translation briefs and glossaries or detailed translation or transcription/translation practice protocols. In some cases, much thought has been given to the types of qualifications that translators should have and how these qualifications may not necessarily coincide with court interpreter qualifications. All of this is evidence of considerable progress being made in court-related translation in the US context.

Nevertheless, more consideration may be given to how court-related translations might be optimally completed and by whom. As shown earlier, translation standards, guidelines and practices may vary considerably across courts in the US. Some courts invest more than others in their own capacity and infrastructure to meet their translation needs. Courts might go as far as to manage their own translation needs and translate both outbound and inbound materials internally with staff translators or individual contractors, while others may limit their translation scope to outbound needs and partially or fully rely on company outsourcing. Managing translation needs and production internally may be cost-efficient and produce levels of quality over which courts might have more control than if they place their trust in a third-party. Staff positions, however, will understandably be more scarce for translators than for interpreters. Outbound translation projects are often one-offs, translations are used over and over again and continuous funding primarily exists to support federally mandated interpreting activities. True, court materials and forms are often updated, which, in turn, necessitates translation revisions, but performing these in a consistent fashion and obtaining, creating and organizing the resources whereby it would be possible to do so efficiently requires solid planning. Maryland, as already pointed out, outsources all of its translation needs to a professional translation company as a means "[t]o ensure quality and consistency" without having to invest in internal translation processes (MJ 2019, 26). Nevertheless, translation outsourcing in institutional contexts allows for communication gaps to occur between vendors and the institution, as well as quality control complications (Scott 2019; Sirovec 2020).

But in a case like that of New Mexico, where outsourcing is being used to handle not only one-time outbound needs but also continuous inbound translations of pleadings completed by litigants in another language, it seems that at least the continuous inbound translation needs could be primarily handled in-house. Perhaps such a solution would be more cost-effective and efficient, facilitating not only more leverage over quality control but also adjustments to production in a more directly informed and speedier way that takes account of the larger context of the court's and LEP individuals' needs. Maricopa County is a good example of how its previous continuous flow of inbound translation commitments to a wide variety of local agencies gave way to the creation of its in-house CITS unit in the early eighties and its employment of multiple staff translators.

One final area worthy of additional reflection is that of court translator qualifications. As previously discussed, the NJITCE existed for both court translators and interpreters until somewhat recently. Palma (2015) cites the exam's inclusion of translation as a key reason to re-launch the exam, but recognizes how expensive it was to develop and maintain according to national credentialing standards. An additional concern is its very low pass rate (Korp-Edwards 2015), with only 30 individuals attaining the credential during its almost 12 years of existence (González-Hibner 2015).

The ATA exam is recognized and regularly available though it is not legal-specific. The State Department, UN and FBI exams might be more applicable in terms of contents, especially in the first two cases, but such exams may only be available when an applicant has arrived at a specific stage of consideration for employment with such entities or when the entities are accepting or in need of tenders for contractors in specific languages. Ideally, generalist translator certification like the ATA certification would be complemented with court interpreter certification to ensure court or legal specialization.[8] Moreover, court interpreter certification features two sight translations of texts that are 225–230 words in length (i.e. similar in length to the texts in the aforementioned translation examinations) and cover both language directions (NCSC 2017, 3; USC 2019, 36).[9] Candidates will need to study for this sight translation component with materials such as reports, affidavits or formal legal documents such as contracts or wills.

In any event, court interpreter certification is recommendable for the "hybrid specialty" work of transcription/translation (NAJIT 2019), which has received considerably less attention from a professionalization standpoint (Dueñas González, Vásquez and Mikkelson 2012, 1220). While interpreters may lack proficiency in converting spoken language to written language with utmost precision, translators may be underprepared to work with "live recorded extemporaneous speech," "nonstandard usage and jargon" or "the errors and misspeaks that often color the speech of individuals with limited or no formal education" (NAJIT 2019, 2).

There is potential value in establishing court interpreting credentials that include translation within their purview. As court interpreters traditionally have been tapped to do court-related translation or transcription/translation work and many are inclined to accept (Dueñas González, Vásquez and Mikkelson 2012, 907; Ortega Herráez, Giambruno and Hertog 2013, 114; Vigier, Klein and Festinger 2013, 47), such a translation test would compel them to engage in translation training or hone their translation skills through self-study. Their doing so may also help them better prepare for the sight translation component of the oral exam. Among the common interpreting deficiencies recorded in the NCSC oral exam are candidates' underdeveloped document analysis abilities and literalness tendencies in the sight translation section (NCSC 2020, 1–2). Focusing more on the translation of documents and written communication might help candidates mitigate such deficiencies.

Interpreters working in legal contexts where oral proceedings and documentation are intricately intertwined may be able to add a good deal of value to the services they offer by being able to effectively translate (Killman 2020). Having the same individuals actively engaged and adequately prepared to work in aspects of both the court document chain and ongoing proceedings may provide these practitioners with additional insights to better serve the interests of both LEP individuals and the courts.

## Notes

1 "Translation," unless otherwise specified, may refer to both the traditional translation of documents or text and the transcription/translation of recordings.
2 "LEP" in this chapter refers to anyone five years and over reporting they "speak English less than 'very well'" (USCB 2018).

3 https://www.uscourts.gov/rules-policies/judiciary-policies/court-interpreting-guidance.
4 Outbound translation in the context of state courts may be contingent upon one-time funding or grant awards (Mellinger 2017, 313).
5 In addition to these four staff translators, CITS has 28 Spanish interpreters, one American Sign Language interpreter and three supervisors (ASC 2017).
6 New Mexico is not alone in using a company vendor for translation. For instance, California recently contracted with a company to perform Spanish and Chinese translations with turnarounds of 6–24 hours for COVID-19 communications (JCC 2020a). In the case of the Judiciary of Maryland, all of its outbound translation needs are handled by a company vendor "[t]o ensure quality and consistency in the translation process" (MJ 2019, 26).
7 New Mexico, given its constitution and long history of multilingualism, is the only state that seats LEP jurors.
8 In an Ohio project to translate court forms to several languages, bios of the translators and translation reviewers are included (OSC 2020). The Spanish translator, for example, has state and federal court interpreter certifications and bi-directional, generalist English-Spanish translator certification from the Canadian Translators, Terminologists and Interpreters Council.
9 In the case of New York, however, the sight translation texts are considerably shorter by as much as 38% (NYSUCS 2020a).

# References

ABA (American Bar Association). 2008. *Law & the Courts: Volume I: The Role of the Courts*. Chicago: ABA Publishing.

ABA. 2012. *Standards for Language Access in Courts*. Chicago: ABA Publishing.

AOUSC (Administrative Office of the United States Courts). 2014. *Federal Court Interpreter Orientation Manual and Glossary*. www.uscourts.gov/services-forms/federal-court-interpreters

ASC (Superior Court of Arizona). 2011. *Administrative Order No. 2011 – 96: In the Matter of Language Access Planning*. www.azcourts.gov/Portals/22/admorder/Orders11/2011-96.pdf

ASC. 2017. *Court Interpreter Recruitment*. www.youtube.com/watch?v=NcCpOLQuMuc

ASCMC (Superior Court of the State of Arizona in and for the County of Maricopa). 2016. *Administrative Order No. 2016 – 034: In the Matter of Language Interpreters and Access to Courts by Persons with Limited English Proficiency*. https://superiorcourt.maricopa.gov/court-interpretation-and-translation-services/

Brau, Maria M. 2014. *The FBI Develops a Translation Aptitude Test*. https://www.govtilr.org/Publications/TAT%2020140512.pdf

Department of Justice. 2010. *Letter from the Assistant Attorney General to Chief Justices/State Court Administrators Regarding Language Access: 16 April 2010*. https://najit.org/wp-content/uploads/2016/09/AAGLEPLetter.pdf

Department of Justice. 2014. *Language Access Planning and Technical Assistance Tool for Courts*. www.lep.gov/sites/lep/files/resources/February_2014_Language_Access_Planning_and_Technical_Assistance_Tool_for_Courts_508_Version.pdf

Dueñas González, Roseann, Victoria F. Vásquez and Holly Mikkelson. 2012. *Fundamentals of Court Interpretation: Theory, Policy, and Practice*. 2nd ed. Durham, NC: Carolina Academic Press.

FBI (Federal Bureau of Investigation). 2020. *FBI Jobs: Language Analysts*. Accessed May 5, 2020. https://www.fbijobs.gov/career-paths/language-analysts

Feuerle, Lois. 2013. "Testing Interpreters: Developing, Administering, and Scoring Court Interpreter Certification Exams." *Translation & Interpreting* 5 (1): 80–93.

González-Hibner, Melinda. 2015. *From the NAJIT Board: The Future of the NJITCE: Part I: Big Decisions Ahead*. https://najit.org/from-the-najit-board-the-future-of-the-njitce/

Jang, Deeana. 2014. *Providing Language Access in the Courts: Working Together to Ensure Justice*. www.justice.gov/archives/opa/blog/providing-language-access-courts-working-together-ensure-justice

JCC (Judicial Council of California). 2015. *Strategic Plan for Language Access in the California Courts*. www.courts.ca.gov/languageaccess.htm

JCC. 2016. *Translation Protocol: Judicial Council of California*. www.courts.ca.gov/documents/lap-Translation-Protocol.pdf

JCC. 2020a. *Master Agreement 2019-01: Avantpage Rapid Fire Service*. www.courts.ca.gov/languageaccess.htm

JCC. 2020b. *Self-Help Glossary: Spanish*. www.courts.ca.gov/selfhelp-glossary.htm?rdeLocaleAttr=es

Killman, Jeffrey. 2020. "Interpreting for Asylum Seekers and their Attorneys: The Challenge of Agency." *Perspectives* 28 (1): 73–89.

Koby, Geoffrey S., and Gertrude G. Champe. 2013. "Welcome to the Real World: Professional-Level Translator Certification." *Translation & Interpreting* 5 (1): 174–210.

Korp-Edwards, Bethany. 2015. *From the NAJIT Board: The Future of the NJITCE: Part III: Why We Don't Need the NJITCE Anymore*. https://najit.org/from-the-najit-board-the-future-of-the-njitce/

KSC (Supreme Court of Kentucky). 2017. *Kentucky Court of Justice Language Access Plan and Procedures*. https://kycourts.gov/courtprograms/CIS/Pages/guidelinespolicies.aspx

MCJBA (Maricopa County Judicial Branch of Arizona). 2020a. *Guidelines for the Transcription and Translation of Spanish Audio and Video Recordings*. Accessed May 5, 2020. https://superiorcourt.maricopa.gov/purchasing/open-and-continuous-solicitations/

MCJBA. 2020b. *Review of Qualifications for Transcription and Translation Services*. Accessed May 5, 2020. https://superiorcourt.maricopa.gov/purchasing/open-and-continuous-solicitations/

Mellinger. Christopher D. 2017. "Equal Access to the Courts in Translation: A Corpus-Driven Study on Translation Shifts in Waivers of Counsel." *Perspectives* 25 (2): 308–322.

Mikkelson, Holly. 2013. "Universities and Interpreter Certification." *Translation & Interpreting* 5 (1): 66–78.

MJ (Maryland Judiciary). 2019. *Language Services in the Maryland Courts*. www.mdcourts.gov/sites/default/files/import/accesstojustice/pdfs/languageservicesreportfy19.pdf

MJ. 2020. *Translation Services*. https://mdcourts.gov/interpreter/translationservices

MPI (Migration Policy Institute). 2011. *LEP Individuals in the US: Number, Share, Growth, and Linguistic Diversity*. https://justiceindex.org/2016-findings/language-access

MPI. 2015. *Number and Share of the Limited English Proficient (LEP) Population in the United States, 1990 to 2013.* www.migrationpolicy.org/

NAJIT (National Association of Judiciary Interpreters and Translators). 2011. *National Judiciary Interpreter and Translator Certification (NJITCE).* https://web.archive.org/web/20110123210831/http:/najit.org/certification/NJITCE.php

NAJIT. 2019. *General Guidelines and Requirements for Transcription Translation in a Legal Setting for Users and Practitioners.* https://najit.org/wp-content/uploads/2016/09/Guidelines-and-Requirements-for-Transcription-Translation.pdf

NCAOC (North Carolina Administrative office of the Courts). 2017. *Standards for Language Access Services in North Carolina State Courts.* www.nccourts.gov/documents/publications/spoken-foreign-language-interpreters

NCAOC. 2020. *Court Interpreter Written Screening Test – Translation Section.* Accessed May 5, 2020. www.nccourts.gov/assets/inline-files/overview_writtentranstest.pdf

NCSC (National Center for State Courts). 2011. *Guide to Translation of Legal Materials.* www.ncsc.org/Services-and-Experts/Areas-of-expertise/Language-access/Resources-for-Program-Managers.aspx

NCSC. 2012. *Court Interpreter Written Examination: Overview.* www.ncsc.org/~/media/Files/PDF/Services%20and%20Experts/Areas%20of%20expertise/Language%20Access/Written%20and%20Oral/2014%20January_Written%20Exam%20Overview%201%2029%2014.ashx

NCSC. 2017. *Court Interpreter Oral Examination: Overview.* www.ncsc.org/~/media/Files/PDF/Services%20and%20Experts/Areas%20of%20expertise/Language%20Access/Resources%20for%20Program%20Managers/2017%20August%20Oral%20Exam%20Overview%20for%20Candidates%208%2018%2017.ashx

NCSC. 2020. *Common Oral Interpreting Exam Performance Deficiencies.* Accessed May 5, 2020. https://www.ncsc.org/~/media/Files/PDF/Services%20and%20Experts/Areas%20of%20expertise/Language%20Access/Written%20and%20Oral/CommonoralexamdeficienciesFINAL22415.ashx

NMJ (New Mexico Judiciary). 2013. *State Justice Institute Grant: SJI-10-TA-179: Language Access Planning for New Mexico State Courts Final Grant Report.* https://ncsc.contentdm.oclc.org/digital/collection/accessfair/id/315

NMJ. 2017. Language Access Plan. https://languageaccess.nmcourts.gov/language-access-plans.aspx

NMJ. 2018. *Language Access Services Annual Report: 2018 Issue IV.* https://nmcourts.gov/Language-Access-Services/annual-report.aspx

NMJ. 2019. *Language Access Services Annual Report: 2019 Issue V.* https://nmcourts.gov/Language-Access-Services/annual-report.aspx

NMSC (Supreme Court of New Mexico). 2016. *Guidelines for Audio Recorded, Video Recorded, or Written Materials in Languages other than English – Rule 1103(E)(8) NMRA.* https://nmcenterforlanguageaccess.org/cms/en/courts-agencies/judges-portal

NYSUCS (New York State Unified Court System). 2017. *Ensuring Language Access: A Strategic Plan for the New York State Courts.* http://ww2.nycourts.gov/COURTINTERPRETER/policies.shtml

NYSUCS. 2018a. *Bilingual Orders of Protection: Translation and Interpretation Services in Criminal Courts.* http://ww2.nycourts.gov/sites/default/files/document/files/2018-06/Bilingual_Orders_Protection.pdf

NYSUCS. 2018b. *Court Interpreter Manual and Code of Ethics.* http://ww2.nycourts.gov/sites/default/files/document/files/2018-05/CourtInterpreter Manual_1.pdf

NYSUCS. 2020a. *Practice – Part I – Sight Translation (English to Spanish).* Accessed May 5, 2020. http://ww2.nycourts.gov/COURTINTERPRETER/ ExamInformation.shtml#Oral

NYSUCS. 2020b. *Written Examination of Language Proficiency and Legal Terminology for Per Diem Court Interpreters in Spanish.* Accessed May 5, 2020. http://ww2.nycourts.gov/COURTINTERPRETER/ExamInformation. shtml

Ortega Herráez, Juan Miguel, Cynthia Giambruno, and Erik Hertog. 2013. "Translating for Domestic Courts in Multicultural Regions: Issues and New Developments in Europe and the United States of America." In *Legal Translation and Context,* edited by Anabel Borja Albi and Fernando Prieto Ramos, 89–121. Oxford: Peter Lang.

OSC (Supreme Court of Ohio). 2020. *Language Services Program Forms Translation Project.* Accessed May 5, 2020. www.supremecourt.ohio.gov/JCS/ interpreterSvcs/forms/default.asp

Palma, Janis. 2015. *From the NAJIT Board: The Future of the NJITCE: Part II: Why We Need the NAJIT Certification.* https://najit.org/from-the-najit-board-the-future-of-the-njitce/

Pym, Anthony, François Grin, Claudio Sfreddo, and Andy L. J. Chan. 2012. *The Status of the Translation Profession in the European Union.* Luxembourg: EU Publications Office. doi:10.2782/63429

Scott, Juliette R. 2019. *Legal Translation Outsourced.* New York: Oxford University Press.

Sirovec, Saša. 2020. "Achieving Quality in Outsourcing." *Babel* 66 (2): 193–207.

Spohn, Cassie, Craig Hemmens, and Wesley S. McCann. 2019. *Courts: A Text/ Reader.* 3rd ed. Thousand Oaks, CA: Sage.

SSCC (Sacramento Superior Court of California). 2020. *Legal Glossaries.* www.saccourt.ca.gov/general/legal-glossaries/legal-glossaries.aspx

TAOC (Tennessee Administrative Office of the Courts). 2018a. *Tennessee Court Interpreter Credentialing Program.* www.tncourts.gov/sites/default/files/docs/ court_interpreter_manual_june_2018.pdf

TAOC. 2018b. *Tennessee Spoken and Written Language Assistance Plan.* www.tncourts.gov/sites/default/files/docs/final_tn_statewide_lep_plan_ july_2018.pdf

UN. 2017. *Competitive Examinations for Language Professionals.* https:// languagecareers.un.org/dgacm/Langs.nsf/files/english_lce_2017_information. pdf/$FILE/english_lce_2017_information.pdf

USC (United States Courts). 2019. Federal Court Interpreter Certification Examination for Spanish/English: Practice Tests. www.prometric.com/sites/ default/files/2019-09/fcice_practiceexam.pdf

USCB (United States Census Bureau). 2018. *American Community Survey: 2018.* www.census.gov/acs/www/data/data-tables-and-tools/

USCB. 2019. *County Population Totals: 2010–2019.* www.census.gov/data/tables/time-series/demo/popest/2010s-counties-total.html

USDS. 2019. *Guidance on Preparing for the Language Services Translation Test.* www.state.gov/wp-content/uploads/2019/06/Guidance-on-Preparing-for-the-Translation-Test.pdf

Vigier, Francisco, Perla Klein, and Nancy Festinger. 2013. "Certified Translators in Europe and the Americas: Accreditation Practices and Challenges." In *Legal Translation and Context*, edited by Anabel Borja Albi and Fernando Prieto Ramos, 27–51. Oxford: Peter Lang.

# 5  Developing an Evaluation Tool for Legal Interpreting Quality Control
## The INTER-Q Questionnaire

*María Jesús Blasco Mayor and*
*Marta Sancho Viamonte*

## 5.1 Introduction

The need for quality legal interpretation is universally recognized as an essential element to ensure the right to effective linguistic assistance, and can be regarded as a fundamental right (Gialuz 2018, XV) in that it places the allophone person on an equal legal footing, is a prerequisite for the right of defense and is fundamental to a fair trial (28). Great strides have been made to promote and protect this fundamental right with the establishment of registers of qualified interpreters and translators in some countries such as Austria, the United Kingdom and Australia (González et al. 2012, 316–324), while others such as the United States have implemented certification exams following the model resulting from the 1978 Court Interpreters Act (Mikkelson 2017, 19–27). In the European Union (EU), Directive 2010/64/EU marked a turning point for the rights of accused persons by ensuring the linguistic presence of the accused in criminal proceedings (Hertog 2015a), stating that quality must be maintained. However, no recommendations, guidelines or standards are suggested as to how this quality needs to be controlled and what evaluation tools should be established to that end. Although some projects have been developed to create accreditation models for legal interpreters and to establish registers in the United States (González et al. 2012; Wallace 2012, 2019; Mikkelson 2017, 13–18) and in the EU (Giambruno 2014; Wallace 2015; Mikkelson 2017, 14), in the countries where this work has been done, no systems have been developed or put into operation to evaluate the real performance of interpreters working in courtrooms and police stations. This quality assurance would seem to be a necessary measure since most of interpreters working in such contexts are unqualified and do not adhere to effective performance protocols (Del Pozo Triviño and Blasco Mayor 2015, 49–51).

Faced with this worrying scenario – which does not show signs of improving as some EU Member States (MS) appear to be avoiding the deployment of measures to counteract it – a quality control tool designed and validated using psychometric principles could prove valuable for

DOI: 10.4324/9780429264894-5

justice administrations to screen substandard performance or malprac-
tice. This study presents the method used to design and validate an evaluation tool for the quality of legal interpretation which contributes to
assessing the performance of legal interpreters in real conditions, including some linguistic factors. The tool is based on objective, quantifiable
parameters from a statistical point of view that provide reliable, valid
and useful tests.

## 5.2 The Many Facets of Legal Interpreting

In Hertog's words, "the fact remains, however, that adequate training
and quality in legal interpreting are far from ensured in many parts of
the world," and "even with the benefit of training and guidance, interpreting in community-based legal settings holds many difficult challenges" (2015b, 231). These challenges can be transposed to research
when it comes to studying quality assurance in legal interpreting, and
the many facets that researchers must take into consideration when em-
barking on a research project on legal interpreting. In this section we
briefly focus on some of them: legal interpreting as an independent specialty, the role of jurists in legal interpreting, legal interpreting performance and competencies and how all these elements impinge upon and
affect legal interpreting and its quality.

As some scholars (González et al. 2012; Mikkelson 2017, 1–4) and
the recently approved ISO 20228 (2019) standard on legal interpreting
argue, for all intents and purposes legal interpreting is an independent
specialty. The fact of having to swear an oath makes a difference (Morris
1999, 21), as does the legal system underlying this activity, since one of
the distinctive features of legal interpretation is that it is explicitly and
strictly regulated by law in many countries (Ortega Herráez 2011, 16).
Different national laws establish differing standards in each country and
a fraudulent interpretation, whether due to omission or to a misrepresentation of the truth, constitutes a criminal offence in some countries like
Spain, as established in Articles 459 and 460 of the Penal Code (Faraldo
Cabana et al. 2017).

In this context, the relevance of legal professionals (judges, lawyers,
prosecutors), as major actors who are present, use and interact with the
activity of legal interpreting, is unquestionable. In some countries such
as the United States, judges are responsible by law for the quality of the
interpreting taking place in their courtrooms (González et al. 2012). In
Spain judges have jurisdiction over their courts and may dismiss an interpreter if they suspect poor performance or deliberate false testimony is
taking place (Blasco Mayor 2015), whereas in Italy they are in charge of
authorizing payments to interpreters (Sancho Viamonte 2018, 54). Some
researchers have advocated that jurists and "government officials or rep-
resentatives of agencies entrusted with tasks of controlling, supervising

and regulating the judicial system" participate in legal interpreting assessment teams (Del Pozo Triviño and Blasco Mayor 2015, 63). They can be considered as "accomplished communicators" since they are already working successfully in the legal system, and thus can "make a huge contribution to the accuracy of the interpretation" (Corsellis, Clement and Vanden Bosch 2011, 317–324). Observation of interpreter performance in courts reveals a number of behaviors that clearly differ from those established in professional codes of conduct (Blasco Mayor 2015), and in many cases they are spotted by legal experts present in the proceedings (Blasco Mayor 2016, Blasco Mayor and Sancho Viamonte 2017, Sancho Viamonte 2018). In fact, Directive 2010/64/EU Art. 6 establishes training of such professionals to work with interpreters, thus acknowledging the impact their interaction may have on a fair trial.

Performance criteria for legal interpreting have been developed by well-known experts in the field (Hertog 2003) and should constitute the basis of any quality assessment such as certification and quality control. According to Pöchhacker (2015, 79), "the notion of 'performance' is used in interpreting studies in relation to both the process and the product of interpreting, as well as to the interpreter's behaviour in interaction." He goes on to admit that a "detailed breakdown of relevant facets of an interpreter's performance is difficult enough," and when referring specifically to situations of dialogic interaction, those most prevalent in legal interpreting, the task becomes huge:

> In face-to-face communication, the interpreter's non-verbal behaviour is not limited to vocal and prosodic characteristics but includes a wide range of visual signals that can impact the interaction, from gaze movement and facial expression to posture and physical positioning. Questions of cultural appropriateness, trust and social identity must be added to the behavioural mix, so that the description and analysis of interpreting performance on dialogic interaction becomes an enormous analytical challenge.
>
> (Pöchhacker 2015, 70)

In theory, legal interpreters should possess a number of competencies (Hertog 2003, 2011; Giambruno 2011) and apply them in their profession; these competencies would eventually make up and shape their performance. However, there is a significant difference between theoretical postulates and real professional performance (Ortega Herráez 2011, 152). Even in some countries with a long tradition of legal interpretation and with established standards like the United States, there are notable variations between the federal level, which uses extremely well-trained and certified interpreters, and the state or county levels (Navarro-Hall 2017). In many countries, more specifically in the EU, the lack of professional recognition and accreditation exams, in addition to the inadequate remuneration, leads to situations in which the real practice of legal interpretation is characterized by the hiring of non-professionals (Blasco Mayor et al. 2013; Ortega Herráez 2013; FRA 2016), while skilled and competent professionals are reluctant to interpret in the criminal justice system due to the low fees (Caciagli, Balletto and Rivezzi 2009). In the light of these facts, well-known scholars advocate that systems of quality control be put in place when interpreting provision cannot guarantee that legal interpreters are trained and certified professionals:

> These systems can combine not only control and direction but also the support and encouragement needed by the individual bilingual professionals, the identification and dissemination of good practice, quality assurance mechanisms, consultation and involvement in incremental forward planning and budgets.
>
> (Corsellis, Clement and Vanden Bosch 2011, 339)

After checking that there seem to be no quality assurance mechanisms available in any EU MS regarding legal interpreting, unless they are not public and are therefore unknown, the idea of designing a quality control instrument that facilitated detection of unprofessional behaviors took shape. From interviews with judges, attorneys and other legal personnel working with interpreters every day, it could be inferred that some of them were certainly able to detect unprofessional behavior when they saw it (Blasco Mayor and Sancho Viamonte 2017). The use of a screening test in courts could be a first step toward achieving at least some quality in legal interpreting within the European area of justice. It would work as one of the many measures that should be applied regarding legal interpreting quality, as advocated in Directive 2010/64/EU.

## 5.3 The Right to Linguistic Assistance and Directive 2010/64/EU as a Milestone in the Pursuit of Quality Legal Interpretation

As noted earlier, one of the distinctive features of legal interpretation is that statutory provisions exist that establish the conditions for appointing interpreters and the right to use the interpreting service (Ortega Herráez 2011, 16). Sometimes the fundamental characteristics of legal interpretation, primarily quality, are structured around these provisions. If this is not the case, the right to due process would be undermined. The protection of the fundamental rights of individuals has moved from the domain of national law, in which each state is responsible for passing its own regulations and establishing its own controls (Fernández Carrón 2017, 19), to the domain of international law. In the international context, the right to an interpreter has become a procedural guarantee of a fundamental right, the right to a fair trial (Jimeno Bulnes 2007, 156), something now integrated into the national and supranational levels.

Directive 2010/64/EU was the first project undertaken as part of the "Roadmap to strengthen procedural rights of suspected or accused persons in criminal proceedings" launched in 2009 by the European Commission's Directorate-General for Justice. Its symbolic value, then, is considerable, as the first explicitly recognized right for suspected or accused persons in a multilingual Europe promoting the free movement of goods, services and capital since its creation. Based on the principle of non-discrimination developed in Article 21 of the EU Charter of Fundamental Rights (CFR) (Gialuz 2014, 84), it was the first Directive under the Treaty of Lisbon related to justice and the first European Directive on translation and interpretation (Hertog 2015a, 73).

Directive 2010/64/EU explicitly mentions the European Convention on Human Rights (ECHR) and the CFR, which enshrines the right to a fair trial and respect for the right of defense. If the accused does not understand the documentation, the attorney or the tribunal, this right becomes relegated to a "sham defence." Two fundamental rights are established: the non-waivable right to interpretation (Art. 2), and the right to translation (Art. 3), waivable if the accused is informed, constituting a meta-right to linguistic assistance (Gialuz 2018, 133–141). The ultimate aim is to safeguard the rights of the suspected or accused person and ensure a fair trial.

The established rights are also to be applied to the execution of a European arrest warrant and the MS must meet the costs, whatever the final ruling (Gialuz 2018, 235). Explicit reference is made to the assistance of an interpreter in any communication between the suspect and their legal counsel in the preparation of the defense. A mechanism must be established to ascertain whether the suspected or accused person speaks or understands the language of criminal proceedings, establishing a subjective sphere of application, to be offered to all suspected and accused persons, whether or not they are citizens of the EU or of a third country, since procedural safeguards are fundamental rights (Arangüena Fanego 2011). It also establishes that the proper authorities must ensure a mechanism to control the adequacy of the interpretation and translation and that the right is only guaranteed when the interpretation service is of sufficient quality. The legal provisions in the Directive are clear; not only is there a right to interpretation, but it is essential that it meet the required quality stipulated (Art. 5). Without quality interpretation and translation, the rights established do not really exist. To that end, the Directive adopts a series of mechanisms, drawing on the AEQUITAS project (Hertog and Vanden Bosch 2001), the Green Paper (Commission of the European Communities 2003)[1] and the Proposal for a Council Framework Decision on certain procedural rights in criminal proceedings throughout the EU. The measures are the following:

1   MS shall ensure that suspected or accused persons have the possibility to complain that the quality of the interpretation and translation is not sufficient (Art. 2.5 and Art. 3.5);
2   MS shall ensure that control can be exercised over the adequacy of the interpretation and translation provided [...] (Recital 24);
3   MS shall endeavor to establish a register or registers of independent translators and interpreters who are appropriately qualified (Art. 5.2.);
4   MS shall request those responsible for the training of judges, prosecutors and judicial staff involved in criminal proceedings to pay special attention to the particularities of communicating through an interpreter (Art. 6); and
5   Interpretations should be recorded (Art. 7) (Commission of the European Communities 2004).

In order to safeguard the precepts established in the Directive, it should have been accompanied by a non-binding document to implement linguistic assistance, which could take the form of "Council recommendations" and be adopted contextually with the Directive (Gialuz 2018, 100). At the moment of writing, ten years after the Directive was passed, no recommendations on the quality of interpreting have emanated from any official body, which shows the Commission's lack of interest in this subject. However, interpreting quality has been and still constitutes an outstanding area of research in interpreting studies. Given the scarcity of research on quality in legal interpreting, we have first looked at the interpreting context where research on quality is more advanced – conference interpreting.

## 5.4 Quality in Legal Interpreting

Generally speaking, quality has been and continues to be a fundamental aspect in studies on interpretation and is considered inherent to the subject, the thread that runs through all specialist studies regarding interpretation (Viezzi 1996) from joining the profession to training, accreditation, the very role of the interpreter (Angelelli 2004; Pöchhacker and Zwischenberger 2015) and ethical implications, in addition to cognitive aspects. The growing attention paid to the social dimension of evaluating quality is reflected in the importance of first impressions (García Becerra 2012) and the application of an evaluation system based on criteria (Collados Aís et al. 2007, 2011) that help to explain the complex relationships that exist between user expectations and the real quality of an interpretation. Although quality can be a dynamic concept whose evolution depends on environmental variables and socially consti-tuted norms (Collados Aís and García Becerra 2015), it is also defined as something objectively and tangibly measurable that is closely linked to the situation, context and general circumstances surrounding the evalu-ation (Grbić 2015; Zwischenberger and Behr 2015, 7–8).

This chapter follows Pöchhacker's sociological view of quality "not as a self-contained topic but as a complex, overarching theme in which all aspects of the interpreter's product and performance—textuality, source-target correspondence, communicative effect, and role perfor-mance—play an integral part" (Pöchhacker 2004, 153). In the specific context of legal interpretation, quality is a crucial factor in ensuring a fair trial. In fact, ISO 20228 on legal interpreting states that speakers of languages other than the language of service used in legal settings can only have access to fair-trial standards when legal interpreting services of a sufficiently high quality are systematically provided (Katschinka 2017). Thus, bearing all these issues in mind, only those aspects of legal interpreting performance that are directly observable have been identi-fied for test construction.

One of the main hurdles to assessing quality in legal interpreting re-sides in the fact that in many countries, unqualified individuals intervene as interpreters in court proceedings and, as legal professionals (judges, attorneys and prosecutors) do not know the languages, they cannot be certain that quality interpretation is being provided. In addition, these professionals are not used to working with interpreters and do not know the peculiarities of the job of interpreting or the protocols to follow in interpreter-mediated communication. For example, a quality interpre-tation is not always accompanied by successful communication (Gile 1983), and legal professionals may be unaware of this state of affairs. As a result, their expectations in some cases are not realistic.

The best way to promote quality interpretation is to establish high-quality standards that must be verified using competency exams and access to a professional register, as established in Directive 2010/64/ EU and advocated by European professional associations and univer-sities. In fact, measuring and evaluating quality is the focus of many studies related to the education and certification of interpreters, whether regarding admission tests, evaluations during the education process, the use of expert interpreters or certification procedures. Consequently, the development of evaluation criteria and specific tools is a highly topical subject (Grbić 2015, 336; Han and Slatyer 2016).

The Directive, however, has been implemented unevenly in the differ-ent EU countries (Giambruno 2014, 149–180; FRA 2016) and although many MS have organized registers and examinations, this is not true for all of them. A review of the literature and official documentation shows that at this time, some countries in the EU do not even have accreditation exams or registers and, accordingly, there is no mutual recognition of certification in MS.[2] Moreover, letting each MS choose the way in which these registers are compiled has led to major disparities and inconsistencies (Giambruno 2014, 182–187; FRA 2016). In Italy and Spain, for example, the implementation has been de jure, but not de facto, thus perpetuating a critical situation of market disorder that has not modified the prior situation (Sandrelli 2011; Garwood 2012; Blasco Mayor et al. 2013). The use of unqualified interpreters is widespread, registers of legal interpreters have not been created and there is an infringement of both rights and the law because the mechanisms to ensure compliance do not exist (Del Pozo Triviño and Blasco Mayor 2015; Ortega Herráez 2016; Alonso Araguás et al. 2018; Bestué Salinas and Orozco Jutorán 2017; Bestué Salinas 2018; Gialuz 2018; Amato and Mack 2015). Moreover, the use of unqualified, untrained interpreters has produced profound distrust, since not only do many of these "ad hoc interpreters" fail to comply with a code of conduct but also some of their behaviors can be said to infringe the law (Alonso Araguás et al. 2018, 11–42; Sancho Viamonte 2018, 50).

## 5.5 INTER-Q: A Quality Control Tool for Legal Interpretation in National Contexts

Considering the imperative need for legal interpretation quality control in the MS as stated in Directive 2010/64/EU, a tool has been designed to measure the professional behavior of legal interpreters in the different settings where they may work. This tool consists of a questionnaire to be given to legal professionals who intervene in criminal proceedings, which should be administered in written form immediately after the interpreter's intervention. This is in no way the only legal interpreting quality control resource that could be applied in the criminal legal context and its use does not exclude the application of other quality control measures. This tool only measures the observable behaviors of the legal interpreter in the specific contexts and circumstances that are described below. As Grbić (2008, 2015) observed, the quality of interpretation in action can and should be measured, as it can objectively define and identify aspects of the work, the interaction and the context.

This questionnaire was created and evaluated by María Jesús Blasco Mayor, Micaela Moro Ípola and Marta Sancho Viamonte, and was the subject of Sancho Viamonte's PhD dissertation. Creating a questionnaire involves a long, detailed process that includes various steps (Meyer 2014, 61): (1) establishing the purpose, (2) defining the construct of interest, (3) drafting the test items, (4) piloting the test, (5) empirical study.

To create the INTER-Q questionnaire, Meyer's method for test design was followed. The term "test" is used in a broad sense and can be applied to many evaluation procedures, whether or not they are called tests. Tests can be used for psychological, educational or occupational assessment, and this particular study falls within the scope of the third type since it evaluates the professional performance of interpreters in legal settings, more specifically criminal proceedings. According to the International Guidelines on Test Use, they should:

- assess both normal and dysfunctional behavior. In this case, normal (adequate and inadequate) behavior and performance are evaluated within a professional setting;
- be administered under controlled, standardized conditions with rigorous scoring protocols. Here, closed (yes/no) questions were used with a coding system for each question that adds up to the total test score;
- provide measures of conduct samples from which inferences can be made; and
- include procedures that allow for qualitative categorization levels for the subjects.[3]

As noted, a solid test must be backed up by empirical data related to its reliability and validity when measuring the proposed objectives (Anastasi and Urbina 1998). Reliability refers to the precision or stability of the measurements, while validity refers to what a test measures and to what extent. Unlike reliability, validity is not studied with correlation coefficients alone, but using broader research designs that include experimental interventions, an analysis of the literature, the judgment of experts and the like. Different aspects of validity are studied using specific methods. Not all evaluation techniques and procedures are equally precise nor do they provide the same guarantees; consequently, it is essential to consider the sources of validity or invalidity in data interpretation (Alonso Tapia 2004). Since the 1950s, the American Psychological Association (APA) has broken down validity into three different types: construct validity, content validity and criterion validity (AERA, APA and NCME 2014).

Determining the content validity of a test fundamentally involves the systematic examination of its contents in order to verify that the instructions, materials, questions and possible answers reflect an important and representative sample of what is being measured. According to Wallace (2019, 116), "content validity has to do with how well items on a test align with what the test is supposed to measure."

### 5.5.1 Purpose and Construct of Interest

The goal, then, was to design a tool to evaluate the behavioral aspects of legal interpreters' performance that could be administered to legal professionals using interpreting services in their everyday work routine in national courts. The use of quality control measures is advocated by Directive 2010/64/EU (Recital 24) and the different projects sponsored by the European Commission's Directorate-General for Justice (AEQUITAS, Aequilibrium, Building Mutual Trust [BMT], Speak out for Support [SOS-VICS] and QUALITAS, among the most important), as well as national and international associations of legal interpreters and translators (the National Association of Judiciary Interpreters and Translators [NAJIT], the National Accreditation Authority for Translators and Interpreters [NAATI], the European Legal Interpreters and Translators Association [EULITA], the Spanish Professional Association of Court and Sworn Interpreters and Translators [APTIJ], and the Italian Association of Legal Translators and Interpreters [AssITIG], among others). In the specific case of Spain, Del Pozo Triviño and Blasco Mayor (2015, 62) have observed that by implementing control mechanisms, it is possible to comply with the procedural safeguards of witnesses and the accused, while also building trust toward the interpreters' work on the part of legal professionals. This should result in greater respect for the work of legal interpreters and recognition of the profession (Corsellis 2011, 2015).

The questionnaire is designed for legal professionals who work with interpreters in different situations and contexts: police officers, prosecutors, attorneys, court clerks, judges and forensic doctors. It evaluates interpreter behavioral aspects of performance using a scientific method based on psychometrics. The evaluation tool is used in legal and quasi-legal settings during all the different stages of the criminal proceedings, from referral and investigation to sentencing. Although these stages share the same underlying legal system and concepts, each one has specific characteristics regarding interaction with interlocutors, the aim of the interaction, the formality of the event, the function of language, the role of the participants and so forth (Hale 2007, 66).

The questionnaire's target group are legal interpreters at work in a national court, usually without the support of any technical resources, in two-way dialogue interpretation situations and without any chance to carefully prepare for a specific situation. According to Meyer (2014), the first step in tool design is defining what is going to be measured. INTER-Q only addresses linguistic aspects that are directly observable such as length, comprehensibility into Spanish/Italian (lexis, pronunciation, grammar), correct use of legal terms in Spanish/Italian, use of the first/third person. So to a certain extent, the test measures the linguistic ability of interpreters in the language of the proceedings, and differences in length of utterances or speaking turns between speaker and interpreter. We considered this a secondary linguistic aspect, but these aspects can certainly signal quality – or absence thereof. However, we totally agree that the main measure of quality is the actual accuracy of content (fidelity, appropriate terminology, lack of omissions, additions or semantic distortions, etc.) which evidently INTER-Q is not able to measure fully. Therefore we firmly believe that further quality control measures should be put in place in any judicial system such as expert assessment of recordings. INTER-Q is only a quality screening test and it should be used as precisely that. It cannot replace a fully-fledged quality assurance system of legal interpretation. In any case, it is a first step and could indicate where further, more in-depth measures need to focus.

### 5.5.2 Drafting the Test Items

Taking the minimum requirements that a legal interpreter should meet and that legal professionals should be familiar with as the starting point, the following sources were consulted to define and classify the interpreter's professional behaviors and competencies in order to design the contents of the questions in the questionnaire:

- codes of ethics from several international and European associations (NAJIT 1988, AUSIT 2010, APTIJ 2010, AssITIG 2012, EULITA 2013);
- a basic bibliography for interpretation in public services (Hale 2007; Corsellis 2008) and legal services (Blasco Mayor 2015; Del Pozo Triviño and Blasco Mayor 2015; Gallai and Rudvin 2015; Rudvin 2015a, 2015b; Rudvin et al. 2015);
- manuals on legal interpretation (González et al. 1998, 2012; Mikkelson 2000; Blasco Mayor 2015);
- Australian and British operating standards for interpreters in legal settings, British and Australian codes, such as that of the London Metropolitan Police Service (London Metropolitan Police 2010), the protocol of the Association of Visual Language Interpreters of Canada (AVLIC 2011) and recently published national recommendations for working with interpreters in Australian courts and tribunals (Martin 2018);
- international legal interpreter accreditation systems;
- results from European DG Justice legal interpretation projects (Corsellis 2001, Katschinka 2008, European Commission 2009, among others);
- position papers from the principal professional associations;
- ISO 13611:2014 standard on community interpreting;
- BA dissertations (Viejo Jovani 2014, Estañ Arellano 2016) and MA dissertations both Spanish (Gascón Nasarre 2015) and Italian (Mometti 2014, Perdicchizzi 2016).

After reading these sources, a classification of the categories on which to base the test was made:

- nonverbal communication and behavior;
- linguistic competency in the language used in the legal setting (the only language the legal professionals are able to judge);
- knowledge of the process, the course of action and legal terminology;
- interpersonal behavior and emotion;
- interpretation competencies: e.g. simultaneous and consecutive competencies, sight translation, notetaking, use of first/third person.

The following legal procedural situations that usually require the assistance of an interpreter were then selected: (1) police questioning, (2) trials, (3) interim hearings such as questionings and depositions, (4) attorney interviews. Questions were devised that cover several behaviors related to the act of legal interpretation in the four different situations. The initial questionnaire was drafted jointly by three researchers and was made up of 34 questions. Table 5.1 shows the number of questions combining each behavior with each situation and context.

A yes/no question format was chosen for the questionnaire both to make it easy to complete in a very short period of time and to obtain the highest possible discrimination in the responses. The process of

*Table 5.1* Situational and contextual categories in the design of the questionnaire

| *Interpreter's behavior and competencies* | *Interpretation contexts and situations* | | | |
|---|---|---|---|---|
| | *Police questioning* | *Trial* | *Interim hearing* | *Attorney interview* |
| Good manners/nonverbal communication | 3, 5, 6, 14 | 3, 5, 6, 14 | 3, 5, 6, 14 | 3, 5, 6, 14 |
| L1 competency | 1, 2 | 1, 2 | 1, 2 | 1, 2 |
| Knowledge of legal terms and procedures | 17, 23, 24, 27, 34 | 17, 23, 24, 27, 34 | 17, 23, 24, 27, 34 | 17, 23, 24, 27, 34 |
| Emotion and behavior | 4, 10, 11, 12, 13, 29, 32 | 4, 10, 11, 12, 13, 29, 32 | 4, 10, 11, 12, 13, 29, 32 | 4, 10, 11, 12, 13, 29, 32 |
| Interpreting competencies | 7, 8, 9, 15, 16, 18, 19, 20, 21, 22, 25, 26, 28, 30, 33 | 7, 8, 9, 15, 16, 18, 19, 20, 21, 22, 25, 26, 28, 30, 33 | 7, 8, 9, 15, 16, 18, 19, 20, 21, 22, 25, 26, 28, 30, 33 | 7, 8, 9, 15, 16, 18, 19, 20, 21, 22, 25, 26, 28, 30, 33 |

drafting the questions took into account the answer format in such a way that the activity being asked about had to occur at least once during the situation under observation (e.g. "yawning") or be permanent (e.g. "carries a notebook to take notes"). If the frequency changes the meaning of the question, this was specified with an adverb (e.g. "interrupts the person being interpreted occasionally to request clarification"). The statements were written in the affirmative and the instructions told the respondents to indicate whether they had seen the interpreter doing what was described in the following question or not. If no specific behavior was recalled or it did not occur, the respondents were told to choose the alternative answer, "not applicable" (n/a).

### 5.5.3 Pilot Test

For the pilot test, contact was made with a group of experts comprising eight judges, eight attorneys and eight interpreters, all with more than seven years of experience working in legal procedures with interpreters. They were asked to fill out the questionnaire twice, first when describing a performance that they remembered as "good" and then when they recalled a "bad" performance, since all of them see interpreters at work on a daily basis. Once the responses to the first questionnaires were received, the experts were asked to answer a second questionnaire, the "Evaluation Questionnaire," on certain aspects regarding the content validity and the apparent validity of the test.

A total of three attorneys, four interpreters and five judges/magistrates responded, providing 24 responses to the INTER-Q first questionnaire and 12 to the later Evaluation Questionnaire. The respondents commented on each of the questions and the Evaluation Questionnaire, allowing to perform a quantitative analysis of the responses, calculating the p-value (difficulty index), the DI (discrimination index), the correlation of the answer to each question and the total questionnaire score.

Finally, the percentage of unanswered responses, considered an indication of the usefulness of the particular question, was calculated. The decision was made to remove the items with an unanswered response percentage above 20%. Using the results from the pilot study, the number of questions was reduced from 34 to 21 and the final version was created, with some correction of the wording of the questions and their order. The change in the question sequence was done to ensure, first, that items from the same category did not follow one another and, second, that two questions with reverse wording did not appear together.

### 5.5.4 Empirical Study

Once the final version was written, a field study was conducted to calculate the metric properties of the questionnaire. This work was done in courts of Italy and Spain, which share certain characteristics with regard to legal interpretation: the need for legal interpretation has become a full-blown emergency due to the steep rise in trials that require an interpreter, the two countries are behind in implementing Directive 2010/64/ EU, they both lack a consolidated register and neither country offers an accreditation exam for legal interpreters. In addition, the people who work in criminal legal settings receive very low pay, whether they are subcontracted or contracted directly, which deters qualified interpreters. Finally, neither Italy nor Spain has protocols for legal professionals working with interpreters that would guide them in their jobs, helping all the parties involved to recognize their role and professional conduct. After presenting requests to several legal and police headquarters, permission was obtained to administer the questionnaire in the courts of Valencia (Spain), Milan and Genoa (Italy).

While the questionnaires were administered, a series of complementary qualitative and ethnographic activities were carried out to obtain valuable observational information that was later used to analyze the results and draw conclusions during the validation phase of the questionnaire. These activities consisted of interviews with judges and interpreters about the role of legal interpreters. Details concerning the interpreters' performance and the conduct of the legal professionals during the various on-site acts were also observed and noted in order to create a description of each situation in which the interpreter intervened, which would later be contrasted with the quantitative data from the finished questionnaires.

All data collected through the questionnaires were processed using SPSS v24 and jMetriks under the guidance of a psychometrician and expert in psychological evaluation and test design.[4]

### 5.5.5 Results

After designing, piloting and validating the questionnaire, the following question arises: is INTER-Q a good tool to evaluate the performance of an interpreter working in a legal context? Different procedures exist to determine the properties of a tool to measure human activity or behavior (Meyer 2014). These procedures are classified into two types: those related to precision, or the absence of error (reliability), and those that indicate the meaning of the measurements and their usefulness with regard to achieving the applied objectives (validity).

This study obtained two types of reliability measurements. The first calculated internal consistency, which informs the degree of error resulting from the selection of questions. Two methods were calculated to obtain internal consistency. The first is the most common, but it has the disadvantage of depending on the characteristics of the sample. In this study, that value is modest (near 0.50). With the second procedure, a significantly higher value was obtained (0.90), indicating that the selection of the items and length of the questionnaire are appropriate. The second reliability measurement calculated was objectivity, or the degree of congruence between different evaluators. This was done in two ways: by calculating a concordance coefficient from four cases where the same researcher and judge were both present and, second, by verifying a high degree of convergence with the cases described in the field notebook.

One important aspect regarding the objectivity of INTER-Q is that it compares evaluations made by a professional from the world of interpretation (the researcher) and legal professionals with more or less experience working with interpreters, who are not necessarily familiar with that work. Both the coefficient value and the case analyses based on the field notebooks indicate high congruence between the evaluators. Therefore, it can be reasonably argued that the INTER-Q questionnaire is an objective evaluation tool that can be used by people who are unfamiliar with interpretation (although they need to know legal procedures and terms, since several of the questions concern these aspects). However, in no way does this suggest that legal professionals should not be trained to work with interpreters as an essential part of their job. Rather, the questionnaire provides reliable, valid data regardless of whether or not the respondent is familiar with the work of the interpreter.

The language used in the questionnaire and the differences between the Italian and Spanish legal systems did not significantly influence the scores. This would suggest that translating and adapting the questionnaire to the other languages used in the EU would produce equivalent results. In short, the results of this study indicate that INTER-Q is quite an objective evaluation tool that requires only minimal training to use.

The second question concerning the measurement properties of a questionnaire is perhaps the most important, since it concerns validity. The results suggest that INTER-Q does discriminate well between good – as in those whose conduct follows professional protocols and codes of conduct – and bad interpreters – those who do not abide by professional codes of conduct –, even when the evaluators are legal professionals.

The analysis of the items indicates that there are different levels of questions (clearly, some of the activities analyzed do not only depend on the knowledge, skills or attitudes of the interpreter, but on the conduct of the judge and other professionals as well such as reading the rights or other documents). The first group contains eight very easy questions, with a low capacity to discriminate between "good" and "bad" interpreters. The questions in this group address the basic skills and behaviors that are expected from a professional in a work setting that follows specific protocols and where fundamental decisions are taken that affect people. There are three questions related to good manners (1, 5 and 11), three to verbal and paraverbal expressive capacity (3, 4 and 12) and, finally, two regarding neutrality with respect to the procedure (18 and 21). Examples of these questions are the following:

> *Question 1: The interpreter's appearance (personal grooming, attire, chewing gum) is adequate to the situation.*
> *Question 11: The interpreter addresses legal professionals in an appropriate manner.*

Most of the interpreters scored correctly on these questions, but they could serve to isolate or identify people who should be rejected as interpreters. In other words, when the INTER-Q questionnaire is used in the future, a low score on these questions would quite likely indicate that this person has neither the training nor the qualifications to work as a legal interpreter. However, it is also true that those who obtain a high score may not have had training, but may have acquired this behavior due to common sense, good instinct or work experience. Despite the fact that the responses to these questions in most of the questionnaires were affirmative, the field notebooks captured cases of interpreters who were chewing gum, were inappropriately dressed for the context or who behaved in some other unseemly way, as described in the questions in this part of the questionnaire. In any case, these behaviors can be interpreted as pointers that signal possible lack of competence in other areas. These aspects may not be infallible but they are a start.

A second group contained six medium difficulty questions with a mid-level capacity for discrimination. These questions were related to compliance with the protocols established in the codes of conduct cited earlier, such as whether the interpreter engaged in parallel conversations with the declarant, if legal jargon was used correctly and whether the interpretation was much shorter than the original declaration. The last question is especially important, since it may be indicative of an incomplete interpretation:

> *Question 13: There is a clear difference between the length of the deponent's utterance and that of the interpreter's rendition.*

In this context, codes of conduct specifically state that it is essential to faithfully translate the statement in such a way that permits communication between the parties involved in the legal procedure without omitting, adding or modifying anything. Only in this way can an allophone or hearing-impaired person be on equal legal footing with a person who speaks the procedural language, a condition known as "linguistic presence."

Finally, the seven questions regarding the interpreters' technical skills indicate that few interpreters demonstrated them, although they have the highest correlation with the total score. Legal professionals in general appear to be unaware of the technical skills associated with interpreters and even believe that acting in a way that runs counter to them is appropriate. These questions are related to the technical skills expected of a qualified interpreter such as carrying a notebook to take notes, using the first person when interpreting the subject's discourse and reproducing the tone of the original message. Indeed, a question related to the final point was added to the original version of the questionnaire on the advice of one of the judges interviewed in the qualitative study. The quantitative analysis now also includes this question among those that best identify a good interpreter.

## 5.6 Conclusion

The EU framework for legal interpreting is still underdeveloped in some MS, namely Spain and Italy, jeopardizing the right of citizens to a fair trial. The mechanisms that would eventually guarantee the minimum interpreting quality required by law to be achieved in criminal proceedings, namely interpreter training, the creation of professional registers and the certification or accreditation of interpreters, are yet to be developed in these two countries. In this irregular situation, we have designed and validated a quality control tool for interpreting in legal settings, following the scientific method of test construction to measure behavior in a professional setting. It has demonstrated its validity and reliability, and can be used in the courts with minimal training by legal professionals. Although the tool still requires fine-tuning, it has already proven to be useful in contributing to discriminate between professional and unprofessional interpreters.

When applying INTER-Q in legal settings, we recommend the following procedure to prevent misuse of the tool and promote good practices in justice administrations: the ideal evaluator would be a senior qualified legal interpreter, preferably a service coordinator from the justice administration or an external auditor. INTER-Q is by no means intended to be the only measure for quality control of interpretation in legal settings. Rather, its main purpose is to detect what is considered as professional or unprofessional behavior without explicitly measuring linguistic output content, as part of an overall quality control system together with complementary controls, such as expert assessment of video or audio recordings. In any case, we would like to emphasize that it is a first step toward quality and could serve to indicate where further, more in-depth quality control measures need to focus. Tools like INTER-Q, used as part of a wider quality assurance framework within the justice administration, could contribute to excellence in legal interpreting, safeguarding fundamental human rights in compliance with the law.

## Notes

1 In any case, the Directive has a lower threshold of rigor than the Council Framework Decision (Ortega Herráez 2016).
2 We are referring to a European register, an original idea from DG Justice (European Commission) that was even piloted in an EU Project lead by EULITA, called *LIT Search – Pilot project for an EU database of legal interpreters and translators* (https://eulita.eu/wp/lit-search-pilot-project-eu-database-legal-interpreters-and-translators/).
3 The International Guidelines followed were those translated into Spanish by the Consejo General de la Psicología de España, whose original source is the International Test Commission, available at: https://www.cop.es/index.php?page=directrices-internacionales.
4 Dr. Micaela Moro Ipola (Universitat Jaume I).

## References

AERA (American Educational Research Association), APA (American Psychological Association), and NCME (National Council on Measurement in Education). 2014. *Standards for educational and psychological testing* (Rev. ed.). Washington, DC: American Educational Research Association.

Alonso Araguás, Iciar, Nuria Hernández Cebrián, and Laura Izquierdo Valverde. 2018. "Responsabilidad penal y código deontológico de los traductores e intérpretes judiciales." In *Traducción, interpretación e información para la tutela judicial efectiva en el proceso penal*, edited by María Jesús Ariza Colmenarejo, 11–42. Valencia: Tirant lo Blanch.

Alonso Tapia, Jesús. 2004. *Evaluación psicológica. Coordenadas, procesos y garantías*. Madrid: Universidad Autónoma de Madrid.

Amato, Amalia, and Gabriele Mack. 2015. "The ImPLI Project, Pre-Trial Interpreting in Italy and the Transposition of Directive 2010/64/EU." *TRANS* 19(1): 43–56. http://www.trans.uma.es/Trans_19-1/Trans19-1_043-056.pdf (accessed May 28, 2018).

Anastasi, Anne, and Susana Urbina. 1998. *Tests Psicológicos* (7th ed.). México: Prentice Hall.

Angelelli, Claudia Viviana. 2004. *Revisiting the Interpreter's Role: A Study of Conference, Court, and Medical Interpreters in Canada, Mexico, and the United States*. Amsterdam: John Benjamins.

APTIJ (Asociación Profesional de Traductores e Intérpretes). 2010. Código deontológico para intérpretes y traductores judiciales y jurados. http://www.aptij.es/img/web/docs/codigo-d-aptij.pdf (accessed March 1, 2019).

Arangüena Fanego, Coral. 2011. "El derecho a la interpretación y a la traducción en los procesos penales. Comentario a la Directiva 2010/64/UE del Parlamento Europeo y del Consejo, de 20 de octubre de 2010." *Revista General de Derecho Europeo*, https://www.iustel.com/v2/revistas/detalle_revista.asp?id_noticia=410537&d=1 (accessed March 1, 2019).

AsSITIG (Associazione Interpreti Giudiziari). 2012. Codice Deontologico. http://www.interpretigiudiziari.org/index.php/iscrizioni/codice-deontologico (accessed March 1, 2019).

AUSIT (The Australian Institute of Interpreters and Translators). 2010. Code of ethics. https://ausit.org/code-of-ethics/ (accessed March 1, 2019).

AVLIC (The Association of Visual Language Interpreters of Canada). 2011. Interpreting Legal Discourse & Working in Legal Settings: An AVLIC Position Paper. http://www.avlic.ca/sites/default/files/docs/AVLIC-Interpreting_Legal_Discourse%26Working_in_Legal_Settings.pdf (accessed March 1, 2019).

Bestué Salinas, Carmen. 2018. "Aproximación empírica a la labor del intérprete en los Tribunales de Justicia." In *Traducción, interpretación e información para la tutela judicial efectiva en el proceso penal*, edited by María Jesús Ariza Colmenarejo, 139–158. Valencia: Tirant lo Blanch.

Bestué Salinas, Carmen, and Mariana Orozco Jutorán. 2017. "Resultados del proyecto TIPp (Traducción e interpretación en los procesos penales) a cargo de los investigadores del proyecto TIPp." Paper delivered at the *VII Jornada de Traducción e Interpretación en los Servicios Públicos en Cataluña*. Barcelona, July 7, 2017. http://grupsderecerca.uab.cat/miras/es/node/245 (accessed March 1, 2019).

Blasco Mayor, María Jesús. 2013. "Quality of Interpreting in Criminal Proceedings in Spain under European Directive 2010/64/EU." *Cuadernos de ALDEEU* 25: 165–190.

Blasco Mayor, María Jesús. 2015. "La asistencia de intérprete en el procedimiento penal. Especial referencia a su papel en la vista oral." In *Vistas penales. Casos resueltos y guías de actuación en sala*, edited by María Luisa Cuerda Arnau, 267–286. Valencia: Tirant lo Blanch.

Blasco Mayor, María Jesús. 2016. "Con la venia, señorías. El papel de jueces y abogados en la profesionalización de la figura del intérprete judicial." Paper delivered at the conference *De la Traducción Jurídica a la Jurilingüística: Enfoques Interdisciplinarios en el Estudio de la Lengua y el Derecho*. Sevilla, Universidad Pablo de Olavide, October 27–28, 2016.

Blasco Mayor, María Jesús, Maribel del Pozo Triviño, Cynthia Giambruno, Anne Martin, Emilio Ortega Arjonilla, Nadia Rodríguez Ortega, and Carmen Valero Garcés. 2013. *Informe sobre la transposición de la Directiva 2010/64/UE del Parlamento europeo y del Consejo relativa al derecho a interpretación y traducción en los procesos penales*. (2). http://auneti.org/?s=Informe+sobre+la+transposici%C3%B3n+de+la+Directiva+2010%2F64%2FUE+del+Parlamento+europeo+y+del+Consejo+relativa+al+derecho+a+interpretaci%C3%B3n+y+traducci%C3%B3n+en+los+procesos+penales (accessed March 1, 2019).

Blasco Mayor, María Jesús, and Marta Sancho Viamonte. 2017. "Percepción de la calidad de la interpretación judicial por parte de los jueces." Paper delivered at the *Third International Conference on Interpreting Quality*. Granada, October 5, 2017.

Caciagli, Flavia, Cristina Balletto, and Giovanna Rivezzi. 2009. *Position Paper. L'Interprete giudiziario e il traduttore giuridico*. https://aiti.org/sites/default/files/utenti/position_paper_interprete_giudiziario_traduttore_giuridico.pdf (accessed March 20, 2017).

Collados Aís, Ángela. and Olalla García Becerra. 2015. "Quality Criteria." In *Routledge Encyclopedia of Interpreting Studies*, edited by Franz Pöchhacker, 337–338. London and New York: Routledge.

Collados Aís, Ángela, Emilia Iglesias Fernández, Esperanza Macarena Padras Macías, and Elisabeth Stéveaux (eds). 2011. *Qualitätsparameter beim Simultandolmetschen, Interdisziplinäre Perspektiven*. Tübingen: Gunter Narr.

Collados Aís, Ángela, Esperanza Macarena Padras Macías, Elisabeth Stéveaux, and Olalla García Becerra (eds). 2007. *La evaluación de la calidad en interpretación simultánea: parámetros de incidencia.* Granada: Comares.

Commission of the European Communities. 2003. Green Paper from the Commission. Procedural Safeguards for Suspects and Defendants in Criminal Proceedings throughout the European Union. https://eur-lex.europa.eu/legal-content/EN/TXT/PDF/?uri=CELEX:52003DC0075&from=ES (accessed March 12, 2017).

Commission of the European Communities. 2004. Proposal for a Council Framework Decision on Certain Procedural Rights in Criminal Proceedings throughout the European Union. https://eur-lex.europa.eu/legal-content/EN/TXT/PDF/?uri=CELEX:52004PC0328&from=EN (accessed March 13, 2017).

Consejo General de la Psicología en España. Directrices generales para el uso de los Test. https://www.cop.es/index.php?page=directrices-internacionales (accessed October 15, 2019).

Corsellis, Anne. 2001. "PSTI: Components of the Profession." In *Aequitas: Acces to Justice across Language and Cultures,* edited by Eric Hertog, 73–77. Antwerp: Lessius Hogeschool. https://eulita.eu/wp/wp-

Corsellis, Anne. 2008. *Public Service Interpreting. The First Steps.* Houndmills, UK: Palgrave Macmillan.

Corsellis, Anne. 2011. "Seven EU Projects. A Journey toward a Regulated Language Profession." In *Interpreting Naturally. A Tribute to Brian Harris,* edited by María Jesús Blasco Mayor and Amparo Jiménez Ivars, 143–160. Frankfurt am Main: Peter Lang.

Corsellis, Anne. 2015. "Strategies for Progress: Looking for Firm Ground." *MonTI* 7: 101–114.

Corsellis, Anne, Amanda Clement, and Yolanda Vanden Bosch. 2011. "Training for Members of the Legal Services Working through Legal Interpreters and Translators." In *Building Mutual Trust: A Framework Project for Implementing EU Common Standards in Legal Interpreting and Translation,* edited by Brooke Townsley, 315–350. London: Middlesex University.

Decreto Legislativo 4 marzo 2014 no. 32. Attuazione della direttiva 2010/64/UE sul diritto all'interpretazione e alla traduzione nei procedimenti penali. Gazzetta Ufficiale 18 marzo 2014, n. 64. https://www.gazzettaufficiale.it/eli/id/2014/03/18/14G00041/sg.

Del Pozo Triviño, María Isabel, and María Jesús Blasco Mayor. 2015. "Legal interpreting in Spain at a Turning Point." *MonTI* 7: 41–71.

Directive 2010/64/UE of the European Parliament and of the Council of 20 October 2010 on the Right to Interpretation and Translation in Criminal Proceedings. https://eur-lex.europa.eu/legal-content/EN/TXT/?uri=CELEX:320 10L0064 (accessed March 13, 2017).

Estañ Arellano, Elena. 2016. *Estudio sobre la calidad de la interpretación en la Ciudad de la Justicia de Valencia.* BA dissertation. Universitat Jaume I, Castellón. http://repositori.uji.es/xmlui/bitstream/handle/10234/161749/TFG_2016_Esta%c3%b1ArellanoElena.pdf?sequence=1&isAllowed=y (accessed March 1, 2019).

EULITA (The European Legal Interpreters and Translators Association). 2013.
Code of Professional Ethics. https://eulita.eu/wp/wp-content/uploads/files/
EULITA-code-London-e.pdf (accessed November 7, 2019).

European Commission. 2009. Reflection Forum on Multilingualism and Interpreter Training. Final Report. https://eulita.eu/wp/wp-content/uploads/files/
Reflection%20Forum%20Final%20Report.pdf (accessed May 24, 2018).

European Ombudsman. 2018. Decision in Case 969/2017/LM on the European
Commission's Failure to Prepare a Report, within the Statutory Deadline,
on Member States' Compliance with Directive 2010/64/EU on the Right to
Interpretation and Translation in Criminal Proceedings, 23 March 2018.
https://www.ombudsman.europa.eu/en/decision/en/91729 (accessed March
1, 2019).

Faraldo Cabana, Patricia, María Angeles Catalina Benavente, and Miguel Cle-
mente Díaz. 2017. *Falso testimonio de testigos, peritos e intérpretes*. Valencia: Tirant lo Blanch.

Fernández Carrón, Clara. 2017. *El derecho a interpretación y a traducción en
los procesos penales*. Valencia: Tirant lo Blanch.

FRA (European Union Agency for Fundamental Rights). 2016. *Rights of Suspected and Accused Persons Across the EU: Translation, Interpretation and
Information*. Luxembourg: Publications Office of the European Union.

Gallai, Francesco. 2015. "Il quadro teorico dell'interpretazione in ambito
giuridico-giudiziario." In *L'interprete giuridico. Profilo professionale e metodologie di lavoro*, edited by Mete Rudvin and Cinzia Spinzi, 153–170. Torino: Carocci Faber.

Gallai, Francesco, and Mete Rudvin. 2015. "Aspetti pratici e logistici dell'interpretazione giuridica." In *L'interprete giuridico. Profilo professionale e
metodologie di lavoro*, edited by Mette Rudvin and Cinzia Spinzi, 153–170.
Torino: Carocci Faber.

García Becerra, Olalla. 2012. "First Impressions in Interpreting Quality Assess-
ment: The Incidence of Nonverbal Communication." In *Interpreting Brian
Harris: Recent Developments in Translatology*, edited by Amparo Jiménez
Ivars and María Jesús Blasco Mayor, 173–192. Bern: Peter Lang.

Garwood, Christopher John. 2012. "Court Interpreting in Italy. The Daily Vi-
olation for a Fundamental Human Right." *The Interpreters' Newsletter* 17:
173–189.

Gascón Nasarre, Fernando. 2015. *La percepción de los abogados de oficio de
las actuaciones de intérpretes judiciales en el partido judicial de Zaragoza:
análisis cualitativo de un grupo focal*. MA dissertation. Universitat Jaume I,
Castellón. http://repositori.uji.es/xmlui/handle/10234/152668 (accessed March
1, 2019).

Gialuz, Mitja. 2014. "L'assistenza linguistica nella prassi giudiziaria e la diffi-
cile attuazione della Direttiva 2010/64/UE." In *Traduzione e Interpretazione
per La Società e Le Istituzioni*, edited by Caterina Falbo and Maurizio Viezzi,
83–96. Trieste: EUT.

Gialuz, Mitja. 2018. *L'assitenza linguistica nel processo penale. Un meta-diritto
fondamentale tra paradigma europeo e prassi italiana*. Milano: Wolters Kluwer.

Giambruno, Cynthia. 2011. "Core Modules in Legal Interpreting and Translation Training." In *Building Mutual Trust. A Framework Project For*

*Implementing EU Common Standards in Legal Interpreting and Transla-tion*, edited by Brooke Townsley, 17–22. London: Middlesex University.

Giambruno, Cynthia (ed.). 2014. *Assessing Legal Interperter Quality Through Testing and Certification: The Qualitas Project*. Alicante: Publicaciones de la Universidad de Alicante. http://www.qualitas-project.eu/sites/qualitas-project.eu/files/the_qualitas_project_web.pdf (accessed March 28, 2018).

Gile, Daniel. 1983. "Aspects in méthodologiques de l'évaluation de la qualité du travail en interprétation simultanée." *Meta* 28 (3): 236–243.

González, Roseann Dueñas, Victoria F. Vásquez, and Holly Mikkelson. 1998. *Fundamentals of Court Interpretation Theory, Policy and Practice*. Durham, NC: Carolina Academic Press.

González, Roseann Dueñas, Victoria F. Vásquez, and Holly Mikkelson. 2012. *Fundamentals of Court Interpretation Theory, Policy and Practice*. Second edition. Durham, NC: Carolina Academic Press.

Grbić, Nadia. 2008. "Constructing Interpreting Quality." *Interpreting*, 10 (2): 232–257.

Grbić, Nadia. 2015. "Quality." In *Routledge Encyclopedia of Interpreting Stud-ies*, edited by Franz Pöchhacker, 333–336. London and New York: Routledge.

Hale, Sandra Beatriz. 2007. *Community Interpreting*. New York: Palgrave and Macmillan.

Han, Chao, and Helen Slatyer. 2016. "Test Validation in Interpreter Certifica-tion Performance Testing." *Interpreting* 12 (2): 225–252.

Hertog, Erik. 2003. "From Aequitas to Aequalitas: Equal Access to Justice across Language and Culture in the EU (Grotius Projects 98/GR/131 and 2001/GRP/015)." In *Aequalitas. Equal Access to Justice across Language and Cul-ture in the EU. Grotius Project 2001/GRP/015*, edited by Erik Hertog, 6–23. Antwerp: Lessius Hogeschool.

Hertog, Erik. 2011. "Core Competencies in Legal Interpreting and Transla-tion." In *Building Mutual Trust. A Framework Project for Implementing EU Common Standards in Legal Interpreting and Translation*, edited by Brooke Townsley, 11–16. London: Middlesex University.

Hertog, Erik. 2015a. "Directive 2010/64/EU of the European Parliament and of the Council on the Right to Interpretation and Translation in Criminal Pro-ceedings: Transposition Strategies with regard to Interpretation and Transla-tion." *MonTI* 7: 73–100.

Hertog, Erik. 2015b. "Legal Interpreting." In *Routledge Encyclopedia of In-terpreting Studies*, edited by Franz Pöchhacker, 230–235. London and New York: Routledge.

Hertog, Erik, and Yolanda Vanden Bosch (eds). 2001. *Aequitas Access to Justice across Language and Culture in the EU*. Department Vertaler-Tolk. Lessius Hogeschool. https://eulita.eu/wp/wp-content/uploads/files/Aequitas_Acces to Justice across Language and Culture in the EU.pdf (accessed March 23, 2018).

ISO (International Organization for Standardization). 2014. *ISO 13611: 2014(E) Interpreting – Guidelines for Community Interpreting for 13611:2014 Stan-dard on Community Interpreting*.

ISO (International Organization for Standardization). 2019. *ISO 20228 2019(E) Interpreting Services – Legal Interpreting – Requirements*.

Jimeno Bulnes, Mar. 2007. "Acceso a la interpretación y traducción gratuitas." In *Garantías procesales en los procesos penales en la Unión Europea*, edited by Coral Arangüena Fanego and Silvia Allegrezza, 155–183. Valladolid: Lex Nova.

Katschinka, Liese. 2003. "On Language, Legal Skills and Structures that Should Be Utilized in LIT." In *Equal Access to Justice across Language and Culture in EU Grotius Project 2001/GRP/015*, edited by Erik Hertog, 59–68. Antwerp: Lessius Hogeschool.

Katschinka, Liese. 2017. "DIS 20228 – An ISO Standard on Legal Interpreting." Paper delivered at the EULITA Conference. Vienna, March 31, 2017.

Ley Orgánica 5/2015 de 27 de abril, por la que se modifican la Ley de Enjuiciamiento Criminal y la Ley Orgánica 6/1985 de 1 de julio, del Poder Judicial, para transponer la Directiva 2010/64/UE, de 20 de octubre de 2010, relativa al derecho a interpretación y a traducción en los procesos penales y la Directiva 2012/13/IE, de 22 de mayo de 2012, relativa al derecho a la información en los procesos penales. Boletín Oficial del Estado no. 101, pp. 36559–36568. https://www.boe.es/eli/es/lo/2015/04/27/5 (accessed March 20, 2018).

London Metropolitan Police. 2010. Working with Interpreters & Translators – Standard Operating Procedures. https://www.met.police.uk/SysSiteAssets/foi-media/metropolitan-police/policies/working-with-interpreters-and-translators---policy (accessed March 30, 2018).

Martin, Wayne. 2018. National Standards for Working with Interpreters in Australia's Courts and Tribunal Address by The Honourable Wayne Martin AC Chief Justice of Western Australia. https://www.supremecourt.wa.gov.au/_files/Speeches/2018/National_Standards_Interpreters_Australia_Courts_Martin_CJ.pdf (accessed March 1, 2019).

Meyer, J. Patrick. 2014. *Applied Measurement with jMetrik*. New York: Routledge.

Mikkelson, Holly. 2000. *Introduction to Court Interpreting*. Manchester and Northampton, MA: St. Jerome Publishing.

Mikkelson, Holly. 2017. *Introduction to Court Interpreting*. London and New York: Routledge.

Mometti, Francesca. 2014. "Il diritto all'assistenza linguistica dell'imputato straniero nel procedimento penale. Indagine conoscitiva presso il tribunale di Trieste". In *Traduzione e interpertazione per la società e le istituzioni*, edited by Caterina Falbo and Maurizio Viezzi, 41–57. Trieste: EUT.

Morris, Ruth. 1999. The Gum Syndrome: Predicaments in Court Interpreting. *Forensic Linguistics* 6 (1): 6–29.

NAJIT (National Association of Judiciary Interpreters & Translators). 1988. Code of Ethics. Atlanta. https://najit.org/wp-content/uploads/2016/09/NAJIT CodeofEthicsFINAL.pdf (accessed March 30, 2018).

Navarro-Hall, Esther. 2017. "La interpretación judicial en Estados Unidos y su evolución hasta el momento actual." Keynote speech delivered at the *Jornada sobre traducción e interpretación judicial, jurada y policial*. Madrid, November 3, 2017.

Ortega Herráez, Juan Miguel. 2011. *Interpretar para la justicia*. Granada: Comares.

Ortega Herráez, Juan Miguel. 2013. "La intérprete no solo tradujo lo que le vino en gana, sino que respondió ella a las preguntas que los abogados le realizaban al testigo: requisitos de calidad en la subcontratación de servicios de interpretación judicial y policial en España." *Sendebar* 24: 9–42. http://revistaseug.ugr.es/public/sendebar/sendebar24_completo.pdf (accessed March 20, 2018).

Ortega-Herráez, Juan Miguel. 2016. "En busca de la calidad: el nuevo marco normativo de la interpretación jurídica en la Unión Europea y España." Keynote Speech delivered at the conference *De la Traducción Jurídica a la Jurilingüística: Enfoques Interdisciplinarios en el Estudio de la Lengua y el Derecho*. Sevilla, Universidad Pablo de Olavide, October 26–27, 2016.

Perdicchizzi, Francesco. 2016. *Interpretazione Giudiziaria Osservazione e analisi dal Tribunale di Palermo*. MA dissertation. Genova: Università degli Studi di Genova.

Pöchhacker, Franz. 2004. *Introducing Interpreting Studies*. London and New York: Routledge.

Pöchhacker, Franz. 2015. "Evolution of Interpreting Research." In *The Routledge Handbook of Interpreting*, edited by Holly Mikkelson and Renée Jourdenais, 62–76. London and New York: Routledge.

Pöchhacker, Franz, and Cornelia Zwischenberger. 2010. *Survey on Quality and Role: Conference Interpreters' Expectations and Self-Perceptions*. https://aiic.net/page/3405/survey-on-quality-and-role-conference-interpreters-expectations-and-self-perceptions/lang/1 (accessed August 20, 2018).

Rudvin, Mette. 2015a. "La deontologia professionale." In *L'interprete giuridico. Profilo professionale e metodologie di lavoro*, edited by Mette Rudvin and Cinzia Spinzi, 153–170. Torino: Carocci Faber.

Rudvin, Mette. 2015b. "Indicazioni per gli operatori giuridici per ottimizzare la qualità del servizio." In *L'interprete giuridico. Profilo professionale e metodologie di lavoro,* edited by Mette Rudvin and Cinzia Spinzi, 185–203. Torino: Carocci Faber.

Rudvin, Mette, Elena Tomassini, and María Jesús González Rodríguez. 2015. "Aspetti pratici e logistici dell'interpretazione giuridica." In *L'interprete giuridico. Profilo professionale e metodologie di lavoro*, edited by Mette Rudvin and Cinzia Spinzi, 153–170. Torino: Carocci Faber.

Sancho Viamonte, Marta. 2018. *Diseño de una herramienta de evaluación de la calidad del desempeño del intérprete judicial: INTER-Q*. PhD dissertation. Castellón: Universitat Jaume I.

Sandrelli, Annalisa. 2011. Gli interpreti presso il tribunale penale di Roma. Un'indagine empirica. *IntTRAlinea*. http://www.intralinea.org/specials/article/1670 (accessed March 1, 2019).

Viejo Jovani, Elena. 2014. *La interpretación judicial a juicio: panorama actual*. BA dissertation. Castellón: Universitat Jaume I. http://repositori.uji.es/xmlui/bitstream/handle/10234/106470/TFG_2014_Viejo_E.pdf?sequence=1&isAllowed=y (accessed March 1, 2019).

Viezzi, Maurizio. 1996. *Aspetti della qualità in interpretazione*. Trieste: SERT 2, Università degli studi di Trieste.

Wallace, Melissa. 2012. *Predictors of Successful Performance on US. Consortium Court Interpreter Certification Exams*. PhD dissertation. Universidad de Alicante. https://rua.ua.es/dspace/bitstream/10045/28364/1/tesis_melissa wallace.pdf (accessed March 10, 2019).

Wallace, Melissa. 2015. "Current Dilemmas in Court Interpreting." *MonTI* 5: 217–236.

Wallace, Melissa. 2019. "Competency-Based Education and Assessment: A Proposal for US Court Interpreter Certification." In *Quality Assurance and Assessment Practices in Translation and Interpreting*, edited by Elsa Huertas Barros, Sonia Vandepitte and Emilia Iglesias-Fernández, 112–132. Hersey: IGI Global.

Zwischenberger, Cornelia, and Martina Behr. 2015. "A Look Around and Ahead: Manifestations and Interpretations of Quality in Interpreting." In *Interpreting Quality: A Look Around and Ahead*, edited by Cornelia Zwischenberger and Martina Behr, 7–14. Berlin: Frank & Timme GmbH.

# Part II

# Translation and Interpreting at International Institutions

# 6 Every Second Counts

## A Study of Translation Practices in the European Commission's DGT

*María Fernández-Parra*

## 6.1 Introduction

In-house institutional translation, as opposed to freelance translation or in-house commercial translation, is one of the biggest areas of employment for translators and many studies have focused on a variety of aspects of this type of translation (e.g. Borja Albi & Prieto Ramos 2013; Koskinen 2014; Prieto Ramos 2014; Svoboda *et al.* 2017). However, despite the recent advances in the research into institutional translation, we still do not know enough about this area of Translation Studies, which has given rise to calls for more detailed research into specific institutions, e.g. by Koskinen (2011, 59).

This chapter aims to contribute to bridging that gap by providing some empirical data about the everyday work of translators at the European Commission's Directorate-General for Translation (DGT) as an example of an institutional translation setting. The focus is deliberately broad in order to contribute a bird's eye view of current DGT translation practices and thus this chapter will cover a range of procedural languages and deficit languages as well as other languages. Deficit languages are languages from which few translators can work at the DGT, including Greek, Finnish, Czech, Polish and other Eastern European languages.

The results presented in this chapter aim to highlight several aspects of institutional translation which clearly set it apart from other types of professional translation, e.g. freelance translation and in-house commercial translation, and contribute to the consolidation of institutional translators as a category of translation professional in their own right. Finally, this chapter reviews the implications these findings might have for updating curricula in translator training programs.

## 6.2 The Directorate-General for Translation

Despite some misconceptions, the European Union (EU) is not a single organization. It comprises several inter-connected institutions, "each with

DOI: 10.4324/9780429264894-6

its own responsibilities and its own translation service" (Wagner *et al.* 2012, ii). Overall, the EU institutions employ some "5,000 translators in more than 10 institutions, along with hundreds of interpreters, translating and interpreting in 552 language combinations" (Maslias 2017). In addition, there is support staff and a large number of freelancers.

The DGT is the translation service of one of the main EU institutions, i.e. the European Commission. It is the largest translation service in the EU and indeed one of the largest in the world. The DGT employs some 1,500 in-house translators (Strandvik 2018, 52) and has headquarters both in Brussels and Luxembourg. It also has several field offices in most European capitals. The DGT includes a group of lawyer-linguists in its Legal Service.

At the time of writing, the DGT is organized in 24 language departments, one per official language. For example, the Croatian Department translates into Croatian, the English Department translates into English and so on, although on occasion a department may translate in the reverse language combination, particularly in the case of languages of smaller diffusion, e.g. the Croatian Department may occasionally translate into English. However, this tends to be the exception rather than the rule. It is interesting to note that the English Department necessarily differs from all other departments in that it caters for translation needs from every EU source language into English as a frequent pivot language. This carries staffing implications, as language combinations are much more diverse than in other departments and involve deficit languages more often.

The DGT departments are further grouped into thematic units. Each unit tends to translate for a specific Directorate-General (DG) (e.g. DG Trade, DG Justice) and, when recruited, translators tend to be assigned to a unit based on their thematic expertise wherever possible. Units may be based in Brussels, Luxembourg, or both, depending on several logistics and/or other considerations. Each unit has a head of unit, who is answerable to the head of department. Heads of department do not translate. Their role is purely managerial, and they also represent the department at relevant meetings and events. Heads of unit can delegate translation management work to workflow managers, who act as project managers for larger translation jobs; these jobs often require outsourcing of the work.

The DGT produces over two million pages of translation per year (Strandvik 2018, 52). It works with a wide range of document types, from legislation to brochures, press releases, web pages and citizens' letters, to name but a few. Typically, documents which are not particularly sensitive, urgent or confidential may be outsourced but all documents must be revised in-house to the extent possible. In 2018, for example, almost a third of the DGT's work was outsourced to freelance translators and agencies (ibid., 52).

## 6.3 Data and Methodology

A range of translators from different departments and units, and with various backgrounds and levels of experience, were observed from September to November in 2017. In total, 11 translators from eight departments (out of 24) were observed in their offices as they worked, and data were collected from these observations as explained below. Participants were recruited on the basis of voluntary individual participation following a call for participants for the study. The overview of participants is shown in Table 6.1.

For anonymity purposes, translators[1] are referred to as T1 to T11. The next column indicates their age at the time of participating in the study, which ranges from 28 to 56. In terms of gender, five were female and six were male. The "Qual." column indicates their highest qualification obtained. Except for three translators with a BA, all other translators had obtained an MA, although often their qualifications were not in translation, or even linguistics, e.g. BA in Political Science, MA in HR Management and Employment. The "PT/FT" column shows that they were all full-time, except for one who was part-time. This is probably the reason why one worked in a shared office whereas all the others had their own offices.

Their experience (in years) in various modes of translation was also very varied. On the whole, very few had worked as freelance translators ("Exper. freelance" column) or in other in-house commercial translation capacities ("Exper. commer." column) before being employed by the DGT, except one who had worked for 12 years before joining the DGT.

Language diversity was the main factor in the selection of translators and this was specified in the call for participants. Fortunately, the languages of the translators who volunteered to take part in the study

*Table 6.1* Overview of participants in the study

| ID | Age | M/F | Qual. | PT/ FT | Private/ shared office | Exper. Freelance (years) | Exper. DGT (years) | Exper. commer. (years) | Main lang./ Dept. |
|----|-----|-----|-------|--------|------------------------|--------------------------|--------------------|------------------------|-------------------|
| T1 | 42 | F | MA | FT | Private | – | 4.5 | – | German |
| T2 | 28 | M | MA | FT | Private | 2 | 3 | – | Croatian |
| T3 | 43 | F | BA | FT | Private | – | 8.5 | – | Maltese |
| T4 | 38 | F | MA | PT | Shared | 0.7 | 8 | 5 | French |
| T5 | 40 | F | MA | FT | Private | 3 | 0.5 | – | Spanish |
| T6 | 32 | M | MA | FT | Private | 2 | 0.5 | 2 | Spanish |
| T7 | 46 | F | MA | FT | Private | – | 18 | 18 | English |
| T8 | 56 | M | BA | FT | Private | – | 28 | – | English |
| T9 | 37 | M | BA | FT | Private | 5 | 6 | 2.5 | Slovenian |
| T10 | 30 | M | MA | FT | Private | – | 3 | 3 | Maltese |
| T11 | 40 | M | MA | FT | Private | – | 1 | 12 | Greek |

belonged to the desired categories: procedural languages (i.e. English, French and German), deficit languages (i.e. languages for which there is a deficit in capacity, e.g. Eastern European, Greek, Finnish) and languages that were neither procedural nor deficit (e.g. Spanish). On the whole, this was generally a young to middle-aged sample of translators with a varied mix of experience.

Each translator was observed in situ, with the observer present alongside them as they carried out their daily work, for eight hours over two days. This amounts to 88 hours' observation of translation work in total. For each translator, eight hours of keylogging data (using Translog II v. 2.0.1.222) were collected from their own work computers in order to establish accurate timestamps for their activities. These data were complemented by video recordings of their computer screens and manual notes to fill in any gaps in the data collection.

In addition, the translators completed a questionnaire which aimed to collect metadata about their background, experience, qualifications and other personal information. After the eight hours of observations, retrospective interviews were also carried out with the translators. These were not structured interviews but simply a contingency tool to capture any aspect of the research that could not be envisaged in the original design of the project. However, the interviews were also a method of collecting additional qualitative data and comments from the translators.

This research did not set out to analyze a specific set of activities. Instead, the study took a "blank canvas" approach where meticulous observation and recording of the work of the translators were carried out in the first instance over a set period of time. The aim was to establish which actual activities the translators were involved with in their day-to-day work and classify the activities a posteriori, rather than begin the research with any preconceptions about the work they did. The observations yielded a vast amount of very short activities, i.e. "mini-activities." At first glance, these activities could be grouped under the broad categories of translation, revision and terminology, which are then broken down further and studied in depth in Section 6.4.

Despite the small size of the sample observed (11 volunteers from approximately 1,500 DGT translators, amounting to 0.73%), it is deemed to be representative of trends among DGT translators, especially considering the inclusion of a diversity of language groups and profiles, which range from the more experienced to the less experienced, from those who have been formally trained in translation to those who have not, and in various modes of employment (part-time, full-time).

## 6.4 Results

This section provides a picture of the typical working day of a DGT translator. The standard translation workflow is presented in Section

6.4.1, based on the observations of translators working at the DGT offices in Brussels and Luxembourg, although there are frequent variations depending on several factors. Sections 6.4.2 and 6.4.3 then take a tour of the full range of activities observed. Section 6.4.2 distinguishes between translation-based activities and non-translation-based activities, whereas Section 6.4.3 explores the duration of each activity. These sections also demonstrate the extent to which every second really counts in the work of a DGT translator.

### 6.4.1 How DGT Translators Work

While much is known about the EU institutions, what they do and what resources are available, there is little in the literature about what the day-to-day work of a DGT translator entails, i.e. what does a typical day of the DGT translator look like? Few studies have focused on providing an overview of several or all DGT departments, apart from the DGT's own literature. This section traces the standard journey from the commissioning of a translation to its delivery to the requester, as illustrated in Figure 6.1. For a more in-depth workflow, see DGT (2016, 5). The following sections will present the specific stages of the daily work observed.

All translation work comes in through the e-Poetry platform. Documents and reference documents are uploaded to e-Poetry, and this is called a *request*. At this stage, the original document is automatically processed by EURAMIS (European Advanced Multilingual Information System), the translation memory (TM) repository, in order to find similar earlier translations (DGT 2016). The pre-processing team tracks down any additional reference materials if necessary (ibid.). The job then progresses to the secretariat of a unit. The staff at the secretariat are also

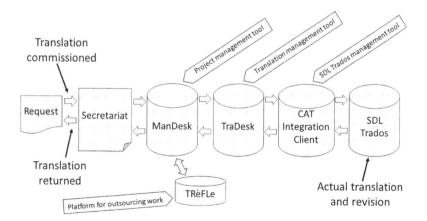

*Figure 6.1* Generic translation workflow at the DGT.

referred to as *workflow assistants* (not to be confused with workflow managers). They do not perform any linguistic or translation work, only management work. For example, they are responsible for negotiating deadlines and specific requirements with the requester. This means that DGT translators are typically not involved in negotiations or in liaising with the client, and that, when receiving a job, translators also receive all additional documentation and reference material with it.

Once the request is processed by the secretariat, it will appear on the interface of ManDesk (Manager's Desk), a project management tool. Once the request is processed in ManDesk, it will then appear on the interface of TraDesk (Translator's Desktop), a translation management tool. If a job needs outsourcing to freelance translators and agencies, it will be processed through the TRèFLe platform, which can be accessed from ManDesk. In some departments, translators can accept the job themselves on ManDesk (i.e. *self-service*), whereas in others the acceptance is processed in TraDesk. Each of these interfaces also supports important tasks such as adding comments, sending a note to the requester, uploading files and consulting any other internal information that might be relevant to a particular job, e.g. translator availability or expertise. A useful feature of TraDesk is that it contains all the translations in all languages in .XLIFF format. These files are also synchronized and can be viewed in real time by any translator, so a translator working from English to Maltese can view the translation of the same document in French or English, for example, in order to make consistent translation or terminology decisions based on the finished translations in other languages.

The file naming of .XLIFF files, which are the bread and butter of the DGT daily translation work, may seem daunting at first glance, e.g. "CLIMA 2017 40020 00 00 00 EN EL 00" or "HOME 2018 80161 00 00 00 EN ES 00." However, this long naming convention can be decoded, as shown in Figure 6.2.

"Part" and "Sub-part" are terms used for document sections and sub-sections. Typically, larger documents are more likely to have sub-parts than smaller documents. For example, a 400-page document may be divided into four 100-page sub-documents, which may then become

*Figure 6.2* File naming at the DGT decoded.

parts or sub-parts of the original document, depending on the specific internal practices of each department. These file-naming conventions are important because the vast majority of documents are named and re-named in this way and help everyone in a specific translation job to trace documents and translations.

Once a translator has accepted a request, whether on ManDesk or TraDesk, the next interface will be activated, i.e. the CAT Integration Client, a management tool for SDL Trados (henceforth *SDL*), the computer-assisted translation (CAT) tool currently used at the DGT, although other CAT tools may be used in future. A range of tasks can be carried out with the CAT Integration Client, from automatically uploading any relevant TMs to SDL to allowing translators to perform several checks, e.g. leverage against previous translations or selecting relevant reference documents, before carrying out the actual translation in SDL. Revision tasks are generally assigned on ManDesk or TraDesk, but can also be managed between translator and reviser through the CAT Integration Client interface, while the actual revision job is carried out in SDL.

Once the translator has completed the translation on SDL, the reviser will also carry out the revision here. However, it will generally be the translator's responsibility to finalize the translation in SDL and complete the job on all the interfaces, from the CAT Integration Client back to ManDesk. Once the translation reaches ManDesk, the secretariat will perform any final checks and return it to the requester. There can be several variations to this basic workflow. For example, for large jobs, especially if outsourcing may be required, a workflow manager (i.e. lead translator) can be assigned to manage the project and deal with any queries (see also the organization and management of departments and units in Section 6.2). By contrast, some very small jobs (e.g. "hot lines," which have a 24-hour deadline, are very short and have no context) may not be recorded on ManDesk or TraDesk or revised by another translator.

### 6.4.2 Types of Activities Carried Out by Translators

After the 88 hours of observation of the volunteer translators, 11,097 activities were recorded, together with their duration in seconds and manually coded using the broad labels shown in Table 6.2, displayed in descending order by the number of activities.

Table 6.2 groups activities under two main umbrellas, that of specialized, translation-based activities and the non-specialized, non-translation-based activities. Under the former, *consistency consultation* refers to checks made by translators to ensure that the term, phrase or wording used was consistent with previous relevant documentation, whereas *terminology consultation* includes all checks made by trans-lators to ensure they employed the most appropriate phraseology for each job. *Translation management* refers to the various tasks involved in accepting a new translation and uploading the finished translation in the various DGT interfaces (as shown in Figure 6.1).

Under the *non-translation-based activities*, the *email management* label groups activities such as reading, replying and archiving emails; *Pauses* refers to brief pauses which were neither a coffee break nor a lunch break, e.g. opening and closing doors and windows, switching the lighting on or off, adjusting ergonomic chair settings and other types of comfort breaks. Coffee and lunch breaks were excluded from the activities analyzed in this research. *Project management* refers to activities such as filing electronic files and folders, opening and closing programs and interfaces and dealing with all the project management settings in SDL, e.g. creating projects, changing settings. Therefore, the *translation* and *revision* labels refer exclusively to the translation and revision activities per se, as all non-linguistic activity was classified under other labels in order to provide a clear picture of the work of these translators.

As would be expected a priori, the vast majority of the translators' work was translation-based (85%). Even if the labels in Table 6.2 were re-arranged in different ways, the duration of the *translation* activities, 35 hours, remains the lion's share of their work time, with revision and terminology tasks making up the bulk of the work. Under the *non-translation-based* activities, project management and email management were the most frequent tasks.

*Table 6.2* Overview of activities and durations

| Translation-based Activities | No. of activities | % of Translation-based | Total duration (hours:mins:secs) |
|---|---|---|---|
| Translation | 4,308 | 45.72 | 35:32:03 |
| Revision | 2,132 | 22.63 | 13:13:36 |
| Terminology consultation | 1,530 | 16.24 | 10:34:39 |
| Translation management | 650 | 6.88 | 05:09:37 |
| Content consultation | 599 | 6.36 | 04:11:40 |
| Colleague consultation (verbal) | 108 | 1.15 | 03:00:44 |
| Consistency consultation | 96 | 1.02 | 00:52:51 |
| Sub-total | 9,423 | 84.91 | 72:35:10 |

| Non-translation-based activities | No. of activities | % of Non-translation-based | Total duration (hours:mins:secs) |
|---|---|---|---|
| Project management | 837 | 50 | 07:05:21 |
| Email management | 721 | 43.07 | 05:49:45 |
| Pauses | 99 | 5.91 | 01:54:08 |
| Solving technical issues | 17 | 1.02 | 00:35:36 |
| Sub-total | 1,674 | 15.09 | 15:24:50 |
| Total | 11,097 | 100 | 88:00:00 |

*6.4.2.1 Translation Activities*

From the 4,308 translation activities, 92% consisted of the actual translation work carried out in SDL Trados Studio 2015, as illustrated in Table 6.3, in descending order by the number of activities.

The remaining 8% included additional source text (ST) consultations, e.g. when the preview feature in SDL was not sufficient because it only covered the immediate surroundings of a specific segment and/or due to personal preferences about reading the ST in paper. This final 8% also included checking the finalized target text (TT), which can be associated to self-revision, together with ST/TT comparisons. The three smallest percentages correspond to comparisons of the finalized (and sometimes printed) TT with the ST, consulting additional reference documents (as the main reference documents or TMs will have already been accessed through SDL) or using additional (non-DGT) resources and reference documents such as WinLexic.

The high percentage of use of SDL is not surprising but the presence of the other 8% suggests that sometimes it was necessary for DGT translators to carry out additional checks outside the CAT environment. In most cases, the reason for these checks lay with the legal nature of the document. For many legal texts, translators had to populate a specific DGT template in MS Word *after* completing the translation and perform additional template and formatting checks (e.g. with MS Word-installed tools such as ProLexis) before signing off the translation. While the figure of 8% for non-SDL tasks seems small in Table 6.3, these activities are nevertheless indicative of a trend that is likely to be recurrent across translators of legal texts throughout the DGT, given that the trends were observed in all the DGT departments involved in this study.

It was also interesting to note that the concept of *translation* at the DGT was not monolithic. It was observed that translators carried out at least three kinds of translation, each involving different attitudes, workflow and perceptions about the task at hand. The most frequent type of translation was what could be termed "translation with revision," where translators knew there would be a reviser checking everything after

*Table 6.3* Specific translation activities

| *Activities under the* translation *label* | *No. of activities* | *% of* Translation |
|---|---|---|
| Translating in SDL Studio | 3,980 | 92.39 |
| Additional ST consultations | 162 | 3.76 |
| Checking finalized TT | 132 | 3.06 |
| ST/TT comparisons | 19 | 0.44 |
| Consulting additional reference documents | 11 | 0.26 |
| Using other resources, e.g. WinLexic | 4 | 0.09 |
| Total | 4,308 | 100 |

them. This meant that the translators did not worry too much if a typo or other kinds of minor error went unnoticed, because they would be easily resolved either by the reviser or by themselves once the translation came back to them after revision. The advantage of this approach is that of time. By not worrying about minor errors, they would spend less time back-tracking and investing time and effort on correcting errors that can be more systematically and efficiently corrected during the revision or post-revision stages. Thus, they would be able to complete the translation more quickly but at the expense of overlooking the minor errors, which would be picked up by the reviser or by themselves eventually.

A second type of translation was one that could be termed "translation without revision." In this type of translation, the translator knows at the start of the project, e.g. through ManDesk or TraDesk, that there will be no reviser assigned to it, which puts the translator under more pressure. The reasons for having no reviser could vary from time constraints to the fact that only a "gist" translation may be required, e.g. briefing for a speaker or short two-paragraph translation. In these cases, the translator would need to ensure that they produce the finalized product, as the safety net of the revision stages would not be available to them. On the whole, they would spend more time on the translation than if they were performing a "translation with revision" task, but the overall time spent on the project would be less than that of the "translation with revision" jobs.

Finally, a third type of translation was that of "recast." This was the term used by the DGT translators when a text would need to be not only translated but also substantially edited, e.g. amalgamating the directives and regulations for passenger cars with the regulations for light goods vehicles in order to combine them into one single set of regulations. This can be considered as a different type to "translation" because it makes additional cognitive demands on translators, who often have to write new text into the translation, and because the use of CAT is also more intricate, e.g. the *autopropagate* feature is typically not used, segments are often color-coded according to whether the segment needs to be translated, recast or whether it is for reference only. In addition, the translators reported that it would normally take them half an hour to set up a recast project in SDL due to the complex nature of this task, e.g. having to remember to change settings in SDL first and then upload files, not the other way around.

### 6.4.2.2 Revision Activities

A closer look at the 2,132 activities grouped under the *revision* label in Table 6.2 also reveals interesting findings about the revision methods in the DGT. These activities are itemized in Table 6.4 in descending order by the number of activities.

*Table 6.4* Types of revision activities

| Activities under the revision label | No. of activities | % of Revision |
|---|---|---|
| Edition of the TT in SDL | 1,726 | 80.96 |
| Comment management in SDL | 169 | 7.93 |
| Visual check by scrolling through segments in SDL | 134 | 6.29 |
| Edition in MS Word | 72 | 3.38 |
| Spell-checking in SDL | 15 | 0.69 |
| Other checks, e.g. ApSIC Xbench | 14 | 0.66 |
| Edition of the TT in paper | 2 | 0.09 |
| Total | 2,132 | 100 |

Practically all of the revision work was carried out in SDL, except for a few edition tasks in MS Word (for reasons explained in the previous section), checking tasks in external programs such as ApSIC Xbench and a couple of occasions where specific tasks were carried out on paper given the personal preferences of the translator. These few exceptions amount to 88 tasks, approximately 4% of the total revision work. The *Edition of the TT* group of activities, by far the most common one under *Revision*, included any change, addition or deletion of TT elements, often in connection with spelling corrections. By contrast, *Spell-checking* refers to spell-checking tasks of the whole text using SDL.

The *Comment management* group of activities include adding or deleting comments or editing the text of the comment within SDL, as different terminological and other queries are solved. Nearly 8% of the revision work was devoted to dealing with comments. The comments would need to be resolved by the translator before finalizing the translation in SDL. It is also worth noting that each of the translators across all languages and departments under observation used the comments feature in SDL.

Finally, the *Visual check by scrolling through segments* category is also worthy of comment. When revising in SDL, if the TT was correct and needed no editing, the revision task would consist of visually scrolling through the already confirmed segments to ensure that they did not contain errors. In these cases, translators would make the most of SDL's highlighting and underlining of any issues in the TT and would only stop to edit the TT if they spotted a problem. Despite a relatively small percentage accounted by this task within the overall amount of revision work, i.e. 6%, this was nevertheless a trend observed across all the translators.

As with the translation tasks, the range of revision activities observed was not homogeneous and depended on the purpose of the revision. The most frequent type of revision among the observed translators was that of revising a translation produced by another translator as part of the usual workflow. Another type of revision was observed among translators in which they would check their own work before passing it on for revision. This could be considered as some form of self-revision and was thus included under translation activities (TT checks and ST/TT comparisons in Table 6.3). A third type of (self-)revision was that carried out by translators after the revision. It is the translator who would need to make the final decisions about the translation. This last type of revision can be associated to various tasks listed in Table 6.4, but more fine-grained data would be needed in order to distinguish between these categories of revision and determine their share within each type of revision activity.

There were also other (less common) kinds of revision involving interns and non-DGT staff. Translators' revision of the work of an intern constituted a different kind of revision because they would need to provide feedback for improvement. On other occasions, translators would need to revise the work of a freelancer. Again, this consisted of a slightly different activity because they would need to score the work of the freelancer anonymously on the basis of an internal scale of scores and provide the justification for having assigned that score. This kind of revision would have implications for freelancers, as only those with the highest scores would likely be employed again.

### 6.4.2.3 Terminology Activities

This section describes the terminology activities observed among the DGT translators, in particular the 1,530 terminology consultation activities recorded in Table 6.2. Since we are dealing with an example of institutional translation, it is not surprising to note that no pre-translation terminological research or documentation tasks were observed. Instead, any terminological or background research was carried out by the observed translators while translating or revising, as queries arose. Although terminology work can take up to 75% of the translator's time according to Dunne (2012), this author was most likely referring to freelance or in-house commercial translation. In the specific case of the DGT, much of the terminology is already contained in the well-known EU institutional resources such as IATE (Interactive Terminology for Europe). However, translators did not always find all the answers to their terminological queries in those resources and they had to consult external resources as well as internal ones. The range of resources for terminological research is detailed in Table 6.5, displayed in descending order by the number of consultations. All kinds of search engines, platforms and tools were considered rather than only terminological resources or institutional repositories.

Overall, translators used DGT or EU institutional resources (75%) to solve terminological queries, but resorted to external resources in almost

*Table 6.5* Types of terminology consultations

| External resources and search engines | No. of consultations | % of external resources |
|---|---|---|
| Google | 221 | 58.31 |
| Non-DGT dictionaries and glossaries | 158 | 41.69 |
| Sub-total | 379 | 24.77% |

| DGT or EU institutional tools and resources | No. of consultations | % of internal resources |
|---|---|---|
| EURAMIS (translation memories) | 491 | 42.66 |
| Concordance feature in SDL | 329 | 28.58 |
| IATE | 118 | 10.25 |
| EUR-Lex | 93 | 8.08 |
| EU webpages | 51 | 4.43 |
| DGT reference documents | 32 | 2.78 |
| QUEST (metasearch tool) | 27 | 2.35 |
| IntraComm (wiki tool) | 5 | 0.43 |
| Information retrieved from body of emails | 4 | 0.35 |
| Terminologist queries | 1 | 0.09 |
| Sub-total | 1,151 | 75.23 |
| Total | 1,530 | 100 |

25% of the consultations. Among the external resources used, there are two main categories: a wide range of dictionaries and Google searches for content/background knowledge, with 41.69% and 58.31%, respectively, of the total number of queries in external sources. Examples of the dictionaries used include the FreeDictionary, WordReference, Oxford dictionaries, dictionaries of linguistic doubts and synonyms dictionaries.

As for DGT resources, the most frequently used one by the observed translators was EURAMIS, the collective repository of DGT TMs. Although all the relevant EURAMIS TMs for a specific job are automatically assigned to an SDL project through the CAT Integration Client prior to translation (including TMs that will be used for leverage and TMs that will be used for reference only; see Figure 6.1) and many TM matches are thus provided within SDL, translators still conducted many searches on the EURAMIS website.

Similarly, despite many TM and machine translation (MT) matches within SDL, the second most frequently used internal source for terminological research was the Concordance feature in SDL, which allows translators to search for terms and their translations throughout the relevant TMs. This type of query amounted to 28% of the total number of consultations. IATE, the EU terminology database of all EU institutions, and EUR-Lex, the repository of EU law, were used 10% and 8% of the time, respectively. It is interesting to note that translators not only made bilingual consultations in their working languages but also made multilingual consultations. For example, the English-Greek translator also had knowledge of German, French and Spanish, which he used to check existing translations of specific terms and phrases in these languages in order to make sure that the phraseology in the Greek translation was current and consistent with the ones in the other languages.

The remaining consultations were divided among a range of EU webpages (4.43%, e.g. InfoCuria), internal DGT documents for reference (2.78%) and QUEST (2.35%), a metasearch tool combining several search engines. Although not used very frequently among our set of translators, the IntraComm proved to be a useful terminological resource too. This consists of an internal wiki page where specific translation requirements for language departments are collected for reference and can be used for communication with the terminologist. For example, the IntraComm can contain specific instructions relating to the translation of weights and measures for a specific client, the spelling conventions for a specific job (e.g. Al-Qaeda or Al-Qaida) or the maximum number of characters allowed for titles of press releases. Occasionally, a department would receive updated terminological information by email. Until that new information is uploaded to the IntraComm, translators would need to access that new information from the body of emails, which explains the four consultations of this kind observed (0.35%).

Finally, it was observed that each department typically has two dedicated terminologists. There are slight differences among departments regarding how the terminologist's services are put to use, but it seems that translators can consult the terminologist if they have a specific query, e.g. a non-existent term in a specific language. Terminologists will work with the translator in order to solve the query and, if necessary, update IATE and/or any other relevant DGT resources. One such query was recorded in our observations, which explains the final 0.09% of the consultations.

## 6.5 Discussion and Best Practices

Overall, the observed translators spent relatively little time in any activity at any one time. Instead, they moved very quickly from one activity to the next, e.g. a few seconds reading an email, followed by a few seconds typing in SDL, followed by a few seconds typing a terminological query in IATE, then going back to typing in SDL, then reading the email again. Of the 2,132 activities observed, a large proportion (9,649 or 88.6%) lasted less than one minute. This included activities such as reading the ST or TT, consulting colleagues and typing emails. Typically, the duration of these 9,649 activities ranged from 2 to 58 seconds. 1,233 activities (11.1%) lasted between 1 and 5 minutes. This included activities such as project management and solving technical issues. By contrast, only 35 activities (0.3%) lasted more than 5 minutes. The three longest activities included a recast (13:57 minutes), the translation of one segment in SDL (19:00 minutes) and a colleague consultation (22:00 minutes). This empirical evidence seems to point to the fact that translators at the DGT are working under tight time constraints and not devoting as much time as they would like to complete each job. This evidence is unanimously supported by each translator's comments during their retrospective interviews.

Despite the tight time constraints, the translators met all the deadlines set by their clients during the four weeks of observations and occasionally they even delivered some translations early. Further, the translations produced were of high quality, as evidenced by the fact that all the revisions observed amounted to relatively minor issues, e.g. fine-tuning a term or correcting typos. At no time during the observations did a reviser need to delete a whole paragraph and start the translation again, for example.

This raises the question of how these translators managed to complete the volume of work required by their clients within the (limited) time allowed and with such high quality. The answer may lie in some additional observations made as translators worked and confirmed during the retrospective interviews. All the observed translators worked in a highly customized, ergonomic environment, e.g. the SDL version used contains some features customized only for DGT (DGT 2016, 11). Translators were also fast typists and expert users of shortcuts, both in and out of SDL. They generally had a very advanced knowledge of the software and had customized their own workplace to suit their own methods of working (for the importance of ergonomics in the translator's workplace, see, e.g., Ehrensberger-Dow and Heeb 2016). Apart from the fact that translators were typically already specialized in the areas in which they were translating, a translation job would typically undergo several revision stages and quality checks, often by more than two people. By contrast, translators were not observed carrying out any preliminary terminological work, since the DGT terminological resources were already kept up-to-date and ready to use by other staff (see Section 6.4.2.3).

These additional observations can also be considered as general examples of best practices from an institutional translation setting and can be generally grouped into two broad categories:

- Ergonomics and IT:
  - Get advanced working knowledge of your equipment (software and hardware)
  - Customize your workplace to suit your own method of working

- Translation, revision and terminology:
  - Specialize in one or two areas
  - Devote time and effort to your specialized terminology
  - Terminological resources should be constantly updated and ready to use at any one time
  - Include more than one revision and quality check in the translation workflow

Beyond institutional translation, these best practices can be applicable to almost any translation setting. They can be used as advice for translator trainees submitting their own work for assessment but also as a gentle reminder in relevant continuous professional development courses for highly experienced freelance translators. In this chapter, these best practices provide an illustration of how DGT translators, as representative professional profiles in institutional translation, strive to make every second count.

## 6.6 Concluding Remarks

This chapter has aimed to shed some light on the everyday work of DGT translators across a representative sample of languages and DGT departments as an example of translation work carried out in an institutional setting. Rather than focusing on one language or department, this chapter has taken the reader on a tour of the current translation practices, drawing on quantitative data from a carefully selected sample of volunteer translators from several language departments, which was supplemented by qualitative data in retrospective interviews with the translators. We have provided an overview of what activities the day-to-day work of a DGT translator involves, gained some insights about their revision and terminology practices and revealed some of the specific labeling used at the DGT.

Despite its size limitations, the analysis of the data collected for this study suggests that terminology and revision practices at the DGT in particular can contribute to raising awareness and updating the profile of institutional translators as a category of professionals in their own right, alongside freelance or in-house commercial translators. Accordingly, the findings of this chapter may be useful for translator trainers wishing to update their translator training programs to include some instruction on the profile of an institutional translator as part of preparing students to embark on an institutional translation career. The findings may also be useful for anyone wishing to join the DGT or a similar institution, as we have discussed the typical DGT translation workflow, which allows a range of variations. In order to expand our results, large-scale studies with larger data sets are necessary. The DGT is only one example of a large institutional setting where multilingual translation work takes place. Further research in this area could be carried out in other institutional translation settings such as intergovernmental organizations.

## Note

1 We would like to extend our grateful thanks to Nikola Kunte and to each of the translators who volunteered to take part in this project. Their participation is greatly appreciated.

## References

Borja Albi, Anabel, and Fernando Prieto Ramos, eds. 2013. *Legal Translation in Context: Professional Issues and Prospects*. Bern: Peter Lang.

DGT. 2016. "Translation Tools and Workflow." Accessed 05/04/19. https://www.scribd.com/document/367837209/Tools-and-Translation-Workflow-DGT-2016.

Dunne, Keiran J. 2012. "Translation Tools." In *The Encyclopedia of Applied Linguistics*, edited by Carol A. Chapelle, 839–843. Hoboken, NJ: Wiley-Blackwell Publishing.

Ehrensberger-Dow, Maureen, and Andrea Hunziker Heeb. 2016. "Investigating the Ergonomics of a Technologized Translation Workplace." In *Reembedding Translation Process Research*, edited by Ricardo Muñoz Martín. Amsterdam: John Benjamins.

Koskinen, Kaisa. 2011. "Institutional Translation." In *Handbook of Translation Studies*, edited by Yves Gambier and Luc Van Doorslaer, 54–60. Amsterdam: John Benjamins.

Koskinen, Kaisa. 2014. *Translating Institutions: An Ethnographic Study of EU Translation*. London and New York: Routledge.

Maslias, Rodolfo. 2017. "Converting the European Terminology Database IATE into the Worlds' Largest Multilingual Data Space." In *Terminological Approaches in the European Context*, edited by Paola Faini, 13–19. Newcastle: Cambridge Scholars Publishing.

Prieto Ramos, Fernando. 2014. "International and Supranational Law in Translation: From Multilingual Lawmaking to Adjudication." *The Translator* 20 (3): 313–331.

Strandvik, Ingemar. 2018. "Towards a More Structured Approach to Quality Assurance: DGT's Quality Journey." In *Institutional Translation for International Governance: Enhancing Quality in Multilingual Legal Communication*, edited by Fernando Prieto Ramos, 51–62. London: Bloomsbury.

Svoboda, Tomáš, Łucja Biel, and Krzysztof Łoboda, eds. 2017. *Quality Aspects in Institutional Translation*. Berlin: Language Science Press.

Wagner, Emma, Svend Bech, and Jesús M. Martínez. 2012. *Translating for the European Union Institutions*. Manchester: St. Jerome.

# 7 Ensuring Consistency and Accuracy of Legal Terms in Institutional Translation

## The Role of Terminological Resources in International Organizations

*Fernando Prieto Ramos*

## 7.1 Introduction

The consistency and accuracy of terminology are central aspects of translation quality and, therefore, key aims of translation-oriented terminology management. For any given context, except for terms that can be considered interchangeable, terminological accuracy is expected to imply a high degree of consistency within the same text and, as far as possible, with other occurrences of the same term in texts that are directly relevant to the translation at hand, especially for the same purposes and users. Accordingly, terminological consistency can be viewed as both an intratextual requirement and an intertextual aspiration. By the same token, high levels of inconsistency for the same concept in a comparable translation context will usually imply some risk of semantic deviation among renderings of the same original term.

It is no coincidence that terminological consistency and semantic accuracy are the first two requirements established for the translation process in the quality standard ISO 17100:2015: "a) compliance with specific domain and client terminology and/or any other reference material provided and ensuring terminological consistency during translation; b) semantic accuracy of the target language content" (ISO 2015, 10). Despite the relevance of these quality requirements, the two main challenges highlighted with regard to terminology management in a survey recently conducted by the International Network for Terminology (TermNet) among practitioners in this field were the lack of awareness of the importance of terminology management and the consistency of terminology, according to 57.65% and 56.47% of 86 participants, respectively. These challenges were followed by the lack of time (45.88%) and human resources (43.53%) for terminology management.[1]

In the case of texts translated in international organizations, interlinguistic concordance and intralinguistic consistency are essential requirements of institutional translation for the sake of semantic univocity (e.g.

DOI: 10.4324/9780429264894-7

Prieto Ramos 2014a, 314; Robertson 2015, 41; Stefaniak 2017, 116). This is particularly sensitive in the process of producing multilingual texts that establish, implement or provide information about rights, conditions or obligations. As expressed by Stefaniak (2017, 117) with regard to translation in the European Commission, consistency "is often more important than any other criterion" in translation decision-making; "[v]arious translations of the same term, especially in legal acts, may mislead the reader to think that these terms denote different concepts and make it difficult to interpret legislation" (ibid., 116). In other words, terminological consistency is also a matter of uniform interpretation and legal certainty (see, e.g., Šarčević 2013). De Saint Robert also refers to consistency or "continuity in a text" as a key aspect of translation quality assessment at the United Nations (UN), and links the assessment of terminological accuracy to consistency "in the use of terms in the database" (2009, 388).

The connection between institutional translation decisions and terminological databases is only logical considering the function of these resources at international organizations. They constitute priority resources for the verification of terminology, and de facto authoritative sources in the case of terms established for institution-specific notions or processes in particular. As they are developed for the highly repetitive and predictable contexts of institutional drafting, they can expedite terminological research and play a vital role in ensuring consistency and accuracy across translation services. This role may be more efficient and practical when the terminological problems are complex and time-consuming for translators. This often applies to legal terms that originated in specific legal traditions and are used in texts translated for international organizations, for example, in reports on the implementation of international legal instruments at national level.

Despite the remarkable development of institutional terminological resources (abbreviated here as "ITRs"), previous research shows that consistency and accuracy issues can be significant in both institutional translation patterns and terminological database records for certain legal terms (see Section 7.2). This study will explore these issues further using quantitative and qualitative analyses of translations of three illustrative legal terms in multilingual documents and ITRs at the European Union (EU) institutions, the UN and the World Trade Organization (WTO). These analyses have been produced by a more extensive research project on legal translation practices at these institutions.[2]

## 7.2 Approach and Hypotheses

As mentioned earlier, previous studies highlight the implications of inconsistencies and inaccuracies in legal terminological decisions within institutional translations, e.g. trade law terms in EU directives (Šarčević

2010, 31–32) and national court names in texts of international organizations (Prieto Ramos 2013, 98–102). The latter study revealed that
approximately two thirds of the translations of "magistrates' court" into
Spanish reproduced the false friend "tribunal de magistrados" in two
major institutions as of October 2012 (ibid., 99). It also showed the inconsistencies found in available terminological resources, particularly
bilingual dictionaries. Similar shortcomings, from the perspective of
translation-oriented legal lexicographical needs, were also detected in
institutional termbank entries on national courts dealing with criminal
cases (Prieto Ramos 2014b).

This study builds on the same preliminary analyses and adopts the
approach of the LETRINT project in distinguishing between multilingual terminology established at international organizations to designate
concepts within the realm of their recognized competences (e.g. human
rights treaties at the UN or international trade rules at the WTO) and
other terminology coined outside international organizations and used
(a) to refer to concepts with generally shared meanings in multiple jurisdictions (e.g. "compliance", "appeal", "evidence") or (b) to designate
concepts more specific to certain traditions or jurisdictions (e.g. singular
proceedings, entities or legal provisions).

The use of the first group of well-established terminology in institutional translations is expected to be highly consistent, and also influential
in the domains of recognized competence of the relevant organizations.
However, consistency and accuracy levels are generally less predictable
for the other groups of legal terminology. It is presumed that higher
degrees of singularity or asymmetry (between the legal traditions associated with the original term and the target language) call for advanced
translation competence and represent more significant challenges to consistency and accuracy in institutional translation settings. This may be
compounded by the fact that these terms are usually less of a priority for
institutional terminology management.

A potential correlation between consistency and accuracy levels was
observed in the Spanish translations of "due process" in the abovementioned institutional settings (Prieto Ramos and Guzmán 2018). Interestingly, the setting with the highest levels of consistency and accuracy, the
WTO, also showed the most marked degree of adherence to terminological recommendations in an internal glossary (93.74% of occurrences),
whereas the EU registered the lowest rates for both indicators and only
22.58% of adherence to IATE (Interactive Terminology for Europe) recommendations for the term. While the EU subcorpus was smaller than
those of the UN and the WTO, the results raise questions about the difficulties in identifying legal terminological nuances and the use of ITRs
for the translation of this kind of terminology.

The lexicometric analyses presented below were also conducted in the
framework of the LETRINT project in order to test the earlier hypotheses

at a larger scale. More specifically, we examine the connections between the levels of legal singularity of terms (and their associated difficulty for translation from English to Spanish) and the degrees of consistency and accuracy of their renderings. Three terms were selected for the following reasons: (1) they are considered representative of groups of terms with varying degrees of legal singularity or asymmetry for translation, as identified in the LETRINT corpora, (2) they are illustrative of recurrent semantic fields within these groups and (3) they occur with sufficient frequency in the three institutional settings for comparative analysis. The three terms are:

- "*prima facie* evidence" (abbreviated as "PFE"): an example of procedural legal terminology adopted at international organizations through the influence of the common law tradition[3] and with closely corresponding *prima facie* standards in civil law systems such as the Spanish-speaking jurisdictions, i.e. the legal singularity is relatively limited but several renderings are possible in Spanish (for example, "prueba *prima facie*" or "prueba indiciaria", also found in national laws), and some previous legal knowledge or verifications are required for translation decision-making;
- "tort": a concept unique to common law that requires a descriptive or partially functional reformulation in Spanish to convey the idea of civil wrong (e.g. "ilícito civil extracontractual") or the legal liability resulting from it (e.g. "responsabilidad extracontractual"), i.e. the significant legal singularity of the term calls for specific attention and comparative legal analysis;
- "magistrates' court" (abbreviated as "MC"): a court name that illustrates system-specific denominations of judicial entities and entails not only a high degree of asymmetry with target-language judicial systems but also a risk of misleading rendering in Spanish due to the false friend "magistrado" (a senior judge, as opposed to "magistrate").

The level of translation difficulty may be perceived differently depending on the translator's previous specialization. Overall, however, it is presumed that the meaning of the first term will be easier to grasp and convey than the other two common law concepts. Advanced competence in legal translation will be critical in detecting these difficulties and making appropriate and efficient translation decisions. The role of terminological resources can be particularly helpful to compensate for specialization gaps in this context. In turn, this strengthens the relevance of observing translation patterns and ITR recommendations for varying levels of legal singularity or asymmetry.

The corpora compiled for the study include all occurrences of the selected terms in English, and their translations into Spanish, in documents published in 2005–2015 and 2016–2019, and retrieved from the following institutional repositories: the EU's EUR-Lex portal, the UN's Official Document System (ODS) and the WTO's Documents Online database. In order to draw a comprehensive overview of recent practices, the corpora comprise three years over a decade (2005, 2010 and 2015) and the subsequent four years (2016–2019). This provides perspective for examining the consistency of decisions over a considerable time span, including patterns of translation precedents and the potential impact of ITR changes or of the increasing automation in translation workflows witnessed in recent years.

After the analyses of consistency and accuracy of translations (Section 7.3), their congruity with ITR recommendations will be examined more closely, with a particular focus on the potential role of these resources in the most statistically significant patterns of terminological decision-making identified (Section 7.4). More methodological details are provided in each section.

## 7.3 Analysis of Consistency and Accuracy Indicators

### 7.3.1 *Overall Translation Variability*

The initial search query results (including singular and plural forms) were screened in order to exclude occurrences that did not refer to the concepts selected for the study, for example, longer terms that deviate from the original concepts or translations of court names from languages other than English (e.g. "administrative tort" or "Federal Magistrates Court"). Table 7.1 shows the total number of occurrences that qualified for analysis and the number of documents from which they were extracted per period and institutional setting. A total of 1,038 occurrences of Spanish renderings of the English terms from 606 documents were considered for the analysis of translation consistency and accuracy. Multiple instances of each term were found in each period and translation setting, except for "magistrates' court", which registered a single occurrence in EU texts compiled for 2016–2019.

The most recurrent textual functions of the documents are related to policy implementation or monitoring at the supranational or national levels, in the areas of trade and judicial cooperation in the EU, human rights at the UN and trade at the WTO. The most frequently used term is "PFE". It was found in the widest range of text types in all the organizations, including EU legal instruments, UN reports and WTO trade policy review and dispute settlement documents. This reflects the widespread adoption of the concept in international jurisdictions, as opposed to more system-specific terms. The largest and most homogeneous subset of documents or "system of genres" (Bazerman 1994, 97), as regards theme, legal framework and genre conventions, is composed of EU texts

*Table 7.1* Number of occurrences analyzed (and corresponding number of documents)

|  |  | PFE | tort | MC | Total |
|---|---|---|---|---|---|
| EU | No. of occurrences (docs) (2005–2015) | 273 (166) | 12 (10) | 20 (7) | 305 (183) |
|  | No. of occurrences (docs) (2016–2019) | 170 (96) | 60 (14) | 1 (1) | 231 (111) |
|  | Total occurrences (docs) | 443 (262) | 72 (24) | 21 (8) | 536 (294) |
| UN | No. of occurrences (docs) (2005–2015) | 54 (42) | 22 (15) | 62 (37) | 138 (94) |
|  | No. of occurrences (docs) (2016–2019) | 75 (48) | 68 (43) | 40 (23) | 183 (114) |
|  | Total occurrences (docs) | 129 (90) | 90 (58) | 102 (60) | 321 (208) |
| WTO | No. of occurrences (docs) (2005–2015) | 80 (36) | 12 (6) | 19 (14) | 111 (56) |
|  | No. of occurrences (docs) (2016–2019) | 36 (26) | 13 (4) | 11 (8) | 60 (38) |
|  | Total occurrences (docs) | 116 (62) | 25 (10) | 30 (22) | 171 (94) |
| TOTAL |  | 688 (424) | 197 (92) | 153 (90) | 1,038 (606) |

on trade defense containing "PFE" (approximately 93% of all the EU corpus components for this term): regulations, implementing regulations, notices and decisions on antidumping, countervailing and safeguard measures. Interestingly, the EU trade defense procedures conform to WTO agreement provisions (and therefore their original terminology) also referred to in the corpus components of this organization. In the case of the most system-specific term, "MC", the name is employed in connection with 33 different national jurisdictions (where English is an official or de facto language of the courts) in documents of the multilateral system (UN and WTO), as opposed to the EU texts, where references to the United Kingdom (more precisely, England and Wales or Northern Ireland) prevail.

A list of translations grouped per lexical clusters is provided in the Annex, including 44 for "PFE", 31 for "tort" and 17 for "MC". If we consider the number of documents where the original terms are used, these figures represent average variability rates of one different rendering in every 15.64, 9 and 6.16 occurrences of "PFE", "MC" and "tort", respectively, or every 9.64, 5.29 and 2.88 documents. In other words, translations of "PFE" are generally more consistent than those of the other two terms. The difference is particularly marked in the EU corpus, with a translation variant of "PFE" in Spanish in every 12.48 documents on average, as opposed to a rate of 3.6 in the UN corpus (see Table 7.2). Only in this organization, the overall variability rate points to slightly higher consistency in the translations of "MC" (one variant per four documents). By contrast, the translations of "tort" are the least consistent in all the settings.

Table 7.2 also shows the three most recurrent translations of each term per setting. The most common ones coincide in the case of "PFE" at the UN and the WTO ("prueba *prima facie*") and "tort" in EU and UN documents ("responsabilidad civil", with the same frequency as

*Table 7.2* Three most recurrent translations (per number of documents and occurrences[1]) and total number of translation variants and documents per term and setting

|  | EU | UN | WTO |
|---|---|---|---|
| PFE | indicio razonable: 226 (336) *(in 86.26% of docs)* | prueba *prima facie*: 45 (58) *(in 50% of docs)* | prueba *prima facie*: 39 (81) *(in 62.90% of docs)* |
|  | indicio a primera vista: 5 (5) | indicio razonable: 15 (18) | prueba de presunción: 5 (5) |
|  | elemento de prueba a primera vista: 4 (7) | principio de prueba: 8 (9) | presunción: 4 (5) |
|  | *Total: 21 translations in 262 docs (average: 1 per 12.48 docs)* | *Total: 25 translations in 90 docs (average: 1 per 3.60 docs)* | *Total: 14 translations in 62 docs (average: 1 per 4.43 docs)* |
| tort | responsabilidad civil: 8 (10) *(in 33.33% of docs)* | responsabilidad civil: 11 (14) *(in 18.97% of docs)* | ilícito civil: 2 (10) *(in 20% of docs)* |
|  | responsabilidad extracontractual: 6 (15) | responsabilidad extracontractual: 11 (14) | responsabilidad civil: 2 (4) |
|  | acto ilícito: 5 (19) | agravio: 7 (20) | delito: 2 (4) |
|  | *Total: 16 translations in 24 docs (average: 1 per 1.50 docs)* | *Total: 21 translations in 58 docs (average: 1 per 2.76 docs)* | *Total: 8 translations in 10 docs (average: 1 per 1.25 docs)* |
| MC | magistrates' court: 4 (16) *(in 50% of docs)* | tribunal de primera instancia: 28 (47) *(in 46.67% of docs)* | tribunal de magistrados: 11 (15) *(in 50% of docs)* |
|  | tribunal de magistrados: 3 (3) | tribunal de magistrados: 11 (16) | corte de los magistrados: 4 (5) |
|  | Tribunal de Magistrados (Magistrates' Court): 1 (1) | juzgado de paz: 6 (13) | juzgado de paz: 3 (4) |
|  | *Total: 3 translations in 8 docs (average: 1 per 2.67 docs)* | *Total: 15 translations in 60 docs (average: 1 per 4 docs)* | *Total: 8 translations in 22 docs (average: 1 per 2.75 docs)* |

1   For each translation, the number of documents is followed by the number of total occurrences between brackets.

"responsabilidad extracontractual" at the UN), but diverge in the case of "MC". For this term, the most commonly coincidental rendering is the false friend "tribunal de magistrados", but only in the WTO subset was it found in more documents than the other translations of "MC". The more generic rendering "tribunal de primera instancia" is more frequent in the UN, and the borrowing is more often accepted in EU translations to refer to court names of one of its Member States during the period covered.

### 7.3.2 *Distribution of Consistency and Accuracy*

In line with the overall variability averages, the most recurrent translation of "PFE" is found in the largest proportion of documents for this term compared to the most popular translations of the other two terms: 86.26% (EU), 62.90% (WTO) and 50% (UN) of each subcorpus for "PFE", as opposed to 33.33% (EU), 20% (WTO) and 18.97% (UN) for "tort" and intermediate values of 50% (EU and WTO) and 46.67% (UN) for "MC". In fact, the question of density or distribution of translation variants emerges as an important aspect to consider in the analysis of consistency. The same average degree of variability may be the result of divergent scenarios, for instance: one in which there is a clearly prevalent translation and other more marginal reformulations, and another where the number of translations is similar to the first scenario but their distribution is much more irregular.

By adding a diachronic dimension to the analysis of these scenarios, it is possible to explore potential patterns of convergence, consolidation or, inversely, sustained terminological dispersion. With this in mind, and to reduce the limitations of statistical analysis of patterns in small subcorpora, an *intertextual variation rate* ("InterVaR") was calculated by applying a multiplicative factor that increases for each translation variant according to the order of frequency (e.g. factor 1 for the occurrences of the most frequent translation, factor 2 for the second most recurrent reformulation, and so on, to produce a cumulative value that is then divided by the total number of occurrences of the source term). Therefore, the closer this rate is to 1 for a particular term, the closer its translations are to total consistency. With a view to offsetting the statistical weight of translations repeated within the same document, and thus refining the values associated with intertextual consistency, an adjusted variation of the same rate was also calculated by considering only one occurrence of each translation variant present in each document.

From a qualitative perspective, two further indicators are of utmost relevance to gain insights on the implications of consistency for institutional translation quality: intratextual consistency and, especially, translation accuracy levels. Both must be read in conjunction with intertextual consistency, as some degree of variation may be possible and justified when several translations are acceptable and considered interchangeable for the same term. However, as mentioned in the introduction, intratextual consistency is particularly critical to ensure univocity in institutional translation, while translation inaccuracies are the most obvious obstacle to sound terminological harmonization and quality in scenarios where multiple translations of the same term coexist in a given setting.

The proportion of documents that include *intratextual inconsistencies* was calculated as a further step for a more qualitative examination of divergent translations. As regards the last indicator, i.e. translation accuracy, the following scale was applied to calculate the average *accuracy rates* ("AccuR") of all renderings of the terms in Spanish:

- Value 0: inaccurate translations that do not reflect the essential content of the original concept; they are too broad, divergent or misleading, or involve unjustified omissions (e.g. "a priori" for "PFE", "materia civil" for "tort" or "corte de los magistrados" for "MC").
- Value 1: acceptable translations considering the context, but not totally accurate (e.g. "elementos de prueba" for "PFE", "responsabilidad" for "tort" or "tribunal inferior" for "MC").
- Value 2: accurate translations that convey the essential content of the original concept and meet communicative adequacy requirements in context (e.g. "prueba *prima facie*" for "PFE", "(acto) ilícito civil" for "tort" or "tribunal de primera instancia (Magistrates' Court)").

In order to reduce any risk of subjective distortion, all the values assigned to translations were verified by two validators, paying particular attention to borderline cases. For four renderings, two different values were confirmed for various occurrences of the same translation depending on the context. As in the case of the InterVaR, AccuRs were calculated for each term, period and setting for the purpose of diachronic comparison. Likewise, a distinction was made between (a) AccuRs for the total amount of occurrences in absolute figures and (b) adjusted AccuRs excluding repeated occurrences of the same translation of a term within the same document. The calculation of averages per period involved using smaller fragmented subcorpora. This means that the values for certain terms and settings are statistically less insightful for the analysis of trends due to the low number of occurrences per period, namely, those for "tort" in WTO texts and "MC" in the EU corpus (see Table 7.1). In the latter case, averages could not be calculated for the period 2016–2019, as this included a single occurrence of the term.

The remaining absolute ("Abs.") and adjusted ("Adj.") AccuRs are provided in Table 7.3, where they are compared to the InterVaR values and the proportion of texts where intratextual inconsistencies ("IntraV.") were detected. The most remarkable commonality found

Table 7.3 Intratextual and intratextual variation indicators and AccuRs per term, period and setting

| | | | EU | | | UN | | | WTO | | |
|---|---|---|---|---|---|---|---|---|---|---|---|
| | | | InterVaR | IntraV. | AccuR | InterVaR | IntraV. | AccuR | InterVaR | IntraV. | AccuR |
| PFE | 05–15 | Abs. | 1.80 | 1.81% | 1.89 | 2.83 | 2.38% | 1.74 | 1.63 | 2.78% | 1.80 |
| | | Adj. | 1.51 | | 1.89 | 2.74 | | 1.67 | 1.70 | | 1.81 |
| | 16–19 | Abs. | 1.11 | 0% | 1.98 | 2.48 | 10.20% | 1.71 | 1.89 | 7.69% | 1.81 |
| | | Adj. | 1.14 | | 1.96 | 2.15 | | 1.83 | 2.11 | | 1.79 |
| tort | 05–15 | Abs. | 1.83 | 0% | 1.33 | 2.18 | 26.67% | 1.45 | 2.00 | 16.67% | 1.16 |
| | | Adj. | 1.91 | | 1.32 | 2.84 | | 1.52 | 1.78 | | 1.25 |
| | 16–19 | Abs. | 3.00 | 42.86% | 1.17 | 2.97 | 11.63% | 1.42 | 1.46 | 0% | 1.76 |
| | | Adj. | 3.23 | | 1.15 | 3.17 | | 1.50 | 2.25 | | 1.50 |
| MC | 05–15 | Abs. | 1.25 | 0% | 1.55 | 3.06 | 13.51% | 0.69 | 1.68 | 7.14% | 0 |
| | | Adj. | 1.63 | | 1.00 | 2.70 | | 0.77 | 1.53 | | 0 |
| | 16–19 | Abs. | N/A | N/A | 0 | 1.48 | 0% | 1.60 | 1.36 | 0% | 0.55 |
| | | Adj. | N/A | | 0 | 1.43 | | 1.48 | 1.50 | | 0.50 |

is that, regardless of the internal variations in each subcorpus, **AccuR** levels systematically rank in the same order in all the periods and settings, and with strikingly similar adjusted average rates: "PFE", the less culture-bound term, has the best scores (between 1.67 and 1.96); it is followed by "tort" (between 1.15 and 1.52) and, finally, "MC" (between 0 and 1.48), which reflects the difficulty of dealing with legal asymmetry and the added risk of the misleading literal rendering "magistrado". Only in the 2016–2019 period and in a single setting, the UN, does the AccuR for this term exceeds 1.

In terms of **InterVaR**, the most significant pattern in common is that "tort" registered the lowest intertextual consistency of the three terms in all periods and settings, per adjusted scores. These results align with the overall variability levels outlined in the previous section, as well as with the lower density of the most popular translations of "tort" per setting in comparison with those of "PFE" and "MC". "Tort" also concentrates the highest proportions of **intratextual inconsistencies** in a single period in all the organizations.

If we compare the three settings, as a general rule, the UN has the lowest consistency indicators, with InterVaR scores above 2, except for "MC" in the last period. It also registered the highest shares of intratextual variation in a single period for each term, with the exception of "tort". For this term, the highest InterVaR and the largest proportion of intratextual inconsistencies are found in the EU subcorpus for 2016–2019. These findings stand out, as the EU registered the lowest intertextual and intratextual variation scores for the other two terms. The results for "tort" reflect the fact that six out of 14 EU documents include several translations of the term, including up to five in one case and four in another.

Overall, the connection between consistency and accuracy is not straightforward, and no rule of thumb can be established from the comparison between terms and settings. For example, the highest accuracy rate in the EU corpus, that of translations of "PFE" in the second period (1.96), is coupled with the best adjusted InterVaR (1.14) of the series for this setting; however, if we observe the best accuracy results in the UN corpus, "PFE" translations also in the second period (1.83), they are less consistent (InterVaR of 2.15) than those of "MC" (InterVaR of 1.43 and AccuR of 1.48 in the same period). The unpredictable nature of internal terminological variations is also illustrated by examples of intratextual inconsistencies. For instance, none of the three translation variants for "PFE" found in the same UN text of 2008 ("indicios", "indicios razonables" and "indicios suficientes" in JIU/REP/2018/4) is inaccurate, while only one of the translations of "MC" in another UN text of 2005 ("juzgados de primera instancia", "Tribunales de Primera Instancia" and "Tribunal de Magistrados" in CERD/C/495/ADD.1) can be judged acceptable.

However, the most systematic (and telling) finding in the parallel examination of consistency and accuracy derives from the analysis of inter-period variations. Changes in InterVaR and AccuR scores for each term and setting generally follow the same patterns: when intertextual variation is reduced, and therefore consistency improves, progress is also detected in terms of accuracy, and the same association is also the norm in the opposite direction. The most marked variation is that of translations of "MC" in UN texts between the first and the second period: the adjusted InterVaR drops by almost half (from 2.70 to 1.43) whereas the adjusted AccuR more than doubles (from 0.77 to 1.48). This trend suggests a process of terminological consolidation that is beneficial for quality and is worth exploring in more detail.

Several factors may contribute to this kind of process. They include the level of translation expertise (and specialized revision) devoted to specific terms and text types over time, as well as the level of coordination between translation professionals, especially when long texts are divided for translation. In institutional contexts, the impact of precedent must also be considered, particularly when it comes to repetitive text segments or literal quotations. Another related factor is the use of terminological resources for the terms under examination. We will focus on this particular aspect in the next section.

## 7.4 The Potential Role of Institutional Resources

It would be difficult (if not impossible) to determine, retrospectively, the extent to which the translation recommendations or interlinguistic associations made in ITRs played a more or less decisive role in each translation of legal terminology that has not been coined at international organizations. As pointed out in the introduction, internal termbanks are a mandatory source for the translation of institutional terminology and priority sources for all other terminology within each institution, even if professional translators tend to consult a diversity of resources as part of their research (see, e.g., Désilets *et al.* 2009). An indicator of the use of ITRs and their potential influence on terminological decision-making is, therefore, the degree of congruity between the renderings extracted from institutional texts and those recommended in ITRs. In turn, this correspondence can be considered indicative of the presumed adherence to such recommendations, even if the translation decisions are also supported by other sources, particularly previous translations in the same context.

For the analysis of congruity, the most relevant ITRs for the English-Spanish translation of institutional texts in each setting were considered, paying particular attention to the dates of creation and modification of the entries that apply to our selected terms.[4] In the case of the EU, the main source is IATE as the terminology database of reference for all EU institutions and agencies. The contents of other EU institution-specific resources were merged into this massive collection in use since 2004. CuriaTerm, the internal database of the Court of Justice of the EU (CJEU), has migrated its contents into IATE until more recently, but with no impact on the records proposed for the terms under examination in this study. Given the predominance of EU documents on trade defense procedures in the analysis of "PFE" translations, the (internal) "Léxico antidumping y antisubvenciones" of 1997 (updated for the last time in 2009 and abbreviated hereinafter as "Léxico") was also considered. As noted by internal informants, this source, where "PFE" is translated as "indicios razonables," was conceived within the European Commission as a mandatory reference for the translation of texts on trade defense.

In the UN, the contents of databases from several bodies were gradually consolidated and integrated into UNTERM from 2013, and this termbank has been integrated into the UN's translation interface eLUNA in recent years. ITRs were previously more fragmented. One of the main databases before merging into UNTERM in 2015 was UNOGTerm, the database of the UN Office at Geneva (UNOG). It included a significant proportion of legal terminology, especially on human rights, which had been populated with a diversity of internal collections. Other popular internal glossaries still available for English-Spanish legal translation were also verified. One of them, the "Glosario provisional de términos jurídicos (E-S)" of 1996 (updated in 2003),[5] includes two recommendations for "PFE" ("principio de prueba", "prueba *prima facie*") and three for "tort" ("acto ilícito civil", "ilícito civil extracontractual", "acto lesivo"), which are also integrated in UNTERM.

In the case of the WTO, two resources were considered: the WTO's dispute settlement glossary English-Spanish ("Términos y expresiones utilizados frecuentemente en el procedimiento de solución de diferencias", abbreviated as "DS Glossary"), which is the main source used by WTO translators for legal terminology, and WTOTERM, which works like a collection of trilingual glossaries. Both provide recommendations for "PFE": "prueba *prima facie*" (since 2002) and "prueba suficiente para justificar la presunción de un hecho" (from the General Agreement on Tariffs and Trade (GATT) glossary of 1988 integrated into WTOTERM), respectively.

We will not elaborate on the amount and reliability of information offered by each resource or entry. We will rather focus on the overall number and relevance of the translation recommendations they make for the three selected terms, and whether these recommendations are reflected in our corpus, particularly in the case of the most statistically significant corpus subsets: those of "PFE" in all settings and "MC" at the UN. Table 7.4 shows the share of occurrences (if any) that match each ITR recommendation available over the entire period covered by the corpus,[6] as well as other ITR recommendations available during a more limited period.

"PFE" translations are, by far, the most consistent with ITRs. These results are in line with the InterVaR and AccuR values for each setting. The translation convention reflected in the European Commission's "Léxico" has prevailed in documents on EU trade defense measures. In only 14 or 5.75% of these documents (244 of the total of 262 EU corpus components for "PFE"), "indicios razonables" is not used in Spanish; inversely, alternative translations are found in 17 of the 18 documents that were not issued in connection with such trade defense measures. In fact, the EU's "PFE" subcorpus contains a significant number of repeated segments whose translations are systematically reproduced, thus greatly contributing to consistency scores (e.g. 63 of 67 slight variations of the segment "the applicant (has) provided (sufficient) *prima facie* evidence (showing) that" include "indicios razonables" in Spanish).

It must be noted, however, that the IATE recommendation for the most frequent translation was only introduced by the language services of the Council of the EU in October 2015 (February 2015 in the case of the other IATE renderings, i.e. long after the recommendation in the "Léxico"). It is presented as reliable (level 3 in a scale of 1 to 4) and refers to the UN's "Glosario provisional de términos jurídicos (E-S)" of 1996 as the source reference, rather than the European Commission's "Léxico" of 1997, and adds a note to indicate that "indicios razonables" in the plural is the most common rendering in trade defense instruments (antidumping and anti-subsidy regulations).[7] Yet, these EU regulations refer to "pruebas" or "elementos de prueba" for "evidence" since Council Regulations (EC) Nos 384/96 and 2026/97 (in line with GATT 1994 provisions on the matter[8]), and "información que contenga a primera vista elementos de prueba" for "information showing *prima facie* evidence" in Council Regulations (EC) Nos 597/2009 and 1225/2009, and their latest amendments, Regulations (EU) 2016/1036 and 2016/1037 of the European Parliament and of the Council. The reformulation of "PFE" employed in these so-called "basic regulations" of 2016 (which are themselves included in our corpus) was only found in a judgment of the General Court (within the CJEU) of 9 September 2010 in connection with Regulation (EC) No 1225/2009 (Usha Martin Ltd v Council of the European Union and European Commission; Case T-119/06) and in Commission Implementing Regulation (EU) 2019/1948 of 25 November 2019 initiating an antidumping investigation.

The other two translations introduced in IATE in February 2015 as reliable options in a list of eight, "prueba de presunciones" and "prueba indiciaria", are functional renderings supported by Spanish case-law but not found among occurrences in EU translations in our corpus. Among the other three IATE suggestions for "PFE", only "presunción" was found in a document of 2005, before the creation of the database entry.[9]

*Table 7.4* Translation recommendations in ITRs and shares of corresponding corpus occurrences (where applicable)

| | EU | UN | WTO |
|---|---|---|---|
| PFE | *Léxico:*<br>indicio razonable<br>(84.42%) | *UNTERM:*<br>prueba *prima facie* (44.96%)<br>principio de prueba (6.98%) | *DS Glossary:*<br>prueba *prima facie*<br>(69.83%) |
| | *IATE (since 2015):*<br>indicio razonable<br>prueba indiciaria<br>prueba de<br>    presunciones<br>prueba suficiente<br>    para justificar la<br>    presunción de un<br>    hecho<br>prueba por presunción<br>prueba por<br>    presunciones<br>presunción | *Second entry since 2015:*<br>prueba *prima facie*<br>prueba indiciaria (0.78%)<br>prueba de presunciones | *WTOTERM:*<br>prueba suficiente<br>    para justificar la<br>    presunción de un<br>    hecho (2.59%) |
| Tort | – | *UNTERM:*<br>responsabilidad<br>    extracontractual<br>    (15.38%)<br>acto ilícito (10.99%)<br>acto ilícito civil (2.20%)<br>daños y perjuicios (2.20%)<br>hecho ilícito<br>    extracontractual (2.20%)<br>acto lesivo<br>culpa civil<br>culpa extracontractual | – |
| MC | *IATE:*<br>juzgado de paz | *UNTERM:*<br>justicia de paz<br>*(only 2014–2018)* | – |

The UN and WTO results for "PFE" also show a marked difference between translation-ITR matches for the most frequent renderings and other translation options. The two UNTERM entries for this term (the second of which was created in August 2015) suggest "prueba *prima facie*" together with other options, of which only "principio de prueba" from the first entry (nine occurrences) and "prueba indiciaria" from the second (one occurrence in a document issued in November 2015) are found in our corpus. No thematic pattern or preference associated with a particular documental subset could be identified.

In the case of the WTO, the prevalence of "*prima facie* evidence" exemplifies the relevance of the organization's DS Glossary for the translation of legal terminology. Considering the direct connection between

WTO and EU trade defense legal provisions and implementation mechanisms, it is interesting to note how translations of "PFE" in Spanish in these two settings diverge systematically, as opposed to the complete consistency of the original English term. In fact, some of the exceptions to the main rendering as "prueba *prima facie*" at the WTO result from reproducing the translation of the applicable EU "basic regulations" in EU notifications on antidumping or countervailing measures to the WTO. As a general rule, notifications and dispute settlement documents for these measures otherwise adhere to the prevalent translation. The other exceptions are found in: (a) a few trade policy review reports (including a diversity of renderings of marginal frequency), (b) in a series of report revisions on the accession of Liberia (a section on special border measures where a recurrent segment contains "pruebas de presunción" in Spanish) and (c) in documents that replicate "presunción" as used in one of the WTO agreements (article 58 of the Agreement on Trade-Related Aspects of Intellectual Property Rights).

The results on translation-ITR congruity for the other two terms are much more scattered, as translation suggestions are only found for "tort" in UNTERM and "magistrates' court" in IATE. The first of these databases contains five entries for "**tort**" in Spanish, four created at UNOG and one at the UN headquarters (with regard to three common areas, among others: law, international law and environment), totaling eight renderings of the term. Four of these translations, all correct in context, are found in the corpus but only represent 30.77% of occurrences. No correlations were observed between the contexts of use and translation choices. All UNTERM renderings refer to the same concept, as expressed in entry 64672, which is explicitly associated with "environmental law; based on the traditional theory of injury in common law." Coincidentally, the only two renderings included in more than one entry, "acto ilícito civil" and "culpa extracontractual", were found in one document (two occurrences) and in none, respectively. This is another sign of the high heterogeneity of translations of "tort".

Finally, "**MC**" is associated with "juzgado de paz" in two IATE entries on the basis of a translation from Spanish suggested by the CJEU's English Translation Division in 1994. This can only be considered a loose conceptual association, as the composition of MCs and the matters they deal with differ from those of *juzgados de paz*. The connection made in IATE for the translation into English is not reflected in the corpus. In practice, the borrowing of national court names of Member States prevails in CJEU documents. In our corpus, an example is found in a reference for a preliminary ruling. The other instances of borrowing are included in annexes to EU legal acts on judicial cooperation. However, the calque in Spanish was also used in a directive and two documents on policy implementation. It is not found in IATE, but it is used in the e-Justice webpages on national judicial systems translated by the

European Commission as "órganos jurisdiccionales de los magistrados" with reference to MCs in England and Wales, and "tribunales de magistrados" in the case of Northern Ireland.[10]

Interestingly, UNOGTerm entry 28240 also associated "MC" with "justicia de paz" (initially influenced by the French "justice de paix") and included a remark to refer to "juez de paz" between 2014 (in UNTERM since June 2015) and 2018. Since then, this entry does not include any rendering of the English term in Spanish, but only in French and Chinese. The reference to "justicia de paz" and "juez de paz" seems too peripheral and short-lived to have any significant impact, but corresponds to a conceptual association that was made more frequently in UN translations in the first period; "juzgado de paz" accounts for 19.35% of 62 occurrences in Spanish (12 instances in five documents) during that period, as opposed to only one in a total of 40 occurrences in 2016–2019. In the second period, occurrences of the borrowing (a translation technique generally avoided at the UN) were also rare (in two documents in 2016–2019 versus three in the first period, including an explanatory addition in one case in 2010), despite the new suggestion to borrow the original court name made in the internal "Orientaciones para la traducción de textos jurídicos (2015)".[11] The trend to discontinue "juzgado de paz" runs parallel to the increase in the use of the more adequate formulation "tribunal de primera instancia", from 27.42% to 75% of occurrences, and to the decrease in the use of the calque "tribunal de magistrados", from 21.67% to 7.5% of occurrences.[12] These patterns explain the accuracy levels provided in the previous section.

As also noted in the previous section, various factors may have shaped this process. The removal of the Spanish reference in the terminological entry for "MC" implies a deliberate action to reduce the risk of confusion and inaccuracy, but the gradual convergence toward "tribunal de primera instancia" (12 of 13 occurrences in 2019) is not reflected in UNTERM or in the internal recommendation of the borrowing issued as part of internal guidelines for legal translation in 2015. It would be necessary to consider other potential factors such as changes in profiles or working procedures, and more particularly whether the increasing use of "tribunal de primera instancia" results from deliberate terminology uniformization supported by automatic retrieval tools or other internal developments.[13] It is apparent, however, that the main terminological database has been lagging behind in this process rather than serving as a reference.

## 7.5 Conclusions

The combined analyses of consistency and accuracy of translations and ITR recommendations for the three selected terms illustrate how concepts of more legal singularity or implying a higher degree of asymmetry with regard to the target-language legal traditions represent a challenge to terminological decision-making and quality in international institutional translation, and tend to be addressed in ITRs less systematically than other established institution-specific terminology. The less system-specific concept of "PFE" is the most frequently found and translated in a consistent and accurate manner in our corpus, and with the greatest correspondence to particular ITR recommendations.

More particularly, EU and WTO translations on antidumping and other trade defense measures show the weight of precedent and the relevance of internal thematic glossaries in ensuring terminological consistency in recurrent standardized institutional proceedings. The same patterns, however, also illustrate that, despite thematic homogeneity, the contents of different ITRs on certain terms are not always mutually consistent or in line with applicable legal provisions within the same setting or international legal instruments more broadly. In the case of "PFE", the prevailing target renderings, "indicios razonables" and "prueba *prima facie*", differ in closely related procedures in the EU and the WTO, respectively, even if the original term is identical. This also leads to a situation in which exceptions to the predominant translation in each context may derive from the reproduction of translation precedents from other settings (e.g. notifications of EU antidumping measures at the WTO). In other words, paradoxically, in order to preserve consistency, certain inconsistencies may have to be reproduced.

The high variability of "tort" translations (as evidenced by their intertextual and intratextual consistency scores, the lowest among the terms analyzed) and their globally acceptable accuracy levels point to a considerable number of valid synonyms in context. In turn, this may be related to the lack of a fully analogous legal concept in the target-language legal systems and the fact that translators may reflect the main defining features of the original concept in several ways. This is also mirrored in the only database where the term appears, UNTERM, which encompasses several overlapping entries and translation variants for "tort" in Spanish. No clear associated thematic or contextual pattern was observed in UN translations, though. These results suggest that the proliferation of synonym translations in ITRs may contribute to preventing inaccuracies, but also to perpetuating terminological fragmentation rather than univocity, as in situations where ITRs provide no guidance on the term.

Finally, the most national system-specific term, "MC", seems to be as problematic for institutional terminologists as it is for translators. It concentrates the lowest accuracy scores in all the settings and periods, and it is the only term for which inaccurate renderings were identified in ITRs.

These findings are certainly explained by the difficulty of dealing with asymmetry between judicial systems and the associated risk of inaccuracy if previous expertise or comparative legal analysis is insufficient to detect key differences between bodies or the false friend "tribunal de magistrados". Nonetheless, translation variation is less marked than in the case of "tort", which suggests that higher inconsistency levels are not necessarily coupled with lower accuracy, as the nature and function of the term in each text may justify more or less tolerance to synonyms. The very idea of variation in denominations of a court name is at odds with translation adequacy since the communicative priority of identifying a judicial body in institutional texts conflicts with the idea of providing a diversity of names for it.

However, the findings of our diachronic analysis of translation patterns point to a clear correlation between changes in consistency and accuracy rates over time, albeit most often minor. The reduction of intertextual variation in the second period (2016–2019) generally coincides with an increase in translation accuracy for any given term and setting, and vice versa, which confirms the positive effects of terminological harmonization on both variables as indicators of translation quality. The most marked positive trend was found in the translation of "MC" at the UN, the organization that otherwise registered the highest variation rates for all terms.

For none of the three terms is there evidence of any major impact of ITR recommendations on translation decisions. Only the results for "PFE" in the EU and the WTO subcorpora can be considered highly indicative of adherence to the relevant glossaries. Yet, it is difficult to determine the extent to which ITRs are consulted and followed by translators in each instance. The most significant cases of terminological convergence identified are clearly influenced by translation precedents in each institution, while other aspects of decision-making fall beyond the scope of this study. As confirmed by the verification of ITRs, the legal terms analyzed, in particular the more system-specific, are not a priority for institutional terminology management and, consequently, ITR recommendations seem to play a peripheral rather than a central role in their translation. The inconsistencies and gaps detected in ITRs do not contribute to the effectiveness of these sources. Addressing them could crucially support new processes of terminological convergence and quality assurance, especially considering the functionalities of integrated online platforms for translation-oriented terminological work.

## Acknowledgments

I would like to thank Diego Guzmán for his valuable assistance with data processing, as well as all institutional informants for their kind cooperation in the framework of the LETRINT project.

# Notes

1 Full results available at: https://es.surveymonkey.com/results/SM-X7FXFJXG/.
2 "Legal Translation in International Institutional Settings: Scope, Strategies and Quality Markers," led by the author and supported by the Swiss National Science Foundation through a Consolidator Grant.
3 Albeit originally inspired by Greek and Roman thought, and not always uniformly used in common law jurisdictions (see Herlitz 1994). For a comparison of *prima facie* standards in national and international jurisdictions, see Pfitzer and Sabune (2009). As they note, "civil law jurisdictions do have presumptions and the concept of *prima facie* proof; however, as in Germany, presumptions arise out of statutory provisions and concepts of *prima facie* evidence are used to rebut such presumptions" (ibid., 10).
4 The relevance and history of ITRs for our corpus analysis were double-checked with institutional informants from each setting. However, it was impossible (and unnecessary for the purposes of the study) to track the origin and dates of all content changes of the relevant ITRs, particularly in the first period.
5 https://conf-dts1.unog.ch/1%20SPA/Tradutek/Recursos%20Juridicos/00 Glos%20Juridico%20Sureda.htm.
6 Unless otherwise specified, our inquiry led to the conclusion that all lexicographical contents included in Table 7.4 existed before the first year of our corpus, 2005, even if they were not necessarily integrated into online databases, where relevant, until later.
7 https://iate.europa.eu/entry/result/1094354/all.
8 Also in the pre-GATT-1994 Council Regulation (EEC) No 2423/88 of 11 July 1988 on protection against dumped or subsidized imports from countries not members of the European Economic Community.
9 This translation is given minimum reliability by IATE, as well as "prueba suficiente para justificar la presunción de un hecho." No references or reliability levels are provided in the entry for the remaining options, "prueba por presunciones" and "prueba por presunción" (as of April 2020).
10 These inaccuracies, first spotted in Prieto Ramos (2013), were still found, respectively, in the following overviews as of April 2020:
  https://e-justice.europa.eu/content_judicial_systems_in_member_states-16-ew-es.do?init=true&member=1 (last update of 12 December 2016)
  https://e-justice.europa.eu/content_ordinary_courts-18-ni-maximize MS-es.do?member=1 (last update of 28 August 2018).
11 https://conf.unog.ch/paginilla/wp-content/uploads/2015/05/Traducci% C3%B3n-de-textos-jur%C3%ADdicos-Orientaciones-2015.pdf.
12 No connection was found between translation decisions and references to specific national judicial systems in previous translations.
13 This translation was also suggested as an acceptable rendering in this kind of context in Prieto Ramos (2013, 99), when the problem of the misleading calque was highlighted.

# References

Bazerman, Charles. 1994. "Systems of genres and the enactment of social intentions." In *Genre and the New Rhetoric*, edited by Aviva Freedman and Peter Medway, 79–101. London: Taylor & Francis.
De Saint Robert, Marie-Josée. 2009. "Assessing quality in translation and terminology at the United Nations." In *CIUTI-Forum 2008 (Enhancing*

*Translation Quality: Ways, Means, Methods)*, edited by Martin Forstner, Hannelore Lee-Jahnke and Peter A. Schmitt, 387–392. Bern, Berlin, Brussels, Frankfurt am Main, New York, Oxford, Vienna: Peter Lang.

Désilets, Alain, Christiane Melançon, Geneviève Patenaude, and Louise Brunette. 2009. "How translators use tools and resources to resolve translation problems: an ethnographic study." In *Proceedings of the Workshop Beyond Translation Memories: New Tools for Translators, Machine Translation Summit XII*. http://mt-archive.info/MTS-2009-Desilets-2.pdf.

ISO. 2015. *ISO 17100. Translation Services – Requirements for Translation Services*. Geneva: ISO.

Herlitz, Georg Nils. 1994. "The meaning of the term 'prima facie'." *Louisiana Law Review* 55 (2): 391–408.

Pfitzer, James Headen, and Sheila Sabune. 2009. "Burden of proof in WTO dispute settlement: Contemplating preponderance of the evidence." ICTSD Dispute Settlement and Legal Aspects of International Trade – Issue Paper No. 9. Geneva: ICTSD.

Prieto Ramos, Fernando. 2013. "¿Qué estrategias para qué traducción jurídica?: por una metodología integral para la práctica profesional." In *Translating the Law. Theoretical and Methodological Issues/Traducir el Derecho. Cuestiones teóricas y metodológicas*, edited by Icíar Alonso Araguás, Jesús Baigorri Jalón and Helen J. L. Campbell, 87–106. Granada: Comares.

Prieto Ramos, Fernando. 2014a. "International and supranational law in translation: From multilingual lawmaking to adjudication." *The Translator* 20 (3): 313–331. doi:10.1080/13556509.2014.904080.

Prieto Ramos, Fernando. 2014b. "Parameters for problem-solving in legal translation: Implications for legal lexicography and institutional terminology management." In *The Ashgate Handbook of Legal Translation*, edited by Anne Wagner, King-Kui Sin and Le Cheng, 121–134. Farnham: Ashgate.

Prieto Ramos, Fernando, and Diego Guzmán. 2018. "Legal terminology consistency and adequacy as quality indicators in institutional translation: A mixed-method comparative study." In *Institutional Translation for International Governance: Enhancing Quality in Multilingual Legal Communication*, edited by Fernando Prieto Ramos, 81–101. Bloomsbury Advances in Translation. London: Bloomsbury. doi:10.5040/9781474292320.0015.

Robertson, Colin. 2015. "EU multilingual law: Interfaces of law, language and culture." In *Language and Culture in EU Law. Multidisciplinary Perspectives*, edited by Susan Šarčević, 33–51. Farnham: Ashgate.

Šarčević, Susan. 2010. "Creating a Pan-European Legal Language." In *Legal Discourse across Languages and Cultures*, edited by Maurizio Gotti and Christopher Williams, 23–50. Oxford, Bern, Berlin, Brussels, Frankfurt am Main, New York, Vienna: Peter Lang.

Šarčević, Susan. 2013. "Multilingual lawmaking and legal (Un)certainty in the European Union." *International Journal of Law, Language & Discourse* 3 (1): 1–29.

Stefaniak, Karolina. 2017. "Terminology work in the European commission: Ensuring high-quality translation in a multilingual environment." In *Quality Aspects in Institutional Translation*, edited by Tomáš Svoboda, Łucja Biel and Krzysztof Łoboda, 109–121. Berlin: Language Science Press. doi:10.5281/zenodo.1048192.

## Annex: Translations of Selected Terms

*prima facie* evidence
- indicio(s): indicio(s); _ razonable(s); _ suficiente(s); _ racionale(s); _ a primera vista; _ preliminares razonables; _ *prima facie*; _ probatorio.
- presunción(-ones): presunción(-ones); _ *prima facie*; _ salvo prueba de lo contrario (*prima facie*); suficiente _; elementos de _.
- prueba(s): prueba(s); _ *prima facie*; principio(s) de _; (elementos de _) a primera vista; _ suficiente(s); _ razonable(s); _ de presunción; _ que permitan concluir *prima facie*; _ que fundamenten / justifiquen la presunción; _ rebatible(s); elementos de _; _ a primera vista; constituir *prima facie* una _; _ iniciales; _ que así lo indican *prima facie*; salvo _ de lo contrario; _ verosímiles; _ indiciaria(s); _ presuntivas; _ concluyentes (*prima facie*); _ suficientes (*prima facie*).
- Other: demostrar *prima facie*; indicios o pruebas que fundamentan la presunción; documentación; acreditar *prima facie*; principios *prima facie*; revelar, *prima facie*; probatorio/a; evidencia a primera vista; *a priori*; elementos de juicio.

tort
- acto(s): _ ilícito(s); _ ilícitos civiles; _ civil ilícito.
- agravio(s): agravio(s); _ civil(es); _ o responsabilidad civil extracontractual.
- delito(s): delito(s); _ civil(es).
- ilícito(s): ilícito(s); _ civil(es).
- responsabilidad: responsabilidad; _ civil; _ extracontractual; _ delictual; _ civil de origen extracontractual; _ civil extracontractual; _ delictiva.
- Other: hecho ilícito; materia delictual; conducta delictual; delictual; daños; infracciones administrativas; infracción; extracontractual; infracción civil; materia civil; erróneamente; culpa extracontractual; daños de origen extracontractual; incumplimiento de contrato.

magistrates' court
- tribunal: tribunal; _ de primera instancia; de magistrados; _ inferior; _ ordinario; _ judicial; _ de Magistrados («Magistrates' Court»); _ de los magistrados; _ de instrucción; _ de primera instancia (Magistrate's Court).
- juzgado: juzgado; _ de paz; _ de primera instancia.
- Magistrate(s|'s|s') Court: Magistrate(s|'s|s') Court; _ (instancias judiciales competentes para el enjuiciamiento de causas penales y demandas civiles relacionadas con reclamaciones de menor cuantía).
- Other: corte de los magistrados; altos magistrados de los tribunales.

# 8 Corrigenda of EU Legislative Acts as an Indicator of Quality Assurance Failures

## A Micro-diachronic Analysis of Errors Rectified in the Polish Corrigenda

*Łucja Biel and Izabela Pytel*

## 8.1 Introduction

The overall objective of this chapter is to approach the topic of translation quality through the lens of corrigenda, an instrument published in the Official Journal which formally rectifies an error in one or more language versions of an EU legal act (cf. Bobek 2009). Corrigenda have been rarely discussed in academic literature and publicly accessible institutional documents; likewise, to the best of our knowledge, they have not been researched empirically so far except for a recent paper by Prieto Ramos (2020). It is surprising, given the potential of corrigenda to give an insight into the nature of those quality issues in high-profile legal documents which were serious enough to require a formal rectification. This chapter intends to fill this niche. We analyze the practice of corrigenda quantitatively and qualitatively, by investigating the correction rates (CRs), the nature of corrigenda and the nature of formally identified and corrected errors (which mainly concern terminology and phraseology) to better understand quality assurance failures in EU translation. Corrigenda are analyzed from a micro-diachronic perspective of 2004–2006 and 2015–2017 to examine their correlation with the maturity of the Polish Eurolect.

## 8.2 EU Law in Translation: Multilingual Concordance and Divergences between Language Versions

The European Union (EU) is now a supranational organization of 27 Member States and 24 official languages, which has legal autonomy. This means that EU law is autonomous and distinct from the Member States' national law and has supremacy over Member States' national laws (Case 283/81 *Srl CILFIT* [1982]; Judgment of the Court of 15 July 1964, Case 6–64 Flaminio Costa v E.N.E.L.; see also Woods, Watson

DOI: 10.4324/9780429264894-8

and Costa 2017). It is drafted by the institutions at the supranational level; yet it is applied in 27 national legal systems (Kjær 2007, 79), either through its directly binding force (regulations) or through transposition (directives) into national legal systems (Biel 2014, 59). As a consequence, it has a considerable impact on national legal systems.

EU law is promulgated in 24 language versions, which altogether contribute to the meaning of a single legal instrument (Šarčević 1997, 64; Derlén 2015, 62). Under Regulation No 1/1958 and the principle of equal authenticity (Šarčević 1997, 64), all language versions are *de jure* authentic, have legal effect and equal status (Derlén 2015, 62). As a result, each language version functions as an independent text in respective Member States: it is used by national drafters to harmonize national legislation and for various official purposes (Robertson 2010, 147).

The fundamental relationship of translations to their source text (ST) – equivalence – is replaced by "multilingual concordance," that is the equivalent relationship among all 24 language versions of a legal act with the same legal effect (cf. DGT 2016b, 4; Drugan, Strandvik, and Vuorinen 2018, 57). In practice, it is predominantly the English[1] version which is an ST – or more precisely a base text subject to rewriting and negotiations. From a legal point of view, it is irrelevant and all language versions are presumed to have the same meaning ("legal accuracy," DGT 2016b, 6). Since language versions are expected to enable the uniform interpretation and application of EU law in all the Member States (Šarčević 1997, 73), it is vital to ensure minimum divergences between language versions. It applies in particular to critical divergences which may favor or disadvantage some citizens, businesses or countries in an unintended way (DGT 2015, 5; Kapko 2005, 2). Yet, considering the political, linguistic and institutional complexity,[2] errors and divergences between language versions are unavoidable (Schilling 2010; Šarčević 2013, 1, 9; Robertson 2010, 155; Somssich, Várnai, and Bérczi 2010, 137–141). Some divergences may be caused by drafting[3] errors (Stefaniak 2013, 59) while others may result from constraints and errors of the translation process. Some errors are corrected before a legal act is published in the Official Journal if spotted by translators or legal revisers (Stefaniak 2013, 60). After the act has been published, an error can be corrected through a corrigendum (see Section 8.4). Second, divergences can be compensated for through judicial interpretation: the Court of Justice of the EU compares language versions through a more flexible teleological approach (Doczekalska 2009, 362–363; Šarčević 2013, 13).

## 8.3 The EU's Renewed Approach to Translation Quality Assurance after the 2004 Accessions

Recently the topic of institutional translation quality has received considerable attention in Translation Studies (cf. Prieto Ramos 2017; Svoboda, Biel, and Łoboda 2017) and EU institutions. What is clearly visible in EU institutions is the critical reframing of the concept of translation quality and its metrics (cf. Biel 2017). Following the doubling of official languages and translation activity after the EU enlargements in 2004–2007, the resulting pressure on cost efficiency and increased outsourcing, the institutions have worked out a more integrated, systematic and structured approach to translation quality assurance in the last 15 years (Strandvik 2017b, 52). It started with the development of quality management policies, guidelines, actions and frameworks to lay the ground for a renewed process-oriented approach (cf. Strandvik 2017b, 54 ff.). It was built around two principles: consistency of approach and consistency of quality (Drugan, Strandvik, and Vuorinen 2018). The new approach focuses on the improvement of processes, quality management through knowledge management (with increased synergies between language units and institutions) and organizational restructuring into "a matrix structure for quality management" with new coordination roles such as quality managers and portfolio managers (Strandvik 2017b, 55–57; DGT 2016a).

Some noteworthy initiatives at the European Commission[4] include: IT investments, prioritization of documents, increased editing of English documents before translation, uniform standards for the evaluation of outsourced translation (Strandvik 2017a), knowledge-sharing and standardization through translation manuals, style guides and clear writing guides (Drugan, Strandvik, and Vuorinen 2018, 44). Key performance indicators were introduced to quantify quality from a process-oriented perspective, including a CR (see Section 8.4), customer satisfaction rate, editing rate and deadline compliance rate (DGT 2016b). The very concept of quality was redefined in line with the EN 15038:2006 standard (ECS 2006) from traditional "faithfulness" to more flexible "fit-for-purpose"; for example, error relevance descriptors in the Commission no longer refer to changes in meaning but to an impairment of "the usability of the text for its intended purpose" (Strandvik 2017a, 125). This redefinition was intended to match quality requirements with text types to prioritize documents and manage resources more effectively (Biel 2017, 35).

Thus, according to the Translation Quality Guidelines (DGT 2015) developed by the European Commission's Directorate-General for Translation (DGT), EU legal acts belong to the prioritized Category A of documents due to the high legal, financial and political risks they entail. They are translated mainly in-house and were initially excluded from outsourcing; however, currently this exclusion is not restrictively applied and ca. 20% volume of legislative translation was outsourced by the Commission in the first quarter of 2014 (Strandvik 2014, 221, 2017b, 53). Legal acts are allocated to the most stringent quality control level with full bilingual revision (DGT 2015, 7) and legal revision by lawyer-linguists. In addition to standard linguistic requirements, they should comply with drafting and other guidelines and have intra- and intertextually consistent terminology of unchanged conceptual scope (DGT 2015, 6). Any new terms created should be consulted with the DGT and ST errors should be flagged to the DGT (DGT 2017, 2). To sum up, EU legal acts are subject to the most rigorous quality assurance requirements.

## 8.4 Corrigenda as a Translation Quality Metric

A corrigendum is a sub-genre in the legislative genre chain. It is a document which formally rectifies an error in one or more already published language versions of an EU legal act and which is published in the Official Journal: "[i]ts purpose is to realign the published legislative text with the original will of the legislative body by removing mistakes that occurred in the publication process" (Bobek 2009, 950).

Corrigenda requests are submitted by Member States, legal persons or EU institutions (EC 2012, 30) to an applicable EU institution which is in charge of a given act. Rectification procedures date back to the 1970s and differ across the institutions. In the case of the European Commission, obvious drafting errors in Commission acts are corrected by the Secretary General, where obvious errors are understood as "easily recognizable errors in the text (e.g. spelling, typing or printing errors, mathematical errors or the omission of one or more words or of part of the text)" (Commission Decision of 12.7.2017, C(2017) 4898 final). Translation errors are corrected by the DGT under the empowerment in SEC(2008)2397. The empowerment lists three cumulative conditions to be met by an error to qualify for rectification: (1) it should appear in translation; (2) it should be "easily recognisable" or identified beyond doubt in comparison to the original; (3) it should not affect "the substance of the text as a whole." The Commission's procedure requires consultations with the author Directorate-General and the positive opinion of the Legal Service. Substantial drafting/translation errors are corrected by way of procedure corresponding to the adoption of the initial act (Somssich, Várnai, and Bérczi 2010, 144).

The rectification procedure of the Council is specified in its Manual of Precedents, which stresses that:

> In practice, a corrigendum (...) is made to those parts of the text that are so lacking in form as to be incomprehensible, as well as to errors liable to produce *undesired legal effects* (obvious typing or language errors that are *unimportant should not be corrected* by a corrigendum).
>
> (Council 2015, 177, emphasis added)

Obvious errors are corrected by way of corrigenda while non-obvious errors can be corrected either by way of corrigendum or by a new act, depending on the delegations' decision (Somssich, Várnai, and Bérczi 2010, 145). In the case of acts adopted in the ordinary legislative procedure, which are analyzed in this study, the corrigendum has to be formally approved by the European Parliament and requires prior consultations with Member States and other stakeholders (see Council 2015, 179–180 for a detailed description of the procedure).

In one of few papers devoted to corrigenda, Bobek distinguishes two types: (1) **purely formal corrigenda** and (2) **meaning-changing corrigenda**. The former are regarded as "genuine corrigenda" as they rectify errors caused during the publication process, including:

> typographic mistakes and omissions, obvious flaws in writing or type-setting. They might include things like omitted letters, small instead of capital letters at the beginning of a sentence, incorrect internal references caused by a typing mistake, wrongly type-set sentences or paragraphs, and so on.
>
> (Bobek 2009, 951)

The meaning-changing corrigenda "substantively alter the content of the legal norm" and are usually caused by translation errors at an earlier stage rather than typing mistakes (Bobek 2009, 951). Such corrections, as pointed out by Bobek:

> include narrowing or broadening of notions in a legal text, changing the nature of a list of conditions to be fulfilled (from enumerative to exhaustive), turning positive sentences into negative ones, or even plainly rewriting of substantive parts of a piece of EC legislation.
>
> (Bobek 2009, 951)

Thus, they effectively change the scope of rule application (Bobek 2009, 252). The recently intensified practice of corrigenda prompts criticism. Bobek criticizes[5] its "inflationary (mis-)use," arguing that EU corrigenda go beyond purely formal corrigenda and often consist in meaning-changing corrigenda, which materially should be treated as amendments, that is, as "*ex post* alterations of the content of the published [...] legal norm" (2009, 951, 960, 962). He also points out that corrigenda are used to belatedly fix translation errors which should have been eliminated much earlier at the drafting stage (Bobek 2009, 958). The European Commission also perceives corrigenda as one of the costs of poor-quality translation which reduce legal certainty due to their retroactive legal effect and may entail a loss of reputation, image risks, litigation risks as well as the costs of handling corrigendum requests from Member States (EC 2012, 12). As a result, the European Commission introduced the CR as one of translation quality metrics in its ex-post quality monitoring. The CR is defined as "the ratio between the number of translations formally corrected during one year and the number of translations of the same year and the preceding two years that can be subject to such corrections," with the 2020 target being below 0.5% and the base rate in 2015 – 0.42 (DGT 2016b, 9).

## 8.5 The Polish Eurolect: Phases of Development and Quality Issues

EU legislation is formulated in 24 Eurolects – translator-mediated supranational varieties of national legal languages, which emerged to cater for the needs of supranational EU law and are hybrid at the terminological, grammatical and stylistic levels (Biel 2020). The Eurolects are in different phases of development, ranging from 10 to 60 years, depending on a country's accession date, e.g. Dutch, French, German and Italian are the oldest Eurolects while Croatian is the youngest one (ibid.).

With Poland's accession to the EU in 2004, the Polish Eurolect is relatively young. Its phases of development can be divided into: the pre-accession formative stage, the transition stage and the mature post-accession stage (Biel 2018, 296). It started to form before the accession in the early 2000s when Poland started to translate the *acquis* and harmonize its national law with EU law. It developed under time pressure in a chaotic manner with insufficient quality assurance on the part of the Polish government, resulting in the low quality of Polish translations and over 4,500 pages of corrections of translations submitted to the EU institutions soon after the accession (Uhlig 2005; Biel 2014, 74–75). This is also confirmed by the findings of the corpus-based Euro-fog project covering the period of 1958–2006, which evidences the low textual fit of the Polish Eurolect to national law and its visible translatedness (Biel 2014, 295). The transition took place after the accession when the EU institutions took control over the translation process and started to build the Polish-language unit and Polish resources. Starting from 2008 to 2010, the Polish Eurolect became stabilized and entered a mature phase of development (Biel 2018).

## 8.6 Material and Method

The study investigates the practice of corrigenda which affected the Polish-language versions of EU legal acts from a micro-diachronic perspective by comparing corrigenda in the early formative stage of the Polish Eurolect 2004–2006 and the mature stage of 2015–2017. The first part of the study adopts a quantitative approach to identify rectification trends in the two periods by analyzing corrigenda to the Polish versions of EU legal acts contained in EUR-Lex,[6] an official database of EU law (refine query option, subdomain – legal acts, type of act – corrigendum, year of document). The second part of the study is qualitative in nature and manually investigates the nature of errors corrected by means of corrigenda. It is narrowed down to a specific type of legislative acts – regulations of the European Parliament and of the Council adopted in ordinary legislative procedure.

The choice of this legal act was dictated by several considerations. First, regulations are directly applicable in Member States; they are self-executing and automatically incorporated into national legal systems as binding law. By contrast, directives require transposition into national law and transposing acts may eliminate translation errors or divergences. Second, legislative acts were selected over non-legislative acts, such as delegated acts and implementing acts, since they are higher in the hierarchy of norms (cf. Curtin and Manucharyan 2015). These basic legal acts serve as a terminological reference for future legislation, in particular non-legislative acts (Stefaniak 2017, 116). Third, the **ordinary legislative procedure**, previously known as a "co-decision" procedure, is the most democratic way of EU decision-making with growing importance.[7] It requires the joint involvement of and balance between three institutions: the Council and the European Parliament adopt a legislative act proposed by the Commission (Lelieveldt and Princen 2015, 82–83). The study does not cover legislative acts adopted in special legislative procedures which are reserved for limited prescribed policy areas.[8] Finally, the ordinary legislative procedure is interesting due to its complexity and negotiations in and between all the institutions, with numerous amendments and up to three readings in the Council and the Parliament. It represents the EU legislative procedure at its fullest, with translators "patching up" the text at its multiple stages.

Some corrigenda have only one correction while others have multiple corrections. One correction point may rectify a single error or a number of errors, usually coming from one editing unit of a legal act. The same errors repeated in one corrigendum were counted only once. However, if the same error was made in two or more regulations, it was counted separately for each act. Errors were classified according to the eight-category error typology used by the DGT to evaluate translations: sense, omission, clarity, grammar, reference documents/materials, term, punctuation and spelling (Strandvik 2017a, 125–126).

## 8.7 The Quantitative Analysis of Polish Corrigenda to EU Legal Acts in 2004–2006 and 2015–2017

The EUR-Lex search for corrigenda to the Polish-language versions of regulations of the European Parliament and of the Council yielded 10 corrigenda for the 2004–2006 period and 82 corrigenda for 2015–2017. These figures indicate a, somewhat surprising, exponential increase in the number of corrigenda in recent years in the mature phase of the

Polish Eurolect. This is contrary to our expectations and we will look into these figures in more detail.

### 8.7.1 Corrigenda According to Error Type: Drafting versus Translation Errors

The analysis of Polish corrigenda shows that they can be divided into ST, target-text (TT) and mixed-type corrigenda, depending on the origin of the errors they rectify, which is whether an error is caused at a drafting or translation stage or both:

a   **ST corrigenda**: rectify errors in the English version which were subsequently mirrored in other language versions, i.e. a drafting error;
b   **TT corrigenda**: rectify errors caused during the translation process from English into the target language, i.e. a translation error;
c   **mixed-type corrigenda**: rectify both English-language ST errors and TT errors.

Table 8.1 shows corrigenda according to the source of error origin. The 2004–2006 period has only one ST corrigendum. It is likely that drafting errors may have already been rectified before translations into Polish began. The 2015–2017 period covers as many as 32 ST corrigenda; hence, although corrigenda are typically associated with translation errors, in the latter period 39% of them concern drafting errors only. This is alarming and raises attention to insufficient institutional efforts to ensure the adequate quality of drafting. ST errors are copied in other language versions since translators have no agency to correct errors in the ST "even if they are obvious" (Stefaniak 2017, 117). On the other hand, as ST errors affect all language versions, they – one could argue – paradoxically do not affect the uniform interpretation and application of the legal act, although they are contrary to the legislator's will.

As illustrated in Table 8.2, ST corrigenda tend to be what Bobek refers to as "meaning-changing corrigenda." They correct wrong dates, e.g. a date of application of the regulation (Examples 1 and 2), intra- and

*Table 8.1* Corrigenda to the Polish versions of regulations of the European Parliament and of the Council

|  | ST corrigenda | TT corrigenda | Mixed-type corrigenda | Total |
|---|---|---|---|---|
| 2004–2006 | 1 | 9 | – | 10 |
| 2015–2017 | 32 | 37 | 13 | 82 |

*Table 8.2* Examples of ST corrigenda

| # | Corrigendum details | EN *initial version* | EN *corrigendum* |
|---|---|---|---|
| 1 | 28.7.2017 to Reg. 2017/1128 | *It shall apply from **20 March 2018*** | *It shall apply from **1 April 2018*** |
| 2 | 21.12.2016 to Reg. 2015/848 | *The provisions of this Regulation shall apply only to insolvency proceedings opened **after** 26 June 2017* | *The provisions of this Regulation shall apply only to insolvency proceedings opened **from** 26 June 2017* |
| 3 | 18.9.2015 to Reg. 1007/2011 | *In the case of the products referred to in Article 9(**4**)* | *In the case of the products referred to in Article 9(**3**)* |
| 4 | 21.12.2016 to Reg. 909/2014 | *Power is delegated to the Commission to adopt the regulatory technical standards referred to in the first subparagraph in accordance with Articles 10 to 14 of **Regulation (EU) No 1095/2010*** | *Power is delegated to the Commission to adopt the regulatory technical standards referred to in the first subparagraph in accordance with Articles 10 to 14 of **Regulation (EU) No 1093/2010*** |
| 5 | 21.10.2016 to Reg. 596/2014 | *a legal person, trust or partnership, the managerial responsibilities of which are discharged by a person discharging managerial responsibilities or by a person referred to in point (a), (b) or (c), which is directly or indirectly controlled by such a person, which is set up for the benefit of such a person, or the economic interests of which are substantially equivalent to those of such a person* | *a legal person, trust or partnership, the managerial responsibilities of which are discharged by a person discharging managerial responsibilities or by a person referred to in point (a), (b) or (c), **or** which is directly or indirectly controlled by such a person, **or** which is set up for the benefit of such a person, or the economic interests of which are substantially equivalent to those of such a person* |

intertextual references (Examples 3 and 4), omissions and additions, e.g. a missing *or* in the enumeration of the definition of *person closely associated* (Example 5). Corrections of the English version required corresponding corrections in other language versions.

To sum up, the increasing number of corrigenda for these EU legislative acts should not be perceived as a merely translation quality issue but also as a drafting problem. The figures suggest the potential overuse of corrigenda, in particular, ST corrigenda which affect all language versions.

## 8.7.2 Correction Rates

To view the corrigenda figures in a broader perspective, we will juxtapose corrigenda to various types of legal acts, calculating their CRs, that is the number of corrigenda in a given year divided by the number of legal acts in that year plus two preceding years (EC DGT 2016a, 4). For this purpose the number of legal acts in respective years was obtained from the EUR-Lex statistics,[9] while the number of corrigenda was retrieved from the EUR-Lex search engine since they were not included in the official statistics. Table 8.3 shows CR calculated for 2006, 2015, 2016 and 2017, excluding the years 2004 and 2005 as the data for two preceding years were not available.

CRs differ considerably for specific types of legal acts and are significantly higher for legislative acts adopted in the ordinary procedure – regulations and directives of the European Parliament and of the Council,

*Table 8.3* Correction rates (CRs) for Polish versions of EU legal acts

| | Legislative acts, ordinary procedure | | | Other legislative acts | Non-legislative acts |
|---|---|---|---|---|---|
| | Regulation | Directive | Decision | | |
| 2006 corrigenda | 4 [3][a] | 7 [4] | 1 | 22 | 39 |
| 2004–2006 acts | 105 | 101 | 39 | 1289 | 4573 |
| **2006 CR** | 3.8% [2.9%] | 7% [4%] | 2.56 % | 1.7% | 0.8% |
| 2015 corrigenda | 25 [14] | 24 [16] | 1 | 41 | 98 |
| 2013–2015 acts | 212 | 82 | 27 | 1195 | 4869 |
| **2015 CR** | 11.79% [6.6%] | 29.3% [19.5%] | 3.7% | 3.4% | 2% |
| 2016 corrigenda | 38 [26] | 14 [10] | 0 | 32 | 85 |
| 2014–2016 acts | 182 | 79 | 18 | 1231 | 4832 |
| **2016 CR** | 20.9% [14.3%] | 17.7% [12.7%] | – | 2.6% | 1.8% |
| 2017 corrigenda | 19 [10] | 7 [3] | 0 | 22 | 83 |
| 2015-2017 acts | 146 | 46 | 13 | 1131 | 4833 |
| **2017 CR** | 13% [6.8%] | 15.2% [6.5%] | – | 1.9% | 1.7% |

a Figures in square brackets exclude ST corrigenda and contain only TT and mixed-type corrigenda. They were calculated only for legislative acts in the ordinary procedure.

ranging from 3.8% (the year 2006) to 29.3% (2015) for all types of corrigenda and from 2.9% (2006) to 19.5% (2015) for TT and mixed-type
corrigenda only. Thus, the CRs for these two types of legislative acts
are much higher than the Commission's impressively ambitious tolerance level for corrigenda to translations of its own legal acts at <0.5%
(DGT 2016b, 9) and they evidence quality assurance failures. This may
be due to the much more complex ordinary legislative procedure as well
as the high status and visibility of these basic acts, which may result in
higher pressure to rectify errors. The lowest CRs were observed for non-
legislative acts and other legislative acts adopted in the special procedure
at the level of ca. 2% on the average. Similar genre-dependent findings
were obtained by Prieto Ramos (2020) in his study of French and Spanish corrigenda in three international institutions (the EU, the United
Nations (UN) and the World Trade Organization (WTO)). In the case
of the EU, his study demonstrates the highest CRs[10] for directives and
regulations of the European Parliament and of the Council, followed by
other non-legislative and legislative acts, soft law instruments and international agreements (2020, 116).

Although we do not have full data for the early period of 2004–2006,
the comparison of 2006 to 2015–2017 confirms a considerable increase
of corrigenda in the latter period for regulations and directives adopted
in the ordinary procedure, but shows similar CRs for other legislative
and non-legislative acts. Yet, in global (absolute) figures, although the
number of Polish-language corrigenda is significantly higher in the latter
period, it decreased from a total of 189 in 2015 to 131 in 2017. What
is also noticeable is the high variation and unpredictability of CRs in
2015–2017: for example, the 2015 CR for the Polish-language regulations in question is 6.6% and it rises to 14.3% in 2016 to fall again to
6.8% in 2017. Furthermore, CRs cannot be correlated with the sub-
genre of a legislative act, that is whether regulations or directives are
corrected more often, as it varies depending on the year. Finally, these
findings may point to the lack of consistency of quality. However, it
should be borne in mind that "[A]s a methodological caveat, it would be
impossible to predict the exact number of corrigenda that legal acts from
a particular year may accumulate after their publication" (Prieto Ramos
2020, 119). While the majority of corrigenda in our study do correct
most recent legal acts, they may correct legal acts from earlier years as
well, which is especially visible for the 2015 and 2016 corrigenda[11] (see
Table 8.4), and hence, may not be regarded as a direct measure of translation quality in a given or preceding year.

We believe that a TT corrigendum should be regarded as a measure of
actions taken to correct errors rather than a measure of error incidence
in itself. In our opinion the growing number of corrigenda in the mature
phase of the Polish Eurolect should not necessarily be interpreted as a
sign of the deteriorating quality of Polish translations but rather, above

*Table 8.4* Breakdown of years of legal acts corrected by corrigenda

| Year of legal act corrected by corrigendum | 2006 | 2015 | 2016 | 2017 |
|---|---|---|---|---|
| 1960s | | | 1 | |
| 1970s | 3 | | | |
| 1980s | | | 3 | 1 |
| 1990s | 3 | 4 | 2 | 2 |
| 2000–2003 | 11 | 6 | 3 | |
| 2004 | 6 | 2 | 5 | 2 |
| 2005 | 23 | 1 | 1 | 1 |
| 2006 | 27 | 5 | 4 | |
| 2007 | | 4 | 2 | 1 |
| 2008 | | 4 | 2 | 2 |
| 2009 | | 8 | 5 | 5 |
| 2010 | | 5 | 0 | 2 |
| 2011 | | 12 | 2 | 4 |
| 2012 | | 10 | 5 | 2 |
| 2013 | | 15 | 24 | 11 |
| 2014 | | 65 | 22 | 12 |
| 2015 | | 48 | 36 | 12 |
| 2016 | | | 52 | 26 |
| 2017 | | | | 48 |
| Total no. of corrigenda | 73 | 189 | 169 | 131 |

all, as evidence of the growing role of this instrument. First, the strikingly low number of corrigenda in the early period may be a result of delays in the translation of *acquis* on the part of the Polish government, as a result of which translation errors might have been corrected by the EU institutions before translations were published with some delays in the Official Journal. Second, a few corrigenda in the mature period rectify pre-accession regulations and a large percentage of corrigenda rectify drafting rather than translation errors. Third, another possible explanation is that corrigenda were not so commonly known to national authorities at that time, which had to find their way of dealing with EU institutions amongst more pressing issues after the accession. In recent years it has become easier to submit corrigendum requests and stakeholders, including Member States, have a higher awareness of corrigenda as an instrument which allows them to take a more active role in the rectification of EU law (cf. EC 2012, 31). Finally, a similar trend of the growing number of EU corrigenda from 2005 to 2015, in contrast to the UN and the WTO, was demonstrated for mature Eurolects – French and Spanish – by Prieto Ramos (2020, 112–113); hence, this increase is not limited to the Polish language only. As will be shown below, corrigenda can be correlated with the phase of Eurolect in terms of their content rather than number.

## 8.8  A Qualitative Analysis of Polish TT Corrigenda to EU Regulations: A Focus on Terminology and Phraseology

This section analyzes the content of TT and mixed-type corrigenda to regulations of the European Parliament and of the Council adopted in the ordinary legislative procedure in the two periods. We first examine error categories and next investigate the most frequent error of terminology and phraseology, based on EUR-Lex, IATE and the Polish Law Corpus (cf. Biel 2014).

### 8.8.1  Error Categories

Main error categories in the 2004–2006 corrigenda are terminological errors (45%), SENS errors, i.e. mistranslations (30%), and clarity/stylistic issues (10%). In respect of the mature 2015–2017 period, the content of corrigenda depends on the year. Over half of the corrigenda from this period were published in 2016 and they mainly correct a batch of regulations, spanning over 600 pages, which were published in the Official Journal on the same date of 20 December 2013. Translation and revision must have taken place under extreme time pressure, which is evidenced by a surprisingly high number of typographic (spelling and punctuation) errors and omissions rectified by the 2016 corrigenda. The typographic errors accounted for 31% of corrections in 2016, which shows that, contrary to the guidelines, corrigenda rectify not only serious but also minor issues. It also indicates insufficient controls put in place to handle such bottlenecks. By comparison, the typographic category represents only 6% of 2017 errors, with main categories being terminological (53%) and phraseological/stylistic issues (28%). The 2015 corrigenda correct a small number of errors from various categories. Still, the overall trend in the mature period is an increased focus on terminology and phraseology, which will be examined below.

### 8.8.2  Corrections of Terminological and Phraseological Errors

An analysis of errors classified as terminology and phraseology has identified the following trends in corrigenda:

- standardization of EU institutional terminology;
- stabilization of equivalents;
- elimination of intra- and intertextual variants to ensure consistency and continuity;
- domestication with terms of national law;
- replacement of an equivalent which triggers an inadequate concept;
- domestication of term-embedding collocations.

Corrections of institutional terminology appear in the early period only. At that time institutional terminology was still taking shape and translators had limited resources at hand. Example 1 in Table 8.5 contains the term *committee procedure* which was wrongly translated as *procedura Komitetu* [procedure of the Committee][12] and rectified into *procedura komitetowa* [committee-ADJ procedure], interestingly, only in one out of ten instances. Example 2 shows a mistranslation of *Community* as *unijny* [of the Union] instead of *wspólnotowy* [of the Community]. Example 3 corrects the terminology related to the subdivision of legal acts since *paragraph* was translated as *punkt* [point] instead of *ustęp* [paragraph]. EU-related terminology is currently highly standardized and controlled through the style guides.

The next – relatively rare – group of corrections stabilizes equivalents and shows how some of them evolved. The initial instability of terminology has been reported for most new EU languages (Bhreathnach, Cloke, and Pháidín 2013, 48–50). Table 8.6 shows attempts at explicitation which was later replaced by literal equivalents or direct borrowings. Example 1 concerns the concise English term *traceability* which was initially explicated into: *przejrzystość ciągu informacji, identyfikujących pochodzenie mięsa i sięgających wstecz aż do daty i miejsca urodzenia zwierzęcia* [transparency of information sequence, identifying the origin

*Table 8.5* Corrigenda standardizing Polish variants of EU institutional terminology

| | Corrigendum | EN | PL initial version | PL corrigendum |
|---|---|---|---|---|
| 1 | 1.5.2004 to Reg. 2700/2000 | committee procedure | procedura Komitetu | procedura komitetowa |
| 2 | 1.5.2004 to Reg. 1760/2000 | a Community framework | jednolite unijne ustalenia | wspólnotowe ramy |
| 3 | 1.5.2004 to Reg. 1760/2000 | paragraph | punkt | ustęp |

*Table 8.6* Corrigenda stabilizing equivalents with literal equivalents and borrowings

| | Corrigendum | EN | PL initial version | PL corrigendum |
|---|---|---|---|---|
| 1 | 1.5.2004 to Reg. 1760/2000 | traceabilty | przejrzystość ciągu informacji, identyfikujących pochodzenie mięsa i sięgających wstecz aż do daty i miejsca urodzenia zwierzęcia | możliwość śledzenia |
| 2 | 19.5.2016 to Reg. 1308/2013 | piquette | napój wzbudzony | piquette |

*Table 8.7* Corrigenda eliminating intratextual terminological variants

| Corrigendum | EN | PL initial version | PL corrigendum |
|---|---|---|---|
| 1  1.5.2004 to Reg. 1760/2000 | *beef* | *mięso wołowe wołowina* | *mięso wołowe* |
| 2  1.5.2004 to Reg. 1760/2000 | *holding* | *gospodarstwo hodowla* | *gospodarstwo* |
| 3  1.5.2004 to Reg. 1760/2000 | *(animal) keeper* | *dozorca hodowca* | *posiadacz* |
| 4  1.5.2004 to Reg. 82/97 | *agricultural levy* | *opłata rolna rolnicza opłata wyrównawcza* | *rolna opłata wyrównawcza -* |
| 5  19.5.2016 to Reg. 1308/2013 | *vine plantings* | *nasadzenia winorośli sadzenie winorośli uprawy winorośli uprawa winorośli* | *nasadzenia winorośli* |
| 6  19.5.2016 to Reg. 1308/2013 | *retention periods* | *okresy zatrzymywania okresy przechowywania* | *okresy przechowywania* |

*Table 8.8* Corrigenda eliminating intertextual variants (discontinuity)

| Corrigendum | EN | PL initial version | PL corrigendum |
|---|---|---|---|
| 1  30.9.2016 to Reg. 952/2013 | *import or export certificate* | *certyfikat przywozowy lub wywozowy* | *świadectwo przywozowe lub wywozowe* |
| 2  30.9.2016 to Reg. 952/2013 | *customs offences* | *przestępstwa lub wykroczenia przeciwko obowiązkom celnym* | *przestępstwa lub wykroczenia celne* |

of meat and going back up to the date and place of birth of an animal]. This clumsy but accurate equivalent was rectified with a more literal and less semantically transparent *możliwość śledzenia* [possibility of tracing], to evolve later into another neologism *identyfikowalność* [identifiability] (IATE ID 1120179). Example 2 concerns a conceptual lacuna (cf. Biel 2018, 306) from the domain of wine-making[13]: a low-alcohol beverage *piquette* with fizz which was explicated as *napój wzbudzony* [activated beverage] to be corrected into a direct borrowing *piquette*.

Tables 8.7 and 8.8 show a very frequent type of corrections which eliminate terminological variants within or across documents. The early period is marked by a considerable intratextual variation of terminology within the same act where a single English term is translated with two or more equivalents. Examples 1–3 illustrate considerable terminological variation in Regulation 1760/2000, where *beef* was translated as *mięso wołowe* [beef meat] and *wołowina* [beef], *holding* as *gospodarstwo* [farm] and *hodowla* [breeding farm], *(animal) keeper* as *dozorca* [caretaker] and *hodowca* [breeder], despite the fact that both *holding* and *keeper* were high-visibility defined terms. The corrigendum eliminates one of the variants or replaces them with a new equivalent in line with the then national usage. Another inconsistency is shown in Example 4, where *agricultural levy* was rendered as *rolnicza opłata wyrównawcza* [agricultural compensatory fee], except for one case when it became *opłata rolna* [agrarian fee]. The latter was rectified into *rolna opłata wyrównawcza* [agrarian compensatory fee] to ensure continuity with the Community Customs Code; yet the first equivalent was left unchanged.

Despite CAT tools,[14] this intratextual variation is, surprisingly, occasionally found in the mature period, as shown by Examples 5 and 6. Example 5 contains as many as four equivalents of *vine plantings*: *nasadzenia winorośli* [vine plantings], *sadzenie winorośli* [planting of vine], *uprawy winorośli* [cultivations of vine] and *uprawa winorośli* [cultivation of vine]. The corrigendum replaced them with the first variant, known in the national agricultural usage. Example 6 shows an inconsistency between an equivalent of *retention periods* used in the preamble, *okresy zatrzymywania* [retention periods], and in enacting terms – *okresy przechowywania* [storage periods].

The mature period has more examples of corrections which eliminate intertextual variation, i.e. discontinuity with terminology in earlier translations. Example 1 in Table 8.8 replaces a literal equivalent of *import or export certificate* – *certyfikat przywozowy lub wywozowy* [certificate of import or export] with domesticated *świadectwo przywozowe lub wywozowe* [certificate of import or export], used in the pre-accession Community Customs Code (Regulation (EEC) 2913/92). Similarly, Example 2 replaces the explicitation of *customs offences* as *przestępstwa lub wykroczenia przeciwko obowiązkom celnym* [offences or minor offences against customs duties] consistent with national usage with more literal *przestępstwa lub wykroczenia celne* [customs offences or minor customs offences], already used in the Modernised Customs Code (Regulation (EC) No 450/2008) and also known nationally as a more informal variant.

Some corrections rectify equivalents which trigger inadequate concepts. This can be well illustrated with Example 2 in Table 8.9 which corrects an equivalent of the civil aviation term *unauthorized interference*

*Table 8.9* Corrigenda adjusting an inadequate conceptual scope of an equivalent

| | Corrigendum | EN | PL initial version | PL corrigendum |
|---|---|---|---|---|
| 1 | 1.5.2004 to Reg. 1760/2000 | *slaughterhouse* | *ubojnia* | *rzeźnia* |
| 2 | 4.2.2016 to Reg. 300/2008 | *unauthorized interference* | *bezprawna ingerencja* | *nieupoważniona ingerencja* |

from *bezprawna ingerencja* [unlawful interference] to *nieupoważniona ingerencja* [unauthorized interference]. The former refers only to intentional access, while the latter covers both intentional and unintentional access (IATE ID 926872, 829246) and is also used in national aviation law.

The largest and most interesting group of changes, which is especially dominant in the recent period, concerns the replacement of EU equivalents with terms of national law (domestication), as was also the case with some examples discussed earlier. These corrections are illustrated in Tables 8.10 and 8.11: the former shows denominative changes while the latter shows non-denominative changes, i.e. minor linguistic modifications. Example 1 in Table 8.10 replaces *pasek informacyjny* [information slip] with *kolczyk* [earring] for *ear tag*. Example 2 replaces the equivalent of *declarant* – *osoba zainteresowana* [person interested] – with *zgłaszający*, a term used in the Polish Customs Code. Example 3 replaces a literal equivalent of *judicial arrangements* – *porozumienia sądowe* [court agreements] – with *ugody sądowe* [court arrangements], a term used in the Polish Code of Civil Procedure. Example 4 also corrects the literal equivalent of *forest holders* – *posiadacze lasów* – into a functional

*Table 8.10* Corrigenda replacing equivalents with terms of national law: denominative changes

| | *Corrigendum* | *EN* | *PL initial version* | *PL corrigendum* |
|---|---|---|---|---|
| 1 | 1.5.2004 to Reg. 1760/2000 | *ear tag* | *pasek informacyjny* | *kolczyk* |
| 2 | 15.2004 to Reg. 82/97 | *declarant* | *osoba zainteresowana* | *zgłaszający* |
| 3 | 8.3.2017 to Reg. 655/2014 | *judicial arrangements* | *porozumienia sądowe* | *ugody sądowe* |
| 4 | 19.5.2016 to Reg. 1305/2013 | *forest holders* | *posiadacze lasów* | *gospodarstwa leśne* |

*Table 8.11* Corrigenda replacing equivalents with terms of national law: non-denominative changes

| | *Corrigendum* | *EN* | *PL initial version* | *PL corrigendum* |
|---|---|---|---|---|
| 1 | 19.5.2016 to Reg. 1305/2013 | *agricultural land* | *grunty rolnicze* | *grunty rolne* |
| 2 | 30.9.2016 to Reg. 952/2013 | *export customs declaration* | *wywozowe zgłoszenie celne* | *zgłoszenie wywozowe* |

equivalent *gospodarstwa leśne* [forest farms] commonly used in Polish, although again only one instance of the term is corrected. This lack of consistency in the corrigendum may have resulted from three spelling variants, *forest holders*, *forest-holders* and *forest-holders*, in the English regulation. The domestication trends may be partly due to the overreliance of EU translators on neologisms and literal equivalents which express autonomous concepts of EU law (Stefaniak 2013, 63) and are easily copied to other concepts which coincide with national concepts.

Corrigenda are also used to fine-tune EU equivalents to national usage also in the case of less confusing non-denominative variants. Example 1 in Table 8.11 concerns *agricultural land* which was translated as *grunty rolnicze* [agricultural land]. This informal variant was replaced by the common term of national law *grunty rolne* [agrarian land], which contains an adjectival morphological variant. Example 2 simplifies the equivalent of *export customs declaration – wywozowe zgłoszenie celne* [export customs declaration] – into *zgłoszenie wywozowe* [export declaration], endorsed by the Polish Ministry of Finance (IATE ID 1568026) and consistent with the long-term national usage.

In respect of phraseology, the early period rectifies mainly grammatical and lexical patterns, including deontic modality, and text-navigation patterns. The mature period shows more interest in legal collocations, in particular by domesticating term-embedding collocations and

*Table 8.12* Corrigenda pertaining to phraseology: domestication

| | Corrigendum | EN | PL initial version | PL corrigendum |
|---|---|---|---|---|
| 1 | 1.5.2004 to Reg. 82/97 | *placed under a customs procedure* | *umieszczone pod procedurą celną* | *objęte procedurą celną* |
| 2 | 30.9.2016 to Reg. 952/2013 | *removed from customs supervision* | *wyprowadzone spod dozoru celnego* | *usunięte spod dozoru celnego* |
| 3 | 8.3.2017 to Reg. 655/2014 | *bankruptcy/ insolvency proceedings have been opened* | *zainicjowano/ wszczęto postępowania upadłościowe* | *wszczęto postępowania upadłościowe* |
| 4 | 8.3.2017 to Reg. 655/2014 | *exempt from seizure* | *wyłączone z/spod zajęcia* | *wyłączone spod zajęcia* |
| 5 | 8.3.2017 to Reg. 655/2014 | *proceedings to obtain a Preservation Order* | *postępowanie o uzyskanie/ wydanie nakazu zabezpieczenia* | *postępowanie o wydanie nakazu zabezpieczenia* |

eliminating intratextual phraseological variants. Example 1 in Table 8.12 comes from an early period and corrects the clumsy calque *placed under a customs procedure* from *umieszczone pod procedurą celną* [placed under a customs procedure] to *objęte procedurą celną* [covered by the customs procedure], a collocation used in Polish law. Similar domestications were made in Examples 2–5 from the mature period. Example 2 adjusts the collocation *wyprowadzone spod dozoru celnego* [carried out from customs supervision] to its national variant *usunięte spod dozoru celnego* [removed from customs supervision]. Examples 3–5 eliminate the inconsistent use of term-embedding collocations in the same act, opting for variants used in Polish law: *wszczęto postępowania upadłościowe* [insolvency proceedings have been instituted], *wyłączone spod zajęcia* [exempt from under seizure] and *postępowanie o wydanie nakazu zabezpieczenia* [proceedings concerning the issuance of a preservation order].

To sum up, the early corrigenda more frequently deal with unstable terminology and a lack of consistency within a single document. The continuity of terminology with previous translations is an issue, quite surprisingly, also in the mature period, despite the technology and resources available. A considerable batch of corrections adjusts the terminology and phraseology to the national usage. Since Polish-language versions of regulations automatically become part of the national legal system, domestications increase their "fit" to the national terminology and eliminate confusing terminological variants where they refer to the same legal concept. There were also instances of a reverse process replacing a national term which evokes an inadequate concept. This delicate interplay between supranational and national conceptual layers is one of the major challenges in EU legal translation.

## 8.9 Conclusions

As shown by our study, corrigenda contain a wealth of information on quality failures in EU legal acts. First, they raise attention to the inadequacies of both drafting and translation, and some findings are alarming (a considerable number of drafting errors, high CRs for basic legal acts). Second, the findings indicate a lack of predictability and stability of those processes, and such inconsistent quality of drafting and translation may adversely affect the certainty of law. The findings also raise attention to the quality of corrigenda themselves which is not always consistent: in some cases corrections rectify a few rather than all occurrences of an error. Finally, more reflection on the nature and function of corrigenda is needed: they include "meaning-changing" corrigenda and, on the other hand, they correct not only "serious" errors but also minor language issues.

The data confirm the increasing use of corrigenda in recent years. This should not be construed as evidence of the deteriorating quality of Polish translations but rather as a heightened awareness of this instrument and a more active role of stakeholders in eliminating translation errors to ensure multilingual concordance, improve consistency and increase the coherence of EU translations with national terminology. From a micro-diachronic perspective, corrigenda may be correlated with the phase of Polish Eurolect in terms of their content rather than number. The largest group of corrections pertains to terminology and phraseology, in particular in the domain of agriculture, food, finance and customs law. The formative period is marked by unstable terminology and intra- and intertextual inconsistencies. Corrigenda from the mature period also eliminate terminological variants; yet these are mainly intertextual inconsistencies. The mature period is characterized by domestications to the national use, which points to the growing sensitivity of how EU terminology "fits" the national terminology and illustrates the fundamental challenge of the supranational and national interplay in EU translation.

Considering the overall number of official languages in EU translation, our study of Polish corrigenda from two 3-year periods should be regarded as small-scale and exploratory in nature. It confirms that corrigenda may provide new insights into the quality of institutional translations and that they require further larger-scale research both from the quantitative and qualitative perspective, involving more languages.

## Acknowledgment

This work was supported by the National Science Centre (NCN) under Grant 2014/14/E/HS2/00782.

## Notes

1 See Biel, Biernacka, and Jopek-Bosiacka (2018) and Doczekalska (2018) on English as the EU's main procedural and drafting language.
2 See, e.g., Biel (2014, 2019) for discussion.
3 The EU's legislative drafting is multilingual and multistage with a frequent rewriting of drafts; it is intertwined with translation and language switching at all stages (Doczekalska 2009, 360; Koskinen 2001, 293; Robinson 2014, 207). Drafts are often written by non-native speakers of English, which increases ambiguities (Sosoni 2011; Biel, Biernacka, and Jopek-Bosiacka 2018, 252). Translators often work on non-final drafts (Koskinen 2000, 59; Stefaniak 2013, 60).
4 See Hanzl and Beaven (2017) on quality assurance in the Council of the European Union.
5 Another interesting aspect of corrigenda raised by Bobek is that they are not explicitly regulated in EU law, case law or doctrine and their nature is unclear, e.g. whether their application is retroactive or prospective (2009, 955–956).

 6  https://eur-lex.europa.eu/homepage.html?locale=pl.
 7  Its role has increased after the Lisbon Treaty from 49% of legislative propos-
    als in the 2004–2009 parliamentary term to 89% in 2009–2014 (Lelieveldt
    and Princen 2015, 82).
 8  In most cases the European Parliament's role is reduced to an advisory body
    while the Council adopts an act.
 9  https://eur-lex.europa.eu/statistics/legislative-acts-statistics.html, date of
    access 30.10.2019.
10  The study calculates correction rates differently by using two ratios: (1) the
    number of corrigenda to the number of texts of a particular genre; (2) the
    number of corrections in corrigenda to translation volumes (number of words)
    (cf. Prieto Ramos 2020, 114).
11  A similar trend for 2015 was reported in the case of Spanish and French
    (Prieto Ramos 2020, 119).
12  Back translations of Polish examples are in square brackets.
13  Conceptual lacunas were also reported for deep-water sea fish for Czech
    and Slovak and rail transport for Maltese (Bhreathnach, Cloke, and Pháidín
    2013, 43).
14  Although CAT tools offer automatic terminology consistency checks, this
    functionality does not work optimally for inflectional languages (we owe
    this comment to an anonymous reviewer).

## References

Bhreathnach, Úna, Fionnuala Cloke, and Caoilfhionn Nic Pháidín. 2013. *Ter-minology for the European Union. The Irish Experience: The GA IATE Proj-ect*. Fiontar: Dublin City University.

Biel, Łucja. 2014. *Lost in the Eurofog. The Textual Fit of Translated Law*. Frankfurt am Main: Peter Lang.

Biel, Łucja. 2017. "Quality in Institutional EU Translation. Parameters, Poli-cies and Practices." In *Quality Aspects in Institutional Translation*, edited by Tomáš Svoboda, Biel, Łucja; Łoboda, Krzysztof, 31–57. Berlin: Language Science Press.

Biel, Łucja. 2018. "Observing Eurolects: The Case of Polish." In *Observing Eurolects*, edited by Laura Mori, 295–327. Amsterdam, Philadelphia: John Benjamins.

Biel, Łucja. 2019. "Theoretical and Methodological Challenges in Researching EU Legal Translation." In *Legal Translation. Current Issues and Challenges in Research, Methods and Applications*, edited by Ingrid Simonnæs and Mar-ita Kristiansen, 25–39. Berlin: Frank & Timme.

Biel, Łucja. 2020. "Eurolects and EU Legal Translation." In *The Oxford Hand-book of Translation and Social Practices*, edited by Meng Ji and Sara Laviosa. Oxford: Oxford University Press.

Biel, Łucja, Agnieszka Biernacka, and Anna Jopek-Bosiacka. 2018. "Colloca-tions of Terms in EU Competition Law: A Corpus Analysis of EU English Collocations." In *Language and Law: The Role of Language and Translation in EU Competition Law*, edited by Silvia Marino, Łucja Biel, Martina Bajčić and Vilelmini Sosoni, 249–274. Cham: Springer International Publishing.

Bobek, Michal. 2009. "Corrigenda in the Official Journal of the European Union: Community Law as Quicksand." *European Law Review* 34: 950–962.

Council, General Secretariat of the Council of the European Union. 2015. *Manual of Precedents for Acts Established within the Council of the European Union*. SN 1250/6/10 REV 6.

Curtin, Deirdre, and Tatevik Manucharyan. 2015. "Legal Acts and Hierarchy of Norms in EU Law." In *The Oxford Handbook of European Union Law*, edited by Anthony Arnull and Damian Chalmers, 103–125. Oxford: Oxford University Press.

Derlén, Mattias. 2015. "A Single Text or a Single Meaning: Multilingual Interpretation of EU Legislation and CJEU Case Law in National Courts." In *Language and Culture in EU Law. Multidisciplinary Perspectives*, edited by Susan Šarčević, 53–72. Farnham: Ashgate.

DGT, Directorate-General for Translation, European Commission. 2015. *DGT Translation Quality Guidelines*. https://ec.europa.eu/translation/maltese/guidelines/documents/dgt_translation_quality_guidelines_en.pdf.

DGT, Directorate-General for Translation, European Commission. 2016a. *Management Plan 2016 DGT*. Ref. Ares(2016)2103398-03/05/2016, https://ec.europa.eu/info/sites/info/files/management-plan-2016-dg-dgt-may2016_en.pdf.

DGT, Directorate-General for Translation, European Commission. 2016b. *Strategic plan 2016–2020. DG Translation*. Ref. Ares(2016)1329034-16/03/2016. https://ec.europa.eu/info/sites/info/files/strategic-plan-2016-2020-dg-t_march 2016_en.pdf: European Commission.

DGT, Directorate-General for Translation, European Commission. 2017. *Translation Quality Info Sheets for Contractors*. https://ec.europa.eu/info/sites/info/files/freelance_info_en.pdf.

Doczekalska, Agnieszka. 2009. "Drafting and Interpretation of EU Law – Paradoxes of Legal Multilingualism." In *Formal Linguistics and Law*, edited by Günther Grewendorf and Monika Rathert, 339–370. Berlin: de Gruyter.

Doczekalska, Agnieszka. 2018. "Legal Languages in Contact: EU Legislative Drafting and Its Consequences for Judicial Interpretation." In *Language and Law: The Role of Language and Translation in EU Competition Law*, edited by Silvia Marino, Łucja Biel, Martina Bajčić and Vilelmini Sosoni, 163–178. Cham: Springer International Publishing.

Drugan, Joanna, Ingemar Strandvik, and Erkka Vuorinen. 2018. "Translation Quality, Quality Management and Agency: Principles and Practice in the European Union Institutions." In *Translation Quality Assessment: From Principles to Practice*, edited by Joss Moorkens, Sheila Castilho, Federico Gaspari and Stephen Doherty, 39–68. Cham: Springer.

EC, European Commission. 2012. *Quantifying Quality Costs and the Cost of Poor Quality in Translation. Quality Efforts and the Consequences of Poor Quality in the European Commission's Directorate-General for Translation*. Luxembourg: Publications Office of the European Union.

ECS, European Committee for Standardization. 2006. *EN 15038:2006 Translation Services—Service Requirements*. Brussels: European Committee for Standardization.

Hanzl, Jan, and John Beaven. 2017. "Quality Assurance at the Council of the EU's Translation Service." In *Quality Aspects in Institutional Translation*, edited by Tomáš Svoboda, Łucja Biel and Krzysztof Łoboda, 139–153. Berlin: Language Science Press.

Kapko, Mirosława. 2005. "Konsekwencje błędów w tłumaczeniu aktów prawa wspólnotowego na język polski [Consequences of Errors in Translations of Community Legislation into Polish]." *Prawo i Podatki Unii Europejskiej* 11: 2–8.

Kjær, Anne Lise. 2007. "Legal Translation in the European Union: A Research Field in Need of a New Approach." In *Language and the Law: International Outlooks*, edited by Krzysztof Kredens and Stanisław Goźdź-Roszkowski, 69–95. Frankfurt am Main: Peter Lang.

Koskinen, Kaisa. 2000. "Institutional Illusions. Translating in the EU Commission." *The Translator* 6 (1): 49–65. doi:10.1080/13556509.2000.10799055.

Koskinen, Kaisa. 2001. "How to Research EU Translation?" *Perspectives* 9 (4): 293–300. doi:10.1080/0907676X.2001.9961425.

Lelieveldt, Herman, and Sebastiaan Princen. 2015. *The Politics of the European Union. Cambridge Textbooks in Comparative Politics*, 2nd ed. Cambridge: Cambridge University Press.

Prieto Ramos, Fernando. 2020. "Facing Translation Errors at International Organizations: What Corrigenda Reveal About Correction Processes and Their Implications for Translation Quality." *Comparative Legilinguistics* 41: 97–133. doi:10.14746/cl.2020.41.5.

Prieto Ramos, Fernando, ed. 2017. *Institutional Translation for International Governance: Enhancing Quality in Multilingual Legal Communication.* London: Bloomsbury.

Robertson, Colin. 2010. "EU Law and Semiotics." *International Journal for the Semiotics of Law – Revue Internationale de Sémiotique Juridique* 23. doi:10.1007/s11196-010-9149-x.

Robinson, William. 2014. "Translating Legislation: The European Union Experience." *The Theory and Practice of Legislation* 2 (2): 185–210. doi:10.5235/2050-8840.2.2.185.

Šarčević, Susan. 1997. *New Approach to Legal Translation.* The Hague: Kluwer Law International.

Šarčević, Susan. 2013. "Multilingual Lawmaking and Legal (Un)Certainty in the European Union." *International Journal of Law, Language & Discourse* 3 (1): 1–29.

Schilling, Theodor. 2010. "Beyond Multilingualism: On Different Approaches to the Handling of Diverging Language Versions of a Community Law." *European Law Journal* 16 (1): 47–66. doi:10.1111/j.1468-0386.2009.00496.x.

Somssich, Réka, Judit Várnai, and Anna Bérczi. 2010. *Lawmaking in the EU Multilingual Environment.* Brussels: European Commission.

Sosoni, Vilelmini. 2011. "Training Translators to Work for the EU Institutions: Luxury or Necessity?" *The Journal of Specialised Translation* 16: 77–108.

Stefaniak, Karolina. 2013. "Multilingual Legal Drafting, Translators' Choices and the Principle of Lesser Evil." *Meta* 58 (1): 58–65. doi:10.7202/1023809ar; https://id.erudit.org/iderudit/1023809ar.

Stefaniak, Karolina. 2017. "Terminology Work in the European Commission. Ensuring High-Quality Translation in a Multilingual Environment." In *Quality Aspects in Institutional Translation*, edited by Tomáš Svoboda, Łucja Biel and Krzysztof Łoboda, 109–121. Berlin: Language Science Press.

Strandvik, Ingemar. 2014. "Is there Scope for A More Professional Approach to EU Multilingual Lawmaking?" *The Theory and Practice of Legislation*

2 (2): 211–228. doi:10.5235/2050-8840.2.2.211; https://www.tandfonline. com/doi/abs/10.5235/2050-8840.2.2.211.

Strandvik, Ingemar. 2017a. "Evaluation of Outsourced Translations. State of Play in the European Commission's Directorate-General for Translation (DGT)." In *Quality Aspects in Institutional Translation*, edited by Tomáš Svoboda, Łucja Biel and Krzysztof Łoboda, 123–137. Berlin: Language Science Press.

Strandvik, Ingemar. 2017b. "Towards a More Structured Approach to Quality Assurance: DGT's Quality Journey." In *Institutional Translation for International Governance: Enhancing Quality in Multilingual Legal Communication*, edited by Fernando Prieto Ramos, 51–62. London: Bloomsbury.

Svoboda, Tomáš, Łucja Biel, and Krzysztof Łoboda, eds. 2017. *Quality Aspects in Institutional Translation*. Berlin: Language Science Press.

Uhlig, Dominik. 2005. "Błąd na błędzie w tłumaczeniach unijnych aktów [Multiple Errors in Translations of EU Acts]." *Gazeta Wyborcza*, 2005, 2.

Woods, Lorna, Philippa Watson, and Marios Costa. 2017. *Steiner & Woods EU Law*. 13th ed. Oxford: Oxford University Press.

# 9 The Impact of Translation Competence on Institutional Translation Management and Quality

## The Evidence from Action Research

*Fernando Prieto Ramos and Mariam Sperandio*

### 9.1 Introduction: Researching Translation Management Competence

Despite the key monitoring functions of service and project managers (PMs) in translation processes, the implications of their competences for the implementation and results of quality assurance actions remain under-researched. In an earlier study on the roles and challenges of institutional translation service managers in quality assurance, the following most common duties were identified as particularly crucial for translation quality: (1) competence management, especially selection of translation professionals and training initiatives, (2) workflow coordination to ensure optimal job assignment and monitoring, (3) input into procedural and material conditions such as resource development and (4) contributions to quality control tasks (Prieto Ramos 2017, 68–70). These duties are all conditioned by strategic, administrative and financial factors, i.e. the most typically managerial dimension of these positions.

Based on the analysis of 12 management structures, 14 job descriptions and 24 interviews with language-specific translation managers, the study revealed significant variability in their common duties, depending on the size and division of work within each service. In the largest services, translation unit managers do not necessarily contribute to quality control tasks and, in certain cases, they are not even required to have translation expertise, as more technical tasks are often delegated, e.g. job assignment and quality monitoring. In small services, however, the manager may be the only staff member devoted to translation into the relevant language and may concentrate all the duties previously identified, including regular revision tasks, into a single profile.

DOI: 10.4324/9780429264894-9

In the second type of setting, translation expertise is not an option but a prerequisite to manage all aspects of translation quality. In practice, the translation service manager also works as the only PM and reviser for the target language, and their influence on the product is more direct. ISO standard 17100:2015 on "Translation services – Requirements for translation services" explicitly refers to translation competence requirements for translators and revisers, but not for service managers or PMs. For the latter, however, it requires "[a]appropriate translation project management competence" that "can be acquired in the course of formal or informal training (e.g. as part of a relevant higher educational course or by means of on-the-job training or through industry experience)" (ISO 2015, 7). While this standard is not binding for institutional translation services, it constitutes an important reference on workflow procedures and professional translation profiles, as "[i]t includes provisions for translation service providers (TSPs) concerning the management of core processes, minimum qualification requirements, the availability and management of resources, and other actions necessary for the delivery of a quality translation service" (ibid, vi).

No explicit consideration is made of the concentration of functions in small translation services, let alone of situations where there is no fully-fledged translation service as such. We will focus on two examples of this kind of setting in order to determine the extent to which introducing translation expertise into translation management can make a difference for translation quality. We will describe an action research project conducted in an organization without a translation service, and its subsequent replication in a second similar setting. The approach, results and impact of these cases of action research are presented in the next few sections.

## 9.2 Approach: The Case for Action Research

The central aim of the research was to measure the effects of advanced translation competence on translation workflow management and product quality in real international institutional settings. The initial project, subsequently replicated in a second study (see Section 9.5), was conceived with a view to analyzing and correcting translation management and quality deficits detected in an organization where translations were outsourced without any planning or revision by in-house translation professionals. It involved an in-depth review of practices and active involvement to improve these practices and subsequently measure the impact of the changes introduced.

The study can thus be viewed as an example of action research in that it combined an intervention for practical improvements and research into the impact of this intervention. As rightly reminded by Reason and

Bradbury (2008, 1), action research "is not so much a *methodology* as an *orientation to inquiry*" (original emphasis). In this case, a diversity of methods was applied, including:

- describing existing translation management practices and recurrent quality problems through interviews and text analysis;
- proposing and implementing new measures to improve the quality of English-Spanish translations of a particular department (the "intervention"), encompassing translation project management, resource development and revision by an in-house professional translator;
- measuring the impact of the intervention by compiling and analyzing a corpus of translations for a comparative error analysis of target texts produced with and without expert translation management in several departments of the same organization.

Drawing on a holistic approach to translation quality (Prieto Ramos 2015), it was hypothesized that entrusting a qualified translator with the management of all other competence and process components of translation service provision would have a positive bearing on the product. In line with the "midway" approach to action research in Translation Studies advocated by Cravo and Neves (2007, 96), a balance was sought between active commitment and scientific rigor in the critical analysis of findings, especially as the practitioner (translation manager and reviser in the intervention) would subsequently look into previous errors as part of a supervised research project, which unfolded while implementing the new measures. It was therefore crucial to place some distance between each role and stage, and accept critique on the previous translation performance, including the intervention period. The significant volume of translations compiled for systematic error analysis (see Section 9.4) helped to avert the risk of excessive bias or statistical deviations that can arise when working with smaller corpora.

Last but not least, the active involvement in a real work environment also entailed a commitment to avoid any exposure of errors in publicly accessible material and to protect the identity of the institution and the informants who took part in the interviews. This explains the fact that all references to "the organization" and its staff remain anonymous. Further insight into translation practices in this setting is provided in the next section.

## 9.3  Setting and Intervention: From Diagnosis to Action

The organization under examination has a global membership and scope in the field of economic cooperation. It produces several hundred publications per year, including reports, surveys, press releases and other documents of a predominantly informative nature. Communicating its activities through dissemination of this documentation is a central in-strument to fulfill its mission. This is generally done in its only official language, English, which is also the working language of an editing de-partment devoted to ensuring the quality of documents for large-scale dissemination. Many of these documents are also translated into other international languages, but not by or through a dedicated in-house translation service.

In order to draw a complete picture of translation policies and prac-tices in the organization, interviews were conducted with eight depart-ments that deal with multilingual documents. The following dimensions of their work were addressed, with a particular emphasis on English-Spanish translation, the language pair of the case study:

- annual average of publications in English and translations into other languages;
- annual average of English-Spanish translation needs in particular and number of English-Spanish translations handled by the department;
- arrangements made to outsource translations (individual contrac-tors or agencies), level of satisfaction and stability in outsourcing patterns;
- access to resources provided by the department, if any (for example, glossaries, parallel texts or previous translations);
- procedures for revision or review after delivery of outsourced trans-lations (none, by a professional translator/reviser or by a specialist reader in the target language).

The information assembled through the interviews contributed to a comprehensive overview of the initial approach of the organization to its translation needs. Given the lack of systematic monitoring of translation outsourcing, it was impossible to calculate the yearly aver-age number of texts and words translated. However, it was possible to estimate that approximately 40% of documents were translated into several languages. These languages varied depending on the target au-dience, and often included Spanish. Apart from reports, surveys, press releases, brochures and other documentation for external dissemina-tion, other internal documents such as legal texts were also considered highly sensitive and regularly translated. Each department dealt with its own translation needs on an ad hoc basis. Even if two particular departments were more specialized in publication and communication matters and had greater translation needs, the organization's trans-lation matters were not coordinated through them. These were also handled by the other thematically oriented departments individually, without any inter-department coordination of outsourcing practices. Lack of time was often mentioned as the main reason for this scattered approach.

Most departments often changed TSP (individual freelancer or agency) because they kept no record of previous TSPs or because their staff perceived that the price-quality relationship of prior assignments could be improved. In this initial situation, the *commissioners*, or the persons responsible for requesting translations for a department (i.e. the institutional *initiator* that needs the text for a particular purpose; see distinction made by Justa Holz-Mänttäri, as summarized in Nord [2018, 20]), had no expert knowledge of translation or translation project management. They would therefore not fulfill the competence requirements established in ISO 17100:2015 for translation PMs. They did not provide any institutional resources (in fact, because they did not exist) or technical specifications for the translation job, and did not ask for a revision of the translation when outsourcing it or after its delivery. However, most departments requested that the translation be checked by staff of the target language whenever possible. While this staff had no expertise in drafting or language matters, their role could vaguely fit into the concept of "review" in ISO 17100:2015: "to assess the suitability of the target language content for the agreed upon purpose and domain and recommend corrections to be implemented" including an assessment of "domain accuracy and respect for the relevant text-type conventions" (ISO 2015, 11). Nonetheless, it was not always possible to ensure that the "reviewer" would be a domain specialist as required by the same ISO standard.

These workflow conditions apply to English-Spanish translation within the departments surveyed. In order to establish a more precise diagnosis of the situation, the focus was placed on the four departments that had the most significant needs of translation into Spanish, which were also the most keenly interested in research and actions that could eventually lead to improvements in translation management and quality. Interviewees from these departments were aware not only of the deficiencies of their approach but also of their lack of expertise and capacity to address these issues thoroughly. As an example of frustrating experiences, a particular department once had to re-translate a 40-page document because the quality of the outsourced translation had been judged very unsatisfactory. Indeed, based on the feedback from the interviews, a random analysis of Spanish translations published by the same departments detected quality issues, including inaccuracies, linguistic errors and terminological inconsistencies within and between texts.

With a view to overcoming these deficiencies, a pilot project was proposed to change the approach to translation management in one of the departments. It was agreed that an in-house qualified English-Spanish translator (and also researcher in this case) would carry out the following tasks: (a) coordinate all translations needed into seven target languages, including the selection and monitoring of external translators and the preparation of translation specifications and briefs, (b) create resources for translation into Spanish and provide them to translators, (c) revise translations into Spanish and (d) make the final verifications of the outsourced translations against project specifications. In other words, in the case of Spanish, the translation process and product were handled in a radically different way compared to the situation before the intervention. The person who acted as a PM and a reviser had a suitable profile to take on the relevant tasks according to the ISO 17100:2015 competence requirements (even if this standard did not exist when the project was conceived). These tasks were integrated into a broader job description that also encompassed other coordination responsibilities not related to translation, i.e. translation-related work was not the only content of a full-time position but rather part-time duties to be fulfilled depending on translation needs. During the implementation of the project, which lasted two years, the review of translations by other staff without translation competence was discontinued in the same department.

The ISO standard does not refer to the accumulation of functions in small translation services, but the key procedural and competence aspects of the ISO quality equation were observed in the project, thus reproducing the conditions of translation services composed of a single person qualified in translation. Table 9.1 provides a comparative summary of the profiles involved in the pre-intervention approach, which continued to be in place in the other three departments ("approach A"), and those of the new approach ("approach B"), using ISO 17100:2015 key specifications as a yardstick for this comparison.

If we assume that the concept of TSP can be equated with translation service management, the ISO standard establishes that these decision-makers are responsible for ensuring compliance with process and competence requirements, but it also makes clear that they are supported by PMs in this endeavor. Except for more strategic decisions and structural aspects of the entire service (which would be reserved to the organization or the department in this case study), almost all other aspects of

*Table 9.1* Comparison of profiles involved in translation processes in approaches A and B

| Profiles (according to ISO 17100) | Approach A | Approach B |
| --- | --- | --- |
| PM | No (commissioner not qualified in translation) | Yes |
| Translator | Yes | Yes |
| Reviser | No | Yes (different from translator but same as PM) |
| Reviewer | Often, but not always by domain specialist of the target language | No |

workflow implementation can be coordinated by PMs, including project preparation, task assignment, monitoring and final verifications. PMs may also implement "corrections and/or corrective action" if necessary (ISO 2015, 10). This implies the possibility for PMs to act as de facto revisers if they have the appropriate competence, as long as the TSP conforms to the central condition of assigning the translation and the revision of the same text to different translation professionals.

The bottom line is that, given the necessity to concentrate PM and reviser functions in the scenario at hand, it seems in the interest of quality to reserve the central translation management position for an appropriately qualified translation professional, even if this would only be mandatory for translation and revision tasks. This is also where the main differences between approaches A and B lie: professional PM and reviser tasks, including setting up resources for translation during the pre-production process (glossaries and a repository of translations and parallel texts). By contrast, the most important commonality between approaches was the fact that translations were assigned to professional translators, although only in approach B these were directly screened by the in-house PM (including through preliminary testing), while the qualifications or competence of specific external translators in approach A could not be verified as part of this study. Self-revision (or "checks" as defined in the ISO standard) was also presumed of all professional translators.

## 9.4 Error Analysis: Impact on the Translation Product

What was the impact of the implemented functional and profile changes on translation quality? In order to guarantee the comparability of results of both approaches, a corpus of texts of the same communicative relevance and textual features in all departments, namely press releases, was compiled for translation error analysis. This was also the only genre for which translations could be traced a few years back in each department and could thus populate a corpus of ample scope for the study, i.e. of sufficient volume and thematic diversity (one main theme per department). Due to the inconsistent handling and archiving of translations in previous years, press releases could not be retrieved for the same years in all the departments, which means that the time spam covered by each text group varied per theme, between 4 and 9 years, while the entire corpus included 10 years. The comprehensive approach to text compilation ensured that the four departments more closely examined in the study were represented with a text group, i.e. a set of press releases on a main theme, and therefore any significant variation in quality patterns between departments could be spotted.

Thirty-eight press releases in Spanish (and their originals) of an average length of 1,642 words (67,924 words in total) were analyzed. Table 9.2 provides a breakdown of the number of words in each group

*Table 9.2* Distribution of translation volumes, errors and intertextual
inconsistencies per text group and approach

|  | No. of words (years covered) | Errors per 1,000 words (average) | Brackets of min.–max. yearly average no. of errors per 1,000 words | Intertextual inconsistencies between translations of key terms |
|---|---|---|---|---|
| Text Group 1 | 43,569 (9) | 9.3 | 5–21 | 13 |
| Text Group 2 | 8,439 (5) | 7.5 | 5–10 | 8 |
| Text Group 3 | 6,351 (6) | 11.8 | 7–21 | 5 |
| Text Group 4-A | 4,046 (2) | 12.0 | 10–14 | 6 |
| Approach A average | 62,405 (10) | 9.5 | 5–21 | 28 |
| Text Group 4-B | 5,519 (2) | 2.2 | 2–3 | 0 |

of press releases per department and approach. Group 1 accounts for the
largest translation volume, followed by group 4, which was produced
by the department where the change of approach was implemented. Accordingly, two different sets of data were created for the press releases of
group 4: one for approach A (group 4-A, including two years before the
intervention) and another one for approach B (group 4-B, comprising the
two years of the intervention).

Based on the rubrics proposed by Hurtado Albir (1996: 49–50) and
Angelelli (2009, 40–41) for translation assessment, the following error
categories were applied:

- semantic inaccuracies (deviations from source text meaning);
- style and cohesion (drafting, register and idiomaticity issues);
- language mechanics (including typographical and punctuation errors);
- other appropriateness problems (concerning translation procedures
  applied, terminological choices and intratextual consistency).

Intertextual inconsistencies were considered separately, as this key aspect of institutional translation quality transcends the level of individual
texts and requires an overarching evaluation across periods and departments. Special emphasis was placed on detecting inconsistencies of key
terminology related to the organization's bodies and work.

In order to concentrate strictly on corrections and avoid subjective
distortions based on personal impressions, the severity of errors was not
measured, and highly suitable translation solutions were not assigned
positive points. Despite the double validation of errors, the exclusion
of positive points seemed all the more reasonable in light of the lack of
professional revision and the diversity of reviewers in approach A. In
other words, positive points for good translation solutions could lead to

a wider gap between reviewed versus revised translations in the assessment, as opposed to an error-based approach more focused on acceptability than on adequacy levels. The primary aim was to detect errors as the first priority of quality assurance, without judging additional aspects of expression holistically (on the validity of assessment methods, see, e.g., Waddington 2001).

The results (see Table 9.2) show an enormous difference between averages for approaches A and B, in particular within the department where the intervention took place, from 12 errors per 1,000 words in group 4-A to 2.5 in group 4-B, i.e. a reduction of approximately 80% of errors from group 4 translations outsourced with approach A, and 75% with respect to the overall average for all text groups in this approach (9.5). The significant internal variations detected, as expressed in the brackets of lowest and highest error scores per year within each text group, reflect the unpredictability of quality in approach A. It is clear that scattered outsourcing practices, combined with unsystematic internal review, led to very changeable degrees of quality. The deficits highlighted during the interviews and the preliminary random analysis were empirically confirmed. These went unnoticed by the organization in approach A, so press releases containing up to 20.7 errors per 1,000 words on average were disseminated in some departments and periods, more specifically, during one year in group 1 and another year in group 3. The variations are more pronounced in the case of text sets covering several years, which points to a rough correlation between fluctuations in quality and changes of TSPs over time.

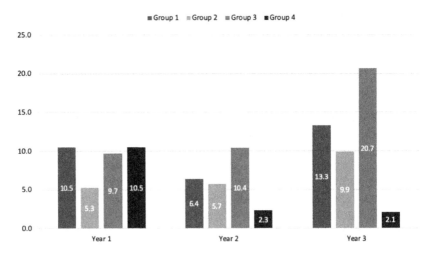

*Figure 9.1* Errors detected in translations of the two intervention years and the previous one.

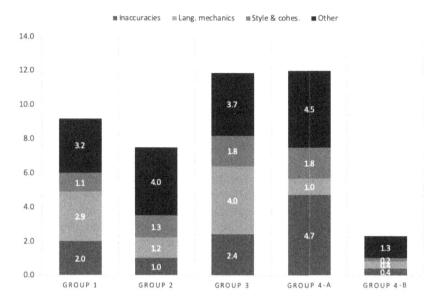

*Figure 9.2* Distribution of error types per text group and approach.

Even in comparison with the best yearly scores in approach A (of between 5 and 6 errors per 1,000 words), approach B results (with averages of 2.3 the first year and 2.1 the second year) represent a reduction of errors by more than half. For a closer look at the impact of quality assurance actions on text group 4, Figure 9.1 captures the evolution of total errors over the three years for which data were available in all the departments examined, including the two years of the intervention (years 2 and 3 in the graph, i.e. group 4-B) and the previous year (year 1 in the graph, corresponding to group 4-A).

As regards error types, Figure 9.2 shows similar proportions of style and cohesion issues and other translation appropriateness problems (including terminology and intratextual consistency) in all text groups of approach A, as opposed to marked variations in the frequency of language mechanics errors (ranging from averages of 1 in group 4-A to 4 in group 3) and inaccuracies (average of 1 in group 2 versus 4.7 in group 4-A). While the severity of errors was not assessed, the high frequency of semantic problems (normally with the most significant impact on meaning) within group 4-A, together with the total error score of this group, confirms that the intervention was particularly needed in this department. In group 4-B, by contrast, only two minor inaccuracies were detected in the translations from the first year of the intervention, and very few errors had otherwise been overlooked in approach B as a whole, including one related to style in the first year and two related to language mechanics in the second year.

The lack of errors of a particular category during an entire year is more rare among the other text groups. When this situation is sustained over more than a year, the results could be indicative of specific strengths among individual translators. For example, no style errors were found in translations from three out of nine consecutive years in group 1 and one year in group 3, no language mechanics problems in one year of group 2 and no inaccuracies in another year of this group.

Finally, between 5 and 13 intertextual inconsistencies were spotted in the translation of key terms within each textual series in approach A, as opposed to none in approach B (see Table 9.2). The inconsistencies include names of programs, bodies and key positions within the organization, which were therefore identified differently in press releases on the same matters and often in the same period. Overall, if the inconsistencies found in several text groups are counted only once, a total of 28 key terms were affected by such inconsistencies in approach A. This aspect of institutional translation quality would be particularly difficult to monitor without a deliberate global approach, not only through consistent revision but also, crucially, by developing and providing relevant resources to translators. The significant number of inconsistencies in group 4-A over only two years suggests, once again, that the intervention to improve quality along those lines was greatly needed in this case.

## 9.5  The Broader Impact: Further Measures and Replication Study

In practice, the extremely positive results of the intervention supported a decision to expand the model to other departments to the extent possible. The approach was therefore maintained after the pilot project in the department that benefitted from it, and as a first step for its gradual expansion, the list of translators and the resources developed during the intervention were shared with other departments. The same PM became the focal point for translation matters until the monitoring of practices for this study came to an end. An important factor in assessing the benefits of the new approach was the fact that the total costs of translations of group 4-B had remained stable compared to group 4-A, even including the part-time support of the PM and reviser. The transition period from approach A into approach B entailed a more significant investment of time at the beginning of the intervention in order to test external translators and develop new resources. This investment, however, gradually evolved into less time-consuming monitoring and updating tasks, apart from revision, which did not necessarily involve more time than a review in approach A.

The same project was subsequently used as a model for a replication study with the same action research approach and supervision, but in a different institutional setting. In this case, the organization is a smaller intergovernmental body integrated into a larger institutional structure where Spanish is one of several official languages. However, it has no translation service or any regular allocation for translation in its operational budgets. In the initial situation examined, ad hoc solutions were sought for specific translation needs through "informal" translations by staff without translation qualifications or experience, and reviews by other staff of the same language, whenever possible. No information was available on the potential use of machine translation by the staff who conducted the translations. In this initial scenario, what we will refer to as "approach C," translations were outsourced very rarely (when texts were considered particularly important), under no translation-specific project coordination and with no institution-specific resources for translation.

If compared to approach A in the first case study, the main difference is that the norm in approach C was non-professional translation rather than systematic outsourcing to professional translators. The translation needs were deemed insufficient to justify any investment in this area, let alone to consider a professional position even partly devoted to translation-related tasks. In sum, the approach can be considered an illustration of "low-cost" informal approaches to institutional translation needs, particularly among very small entities (see, e.g., Tesseur 2018 in connection with international non-governmental organizations). Their translated material, however, can be as critical as that of larger institutions for the achievement of their policy objectives – in this case for global cooperation in an area of great societal relevance. This material included reports, guidelines and website contents such as news items. These texts were eventually selected as the most regular genre for the study on translation quality.

The key action agreed to by the institution, with a view to improving the situation, consisted of entrusting English-Spanish translation matters to a qualified translator who had no previous professional experience in the field. This person, initially hired as a part-time trainee, would translate texts and propose further measures to improve translation quality, in principle, without resorting to external translators or revisers. In-house translations would then be checked by the same staff who had reviewed translations before the intervention, i.e. whenever possible, a target language reader with knowledge of the institution's policies. Consequently, the new approach ("approach D") did not provide for any revision by experienced translation professionals. In practice, the qualified trainee translated all texts needed in Spanish over one year, including self-revision, and gradually became a pro-active adviser on translation matters and set up a glossary and a document repository in order to improve text consistency. The translator's views, however, did not always prevail when disagreement arose with the reviewers, whose suggestions often seemed too arbitrary and inappropriate.

A total of 51 Spanish translations of news items of an average length of 225 words from five years, including the year of the intervention, were subsequently compiled for a comparative error analysis of approaches C and D, along the lines of the first case study. Three texts that had been exceptionally outsourced during the five-year period were excluded from the calculations. The analysis revealed an overall average of 92 errors per 1,000 words in the four years and 41 texts of approach C, compared to an average of 14 errors in the ten translations produced over one year with approach D.[1] This represents a reduction of 85% in errors. The yearly scores during the first four years range between 66 and 113 errors per 1,000 words, but the distribution of error types was strikingly similar, with the following order of frequency: semantic inaccuracies, style and cohesion, language mechanics and other appropriateness problems. Intertextual inconsistencies were also detected in the translations of 12 key terms in the pre-intervention period.

Interestingly, the results for approach D depict quality levels comparable to those of outsourced translations in approach A in the previous study (see Table 9.3). In other words, the introduction of translation competence in-house ameliorated a situation of poor quality communication in Spanish that could seriously damage the image of an institution of its caliber, but there was still room for improvement. While the translator was convinced that many of the mistakes spotted ex post during the error analysis were due to the input of reviewers (without translation expertise), the measures implemented made a marked difference. Despite

*Table 9.3* Comparison of approaches and error scores in each setting (excluding intertextual terminology inconsistencies)

| Approach (setting) | PM | Translation | Revision | Review | Average error score (per 1,000 words) |
|---|---|---|---|---|---|
| Approach A (setting 1) | – | Outsourced (various TSPs) | – | In-house (unsystematic) | 9.5 |
| Approach B (setting 1) | In-house (professional) | Outsourced (screened freelancers) | In-house (professional) | – | 2.2 |
| Approach C (setting 2) | – | In-house (non-professional) | – | In-house (unsystematic) | 92 |
| Approach D (setting 2) | In-house (professional) | In-house (professional) | – | In-house (unsystematic) | 14 |

budget and structural constraints, the project led to increased awareness of the need for a more professional approach to translation. The same qualified translator was eventually employed to perform more translation, revision, editing and PM work, among other tasks, and was thus able to promote progress toward approach A for certain sensitive texts. This later period, however, falls outside the scope of the replication study.

## 9.6 Discussion and Conclusions

Our findings confirm the beneficial multiplying effects of introducing translation competence in managing translation in institutional settings that have limited translation volumes and no matured translation service. The smaller the setting and the budget for translation, the more acute the need will normally be to tackle the most compelling competence and procedural deficits through the concentration of translation-related tasks into a central qualified profile. In line with a holistic approach to quality, the positive impact of profile changes and related workflow adjustments on product quality has been corroborated in the two cases of action research presented in this chapter. ISO 17100:2015 has been a useful yardstick to compare approaches to translation management, while systematic error analysis has proved a reliable way to draw an indicative picture of product quality across settings, even if the severity of mistakes was not measured.

In both settings, the actions undertaken combined translation workflow management with institution-specific resource development and other priority tasks: professional translator screening and revision of outsourced translations (previously replaced by informal internal review) in the first project (move from approach A to approach B); and professional translation of all texts (previously done by unqualified staff), followed by informal internal review, in the replication study (move from approach C to approach D). The error scores of translations carried out before and after these changes depict an almost perfect continuum: PM coordination and revision by a translation professional in the first setting (approach B) led to almost error-free revised translations, representing a reduction of approximately 75% of errors from the previous approach (A); and replacing non-professional translation (approach C) with professional translation, even if by a newly qualified translator (approach D), resulted in a drop of 80% in errors, to levels comparable to the starting situation in the first setting (i.e. approach A, with outsourced professional translation and internal review). In both cases, intertextual inconsistencies between the renderings of key terms in previous translations were detected and corrected as part of terminological harmonization and glossary building. This aspect of translation management, completely neglected in the initial approaches, ultimately yielded similar longer-term benefits for institutional translation quality.

In the first project, the creation of support material for that purpose and professional screening of external translators through competence testing were key factors in fostering quality more efficiently, as opposed to the previous outsourcing of translations without any tailored PM coordination or guidance. In fact, in the initial approach, it would be unrealistic to expect non-experts to have any ability to test potential contractors when non-expert initiators of the translation job are often not competent to formulate translation briefs, as noted by Nord (2005, 10), and much less to judge all aspects of translation quality. The risks of contracting translation services without assessing the competence of individual translators were compounded by the absence of professional revision of their work.

Furthermore, due to frequent changes of TSPs and reviewers, the product quality can be very unpredictable, as shown by the scores in approach A, which ranged between yearly averages of 5 and 21 errors per 1,000 words (between 10 and 14 over two years in the case of the department where the first intervention took place). Likewise, recourse to informal non-professional practices in the initial approach of the second institution was marked by unpredictability, but at much higher error density levels, between 66 and 113 each year on average per 1,000 words, and with a larger proportion of serious semantic errors. Coincidentally, the shift to professional translation brought these levels down to those of mid-range translator performance in approach A of the first organization. According to the translator in the second intervention, the scores could have been much lower without the input of non-expert in-house reviewers.

As in the case of risks associated with outsourcing without proper translator screening and revision, averting the risks of non-professional translation did not entail an increase in translation costs. For both settings, the findings suggest that the quality issues initially identified did not primarily or exclusively derive from budget constraints but from the lack of expertise to tailor translation management solutions to the available budgets in effective ways. This is a crucial aspect of empirically examining the added value of translation expertise in institutional translation processes. It is also a pivotal step in raising awareness of the cost-effectiveness of investing in translation quality assurance in the long term. This is exactly what occurred in the two settings analyzed: practices were subsequently improved based on the action research results. The seed was sown for further recognition of professional translation and its benefits for the quality of communication and, ultimately, for the image and credibility of both organizations.

## Note

1 The intervention included other texts, but news items were considered the most suitable for the diachronic examination of errors. The authors of this chapter would like to thank Ms Marta Godino Rodríguez for her kind co-operation in the process of summarizing the replication study. As in the first case study, all references to the institution are anonymized.

# References

Angelelli, Claudia V. 2009. "Using a rubric to assess translation ability: Defining the construct." In *Testing and Assessment in Translation and Interpreting Studies: A Call for Dialogue between Research and Practice*, edited by Claudia V. Angelelli and Holly E. Jocobson, 13–47. Amsterdam and Philadelphia: John Benjamins.

Cravo, Ana, and Josélia Neves. 2007. "Action research in translation studies." *Journal of Specialised Translation* 7: 92–107.

Hurtado Albir, Amparo, ed. 1996. *La enseñanza de la traducción. Metodología en la formación de traductores e intérpretes*. Castellón: Universitat Jaume I.

ISO. 2015. *ISO 17100. Translation Services – Requirements for Translation Services*. Geneva: ISO.

Nord, Christiane. 2005. *Text Analysis in Translation: Theory, Methodology, and Didactic Application of a Model for Translation-oriented Text Analysis*. 2nd edition. Amsterdam: Rodopi.

Nord, Christiane. 2018. *Translating as a Purposeful Activity. Functionalist Approaches Explained*. 2nd edition. London: Routledge.

Prieto Ramos, Fernando. 2015. "Quality assurance in legal translation: Evaluating process, competence and product in the pursuit of adequacy." *International Journal for the Semiotics of Law* 28(1): 11–30. doi:10.1007/s11196-014-9390-9.

Prieto Ramos, Fernando. 2017. "The evolving role of institutional translation service managers in quality assurance: Profiles and challenges." In *Quality Aspects in Institutional Translation*, edited by Tomáš Svoboda, Łucja Biel and Krzysztof Łoboda, 59–74. Berlin: Language Science Press. doi:10.5281/zenodo.1048188.

Reason, Peter, and Hilary Bradbury, eds. 2008. *The SAGE Handbook of Action Research: Participative Inquiry and Practice*. 2nd edition. London: Sage.

Tesseur, Wine. 2018. "Researching translation and interpreting in non-governmental organisations." *Translation Spaces* 7(1): 1–19. doi:10.1075/ts.00001.tes.

Waddington, Christopher. 2001. "Different methods of evaluating student translations: The question of validity." *Meta: Translators' Journal* 46(2): 311–325. doi:10.7202/004583a.

# 10 Interpreting at the United Nations

## The Effects of Delivery Rate on Quality in Simultaneous Interpreting

*Lucía Ruiz Rosendo, Mónica Varela García, and Alma Barghout*[1]

### 10.1 Speed and Simultaneous Interpreting

Speed is usually put forward as one of the main stressors in simultaneous interpreting (SI) and is considered as a factor that affects the interpreter's processing capacity; thus, it has an impact on the process and the quality of the rendition. Over the years, numerous scholars have studied the variability of speed among different languages and contexts (Roach 1998; Rodero 2012; Baese-Berk & Morrill 2015) and the impact of speed on the interpreter's rendition (Gerver 1969/2002; Barik 1973; Sunnari 1995; Lee 2002; Pio 2003; Meuleman & Van Besien 2009; Pym 2009; Changshuan 2010; Barghout, Ruiz Rosendo and Varela García 2015). According to the latter studies, there is a correlation between delivery rate, short-term memory overload and interpreter performance. Along these lines, Gerver (1969/2002) concludes that any deterioration in interpreter performance is due to the effects of delivery rate on inherent SI processes.

As part of the discussion on the impact of speed on rendition quality, many authors have focused on omissions as a quality indicator (Barik 1971; Noteboom 1973; Garnham et al. 1981; Pio 2003; Napier 2004; Pym 2009; Korpal 2012; Díaz Gálaz & López Portuguez 2016) or as a quality microcriterion. Barik defines omissions as those segments of the source speech that do not appear in the target speech (1975/2002). Some authors consider omissions as errors (Altman 1990; Cokely 1992; Moser Mercer, Künzli & Korac 1998), particularly in early SI literature: for example, Noteboom (1973) and Garnham et al. (1981) consider omissions to be a slip of the tongue. Similarly, Barik (1973), Gerver (1976) and Setton (1999) posit that omissions are a result of a lack of comprehension by the interpreter. Other authors, however, state that it is inappropriate to automatically consider any and all omissions as errors (Galli 1990; Sunnari 1995; Pio 2003; Liu 2009; Meuleman & Van Besien 2009; Pym 2009). Galli (1990) suggests that omissions may be conscious, and Pio (2003) accepts the possibility of some strategic use of omissions to make

DOI: 10.4324/9780429264894-10

the target speech clearer. Pym (2009) even asserts that omissions are necessary in interpreting, and that the key to using them appropriately is to determine beforehand the risk factor associated with the omission of a specific fragment. In the same vein, Korpal (2012) concludes that both trainees and professional interpreters view omission in SI, particularly the omission of redundancies, as a deliberate act.

In their studies on the impact of speed on interpreter performance, Barik (1973), Pio (2003) and Ruiz Rosendo and Galván (2019) conclude that the faster the speed, the greater the number of omissions. Shlesinger (2003), for her part, states that there is an inverse correlation between delivery rate and the interpreter's ability to give an accurate rendition. Korpal (2012) comes to a more nuanced finding: in his study, the positive correlation between delivery rate and number of omissions is to be found among interpreting trainees, but not among professional interpreters. Finally, Ruiz Rosendo and Galván (2019) state that a higher delivery rate has a negative impact on target speech accuracy, both among expert and novice interpreters.

Other authors analyze the impact of high delivery rate on ear-voice-span (EVS) without reaching consensus: according to some authors, EVS is longer at a high delivery rate (Barik 1973; De Groot 1997), while others argue that EVS is shorter when the input rate increases (Lee 2002). Ruiz Rosendo and Galván (2019) conclude that delivery rate does not have an overall significant impact on EVS.

Still other authors have studied the influence of the speaker's delivery rate on the interpreter stress (Korpal 2016). In his experimental study with interpreting trainees, Korpal focuses on the causal relationship between moderate and high delivery rates in SI and psychological stress, operationalized by heart rate and blood pressure (physiological stress markers). The findings show that, while interpreting a fast speech, participants experienced a higher level of stress than when interpreting a speech delivered at a moderate rate, manifested by higher heart rate but not by higher blood pressure. Considering the analysis of heart rate values, the study concludes that delivery rate is a stressor in SI.

### 10.1.1 Recommended vs Actual Delivery Rates

Speed in SI is not to be considered a static factor, but one that has changed with the passage of time, and recommendations for what constitutes a reasonable and feasible speed for interpreting purposes have changed accordingly. Gaiba (1998) tells us that at the Nuremberg trials, speakers were instructed to speak at 60 wpm; whether this was the actual rate at the time, however, is questionable, given that no empirical studies have been carried out to corroborate this claim. In a later publication, Seleskovitch (1965) considers that the comfortable input rate for SI of impromptu speeches is 100–120 wpm, a conclusion also reached by Gerver (1976), who maintains that a higher rate negatively impacts the interpreter's performance. Seleskovitch and Lederer (1984) state that rates between 150 and 200 wpm constitute an upper limit for effective interpreting, although this presumption was not submitted to experimentation. They consider that the standard actual delivery rate in interpreted meetings is generally 150 wpm, although again they did not carry out an empirical study. Professional associations also provide recommendations on speed: in its guidelines, the International Association of Conference Interpreters (AIIC) stipulates that a speaker's average delivery rate should be around 130 wpm.

It is worth noting that some authors have suggested reference values regarding speed. Monti, Bendazzoli, Sandrelli and Russo (2005) categorize these values into low (up to 130 wpm), medium (up to 160 wpm) and high (above 160 wpm). More recently, Setton and Dawrant (2016) have offered different ranges: easy (100–120 wpm), moderate (120–140 wpm), challenging (140–160 wpm) and difficult (above 160 wpm). In this chapter, we will use Setton and Dawrant's framework.

In spite of these recommendations and reference values, few scholars have analyzed the actual (measured) delivery rate with which interpreters are confronted in international organizations. De Manuel Jerez (2014), in his study on the use of real speeches in interpreter training ("Corpus Marius"), measures the actual delivery rate in the European Parliament (EP), among other events. According to his findings, the average delivery rate in the EP is 150–151 wpm in Spanish and in French.

In 2015, we undertook an initial norming experiment to calculate the number of words per minute for speeches delivered at the UN Human Rights Council (HRC) (see Barghout, Ruiz Rosendo and Varela García 2015). The findings reveal that the average delivery rate at the United Nations (UN) is similar to the EP. The study analyzed two weeks of the 16th Session, randomly selecting two speeches delivered in English per day. As a first step, the prepared written statements were downloaded from the HRC website, and the recordings of the delivered speeches were listened to. The written statements were then checked against delivery and the words per minute were calculated. The findings suggest an average delivery rate of 149.12 wpm ($SD = 21.51$), the highest delivery rate being 201 wpm and the lowest 122.17 wpm.

A second analysis was carried out to measure speed in French and English in order to establish whether or not delivery rate varies from one language to another (see Ruiz Rosendo, Varela García and Barghout 2016). In this case, 42 speeches were randomly selected from the 24th Session of the Universal Periodic Review (UPR) Working Group, 21 from the review of Belgium (10 speeches in English and 10 in French, plus the delivery (in French) of the Belgian government's introductory statement) and 21 from the review of Namibia (10 speeches in English and 10 in French, plus the delivery (in English) of the Namibian government's introductory statement). The total number of words per minute was then calculated for each speech. In the review of Belgium, for the French speeches, the highest delivery rate was 193 wpm and the lowest 128 wpm, with an average of 158.9 wpm ($SD$ = 23.63). For the English speeches, the highest delivery rate was 190 wpm and the lowest 133 wpm, with an average of 160.7 wpm ($SD$ = 20). The total average was 160.71 wpm ($SD$ = 20). In the review of Namibia, for the English speeches, the highest delivery rate was 185 wpm and the lowest 121 wpm, with an average of 163 ($SD$ = 13.55). For the French speeches, the highest delivery rate was 191 wpm and the lowest 126 wpm, with an average of 160.4 ($SD$ = 18.43). The total average was 161.76 wpm ($SD$ = 18.28).

With the aim of delving deeper into the actual delivery rate at international organizations, we conducted a third analysis of speeches delivered at the International Labour Organization (ILO), more specifically at the Plenary Session of the International Labour Conference (ILC). We used the same method as in the previous studies. Due to access limitations, the 102nd (2013) and 105th (2016) ILCs were selected. Twenty-six speeches in English and 19 in French were randomly selected (two for each day, to the extent possible). Fewer speeches in French were selected because there were not enough available speeches for some days. For the 102nd ILC, the average speed for English speeches was 141.4 wpm ($SD$ = 15.27) (the highest speed being 172.7 wpm and the lowest 113 wpm). The average speed for French speeches was 143.06 wpm ($SD$ = 13.71) (the highest speed being 159.7 wpm and the lowest 118.1 wpm). The total average was 142.19 wpm. For the 105th ILC the average speed for English speeches was 127.3 wpm ($SD$ = 14.14) (the highest being 148.7 wpm and the lowest 103 wpm). The average speed for French speeches was 134.7 wpm ($SD$ = 14.25) (the highest being 159.13 wpm and the lowest 119.8 wpm). The total average was 130.2 wpm.

These results confirm that the average actual delivery rate is higher than what is usually recommended in the literature. The total values indicate that the delivery rate tends to be higher at the UN and the EP, where the actual speed could be qualified as "challenging," for the HRC and the EP (140–160 wpm), and "difficult" (>160 wpm) for the UPR. The findings show that the average speed at the ILO for the two years examined is moderate (120–140 wpm), according to the same reference values. We believe that the similar results in English and French, and therefore the related speed factors, are due to the style of the speeches and the situation in which they were produced, not the language per se (Roach 1998) – in the different scenarios examined by the authors, speakers had very limited time to deliver their speeches. Also, in all cases they delivered a read discourse; this is an increasingly frequent occurrence at international organizations and is associated with high delivery rates.

## 10.1.2 Read Discourse

The impact of speed on the interpreter's rendition might be increased when the speaker delivers a read discourse rather than an improvised speech. In fact, a speech written to be read aloud poses added challenges, influencing the interpreter's performance. Most authors have emphasized the difference in delivery rate between "off-the-cuff" and prepared speeches, and have concluded that text written to be read aloud is often delivered at a higher rate (Dejean le Féal 1978; Seleskovitch 1978; Seleskovitch & Lederer 1984; Balzani 1990; Messina 1998; Napier 2004; Gile 2009). Barik (1973) even considers that a situation where a speaker reads from a written script is a counter-ideal situation, opposed to a situation in which the speaker does not use a text.

Texts written to be read aloud include dense fragments as well as complex and artificial structures, making them more difficult to comprehend than an improvised speech (Chafe & Danielewicz 1987; Gile 2009). In spontaneous speech intonation, rhythm and the use of pauses are more natural. Regarding pauses, Roach (1998) analyzes the differences in delivery rate between different languages and states that pauses do make a difference. In fact, there are two different measurements of delivery rate, with one including pauses and hesitations and the other excluding them. Speed is arguably higher when pauses are scarce.

Read discourse presents the usual features of written text, including low-frequency vocabulary (Johns, Gruenenfelder, Pisoni and Jones 2012), lexical density (Paltridge 2006), complex syntactical structures, and a high degree of textual coherence and cohesion (Chafe 1982; Balzani 1990; Napier 2004). These features generate an additional processing load during the act of comprehension. In addition, read discourse requires less reflection on the part of the speaker, most frequently resulting in an increased delivery rate. Even when a written speech is recited at a normal rate, interpreters perceive the speech as being faster than it actually is (Chernov 1994), and understanding read discourse delivered at a high speed can be difficult even for source language listeners. Indeed, the unpublished minutes of a UN interpreters' staff meeting (Baigorri Jalón & Travieso Rodríguez 2017, 57) support these views:

> Lately the quality of the service we provide has been compromised due to speed of delivery and lack of texts. This also generates unusual fatigue and a sense of uselessness and frustration. [...]
>
> [...] speakers deliver their texts at such a speed that even listeners in the original language cannot absorb the content. Statements are not acts of communication anymore, since delegates just read for the record.

Indeed, speed has become an intrinsic element of SI at the UN. In his survey with UN interpreters, Baigorri Jalón and Travieso Rodríguez

(2017) explain that speed, usually associated with a growing frequency of read speeches, is mentioned as one of the major changes which interpreters have experienced in their working conditions and which have an impact on the quality of interpreted speeches.

## 10.2 Coping with Speed as a Quality Criterion at the UN

At the beginning of the 1990s (Baigorri Jalón 2004), the UN introduced a new testing system, the Language Competitive Examination (LCE), aiming to establish a roster from which to fill present and future staff vacancies. The LCE consists of two parts: an interpreting test (simultaneous[2] only) and an interview. In the first, eliminatory, part, candidates are asked to simultaneously interpret three 5- to 10-minute speeches of progressively increasing difficulty (in terms of complexity and speed of delivery), from (and into, depending on the language combination) each of their foreign languages (see Ruiz Rosendo & Diur 2017, 2018 for more information regarding the LCE).

As can be observed, delivery rate is considered a major challenge and candidates have to show that they can cope with it. Not surprisingly, the ability to keep up with high delivery rates is one of the qualities that candidates must demonstrate and a criterion against which candidates are tested, together with other traditional quality criteria mentioned by some scholars (Bühler 1986; Kalina 2000). Even if quality is considered an elusive construct, sense consistency, logical cohesion, accuracy and completeness, fluency and correct grammar are the traditionally accepted quality criteria in the interpreting community (Chiaro and Nocella 2004; Pöchhacker and Zwischenberger 2010).

There are, however, factors beyond the interpreters' control that may prevent them from meeting these traditionally accepted quality criteria, speed being one of them. Indeed, Altman (1990) states that there are variables that depend on the interpreter (e.g. familiarity with the subject matter, health state and fatigue) and others that do not. High delivery rate is one such factor, together with sound, visibility, the use of a non-native language by the speaker and booth conditions.

The inclusion of speed as a difficulty and of coping with speed as an assessment criterion is not unwarranted given the increasing speed at which speeches are delivered at the UN. Speed has probably become the most relevant criterion, given that only a few candidates are able to cope with it. Along these lines, Diur (2015) and Ruiz Rosendo and Diur (2017) highlight the difficulties that LCE candidates encounter, reflected in the low success rate of all six booths, seldom exceeding 20%. In their study, speed is shown to be the main challenge of the LCE, as it is the challenge most often mentioned by participants. Likewise, participants attribute the low pass rate to the excessive speed of the speeches as it puts pressure on candidates and prevents them from achieving the quality criteria imposed by the UN. Similarly, Diur (2015), in her study with senior interpreters entrusted with selecting candidates and marking the LCE, highlights that speed is the major challenge faced by candidates sitting the LCE; indeed, many of the respondents posit that an excessive delivery rate is one of the main causes of the medium or low success rate.

## 10.3  The Impact of Speed on the Interpreter's Performance

The results of the three analyses on actual delivery rate, described in Section 10.1, confirm that speed is challenging at international organizations and, in particular, at the UN. In addition, coping with speed is a quality criterion in the LCE and has been shown to be a major contributor to its low pass rates (see Section 10.2). In light of these findings, we decided to carry out a study to analyze the impact of high delivery rates on the performance of UN interpreters.

### 10.3.1  Study Design

Our experimental study involved one independent variable – delivery rate – at three different levels. Ten UN staff interpreters were asked to interpret three speeches from English into French. Each of these speeches had three segments with three different delivery rates within one speech: moderate (120 wpm), challenging (160 wpm) and difficult (200 wpm), according to Setton and Dawrant's (2016) reference values. In each of the three speeches, the order of the delivery rates was different (see Table 10.1).

### 10.3.2  Participants

Ten staff interpreters (nine female and one male) working at the United Nations Office at Geneva (UNOG) participated in the study. All were French booth interpreters with passive English and had been working at UNOG for an average of 8.9 years. Participants were divided into

*Table 10.1* Delivery rate by segment in the three speeches

| Speech 1 | Speech 2 | Speech 3 |
|----------|----------|----------|
| 200 | 160 | 120 |
| 160 | 120 | 200 |
| 120 | 200 | 160 |

three groups (of 3, 3 and 4, respectively). This number of participants represents more than half of the French booth interpreters on staff at that time (18). It is also worth noting that the study population is limited to UN staff interpreters; as such the sample size can be considered as reasonable.

### 10.3.3 Materials

Material was selected from a corpus of previously delivered HRC speeches: two speeches delivered by Special Rapporteurs[3] at the 17th Session of the HRC on 1 June 2011, and a speech delivered at the 11th Session of the UPR of the HRC held on 4 May 2011 by the Head of the Delegation of the Republic of Seychelles. The speeches were edited to be equal in length (10 minutes), recorded by a native English speaker, and then manipulated to the three aforementioned rates (120, 160 and 200 wpm) using Sound Studio 3.

### 10.3.4 Procedure

Prior approval from the Chief of the Interpretation Service and the Head of the French Interpretation Section at UNOG was obtained to conduct the project. All French Section staff interpreters were contacted by email to inquire about their availability and willingness to participate in the study. All willing respondents were included in the experiment, a total of ten interpreters out of the 18 in the French Section. The experiment was conducted at the University of Geneva in two sessions. During the first session, one group of three participants interpreted Speech 1 and a second group of three participants interpreted Speech 2 in simultaneous mode. During the second session a group of four participants interpreted Speech 3 in simultaneous mode. The speeches were presented as audio recordings with no live speaker nor audience. The reason for using audio recordings was that they could be manipulated to three specific delivery rates using a software programme, Sound Studio 3, which can only edit audio files. Another reason is that LCE speeches are audio recordings, which means that candidates who sit the examination to become a staff interpreter at the UN are only exposed to audio material. The hypothesis and objectives of the study were not revealed to the participants, who were asked to simultaneously interpret as if they were at a real HRC meeting. Each of them signed an informed consent form and was assigned an individual booth and a number to be used later by the authors for the transcriptions of the renditions to guarantee anonymity. For the sake of anonymity, the transcriptions of the interpretations were carried out by only one of the three authors as she has never worked for the UN.

### 10.3.5 Data Analysis

The first round of data analysis (see Barghout, Ruiz Rosendo and Varela García 2015) focused on the impact of delivery rate on omissions. More specifically we quantitatively explored the impact of high delivery rate on the strategic omission of synonyms and redundant compound conjunctions (RCCs). We hypothesized that when read speeches are delivered at high speed, expert interpreters strategically omit redundant information. The findings of this analysis showed that the faster the input, the more likely the expert interpreters were to omit synonyms and redundant conjunctions.

After this first analysis had been completed, we carried out a second qualitative analysis to explore the impact of delivery rate on the interpreter's performance and rendition quality. More specifically, we focused on the impact of speed on omissions as a quality indicator: even if omissions could be seen as a deliberate strategy, it is important to consider that accuracy and completeness represent quality criteria at the UN. We examined the categories of omissions that interpreters make when confronted with different delivery rates, and whether delivery rate has an influence on the type of omission. Eight of the ten interpreters consented to this additional analysis (two for Speech 1, three for Speech 2 and three for Speech 3).

For the second analysis, the corpus of recordings was qualitatively analyzed. Importantly, the objective was not to provide a statistical analysis but to describe the impact of speed on the interpreters' rendition as operationalized by omissions. Also, the aim was not to generalize the findings to a broader population but to provide an explanation of how the participants to the study behave when confronted with moderate, challenging and difficult delivery rates.

We conceived this second study as a microanalysis, i.e. an open, detailed and exploratory form of coding (Corbin and Strauss 2008), to explore the data in greater depth with the objective of trying to grasp its meaning and to find concepts reflecting that meaning. Initial selective coding allowed all categories to be unified around the core category of "omissions." Open coding was subsequently used to identify different concepts or codes. Every code discovered in the research process was first considered provisional. Its relevance was confirmed after repeated occurrences. Concepts pertaining to the same phenomenon were grouped to form categories. During the analysis of the recordings, memos (i.e. a written record of analysis) and diagrams were used from the first coding session and until the end of the research process to illustrate our ideas (see Corbin and Strauss (2008) for more information about the use of memos and diagrams in qualitative research). Continued discussion among the researchers helped mitigate bias. Group discussions made it possible to open individual analyses to the scrutiny of the other researchers, leading to new insights and increased theoretical sensitivity.

After thorough analysis of the recordings, we identified recurrent codes and categories within the core category "omissions." Initial coding was undertaken between words, informative clauses and phrases, the latter being of particular interest as they may have a major impact on meaning. The two latter categories were then grouped into the category of segments, in line with what Pio (2003) suggests in her study on omissions. Several subcategories were then identified for words: redundancies, adjectives, adverbs, elements of an enumeration, elements of a cluster and links. Another subcategory was added, entitled "omissions with substitution" (OmS), where the interpreter had omitted the original word but replaced it with another. If this word was an equivalent (see example 10 hereunder) the omission was considered an "OmS as a strategy" (the original and replacement words had similar meanings in the target language), and, if it was a word with a different meaning, it was considered an "OmS as an error" (see example 11 hereunder). The subcategory "redundancies" was then divided into further subcategories: synonyms – defined as alternative terms that mean exactly or nearly the same as a certain term in the same language –, RCCs – elements that do not add information and introduce the repetition of a previously expressed idea –, and redundant references to a previously expressed element (see Figure 10.1).

In order to understand what each subcategory entails, some examples from the original read texts are provided:

### Category 1. Words

#### Subcategory 1.1. Redundancies

1   *Synonym*: I would like to <u>stress and highlight</u> the important points of the report.
2   RCC: <u>Put differently,</u> it was a comprehensive and consultative process.
3   *Redundant reference to a previously expressed element*: My annual thematic report focuses on the right to an effective remedy <u>for trafficked persons.</u>

In example (3), the highlighted compound refers to a previously mentioned element and is thus considered a redundancy. The context is presented in the following sentences:

These are fundamental guiding principles in developing and implementing measures aimed at combating trafficking in persons and <u>protecting and promoting the human rights of trafficked persons.</u> My annual thematic report focuses on the right to an effective remedy <u>for trafficked persons.</u>

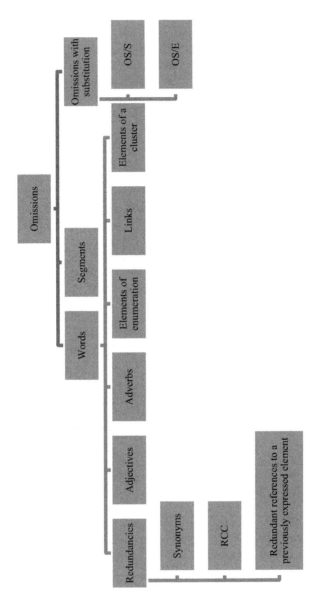

*Figure 10.1* Categories and subcategories of omissions.

*Subcategory 1.2. Adjectives*

4    These were measures aimed at facilitating <u>criminal</u> investigation.

*Subcategory 1.3. Adverbs*

5    At worst, many trafficked persons are <u>wrongly</u> identified as irregular migrants.

*Subcategory 1.4. Elements of an enumeration*

6    Procedural rights of access to remedies such as access to <u>information, counseling and legal aid.</u>

*Subcategory 1.5. Elements of a cluster*

7    States should develop <u>court procedures.</u>

*Subcategory 1.6. Links*

8    I recognize, <u>however,</u> that there are often obstacles in ensuring the provision of services.

## Category 2. Segments

9    I observed that adequate and effective remedies are often out of reach for trafficked persons, <u>despite the egregious human rights violations they suffered.</u>

## Category 3. Omissions with substitution

*Subcategory 3.1. Omissions with substitution as a strategy*

An omission falls under this category when the participant omitted the original reference but replaced it with a similar equivalent from the field:

10    Furthermore, there are common obstacles for <u>trafficked persons</u> (in the French interpretation replaced with the word "victims").

*Subcategory 3.2. Omissions with substitution as an error*

An omission is considered to be of this category when the participant omitted the original reference and replaced it with a reference with a different meaning:

11    My annual thematic report focuses on the right to an effective remedy for trafficked persons and contains <u>recommendations</u> (in the French interpretation replaced with the word "communications").

In qualitative research it is possible to "count the times that one observes or reads about an event or action as indicative of a concept" (Corbin and Strauss 2008, 9). We therefore decided to count the occurrences of the aforementioned categories in each speech, as we considered this useful for the overall qualitative analysis.

### 10.3.6 Results and Discussion

For the first speech, with a speed progression of 200–160–120 wpm, interpreters made a total of 18 omissions of segments and 61 omissions of words in the part delivered at 200 wpm. In the part delivered at 160 wpm, 19 segments and 35 words were omitted. In the part delivered at 120 wpm, three segments and 29 words were omitted. For the second speech, with a speed progression of 160–120–200 wpm, the interpreters made a total of 25 omissions of segments and 67 omissions of words in the part delivered at 160 wpm. In the part delivered at 120 wpm, ten segments and 42 words were omitted. In the part delivered at 200 wpm, 31 segments and 72 words were omitted. For the third speech, with a speed progression of 120–200–160 wpm, the interpreters made a total of seven omissions of segments and 31 omissions of words in the part delivered at 120 wpm. In the part delivered at 200 wpm, 42 segments and 77 words were omitted. In the part delivered at 160 wpm, 16 segments and 96 words were omitted (Table 10.2).

The overall results are similar for all three speeches. In each case, the parts delivered at 160 and 200 wpm register the highest number of omissions of words and segments, which indicates that delivery rate does have an impact on the message transmitted. However, in Speech 1, most segments were omitted at 160 wpm and, in Speech 3, more words were omitted at 160 wpm than at 200 wpm. It is interesting to note that the specific order of delivery rates has an impact on the number and types of omissions made by the interpreter: when the order was 120–200–160 (Speech 3), there were more omissions of segments and words in the fastest part (200 wpm) in comparison with Speech 1, which started at the delivery rate of 200 wpm. This might be due to the abrupt and unnatural change in the delivery rate from 120 to 200 wpm which the interpreters would not have expected. When the speech started at 200 wpm, then changed to 160 wpm (Speech 1), the number of segments omitted at both

*Table 10.2* Omitted segments and words in the three speeches

|  | Speech 1 | | | Speech 2 | | | Speech 3 | | |
|---|---|---|---|---|---|---|---|---|---|
| wpm | 200 | 160 | 120 | 160 | 120 | 200 | 120 | 200 | 160 |
| Segments | 18 | 19 | 3 | 25 | 10 | 31 | 7 | 42 | 16 |
| Words | 61 | 35 | 29 | 67 | 42 | 72 | 31 | 77 | 96 |

speeds was nearly the same but was lower at 120 wpm. This may be due to the unexpected extremely high speed from the very beginning. Therefore, when confronted with a moderate delivery rate in the last part of the speech, fewer segments were omitted, probably due to the reduced stress on processing capacity after experiencing overload when coping with the fast rates at the beginning of the speech.

The results confirm the other authors' findings that there are indeed more omissions when the delivery rate increases (Barik 1973; Pio 2003; Ruiz Rosendo & Galván 2019) even among professional interpreters used to interpreting read-aloud speeches characterized by high delivery rates. Interestingly, participants made longer omissions (of segments) when the speed increased, although the results were similar for the two fastest speeds.

A thorough analysis of the data shows that some categories of elements tend to be omitted at difficult and challenging speed, but also at moderate speed (120 wpm). Interestingly, the findings show that, at all three delivery rates, the interpreters omitted redundancies, these being the most omitted elements. One could argue that the omission of redundancies (synonyms, RCCs and redundant references to previous elements) is not always an error and can be a strategy stemming from the interpreter's analysis of relevance in the target language. Indeed, redundancies are considered to be elements that can be omitted without implying a loss of meaningful information (Sunnari 1995) or causing a disruption in communication. Along these lines, Chernov (1994) states that when communicating the semantic structure of the speech, the interpreter has some leeway for achieving a precise reproduction of the message. As a matter of fact, redundancies, even if they may help the interpreter to better grasp an idea, are, by definition, elements whose inclusion in the target speech is not essential.

The second and third most omitted categories were adjectives and adverbs, which were even omitted at 120 wpm. This could be an additional evidence to the use of omissions by the interpreters as a strategy. At the higher speeds (160 and 200 wpm), in addition to the aforementioned categories, elements of enumerations and elements of clusters were also omitted. Links were the least omitted elements, probably due to their positioning at the beginning of a phrase or a sentence and the possible tailing strategy applied by interpreters when confronted with speed. Importantly, links are considered by interpreters as important elements that have to be kept for the sake of cohesion.

Even if the interpreters made omissions at the three delivery rates, the types of omissions made at each delivery rate varied from one to the other. At 120 wpm, the participants omitted very few long segments that carried meaning, whereas at 160 wpm more segments and words in general were omitted. The results both at 160 and at 200 wpm show a clear increase in omissions of arbitrary segments that imply a loss of or a change in meaning. One might argue that the interpreters did not have enough capacity left to distinguish what was relevant from what was not and had to omit segments in order to keep pace with the speaker.

## 10.4  Conclusions

Although speed is usually put forward as a problem trigger in SI, to the best of our knowledge very few studies have been carried out to confirm the widespread hypothesis that high delivery rate has an impact on interpreter performance and its quality. If omissions are taken as a quality indicator, as mentioned in the literature, very few studies measure and evaluate the types of omissions made by interpreters. This study's findings support the suggestion that a challenging delivery rate has a negative impact on interpreter performance, in that such conditions gave rise to a higher number of arbitrary omissions implying a loss of meaningful information, even among veteran expert interpreters. Therefore, we can suggest that high delivery rate does have an impact on the quality of interpretation: if a speech is delivered at such a high speed that interpreters cannot adequately process the information, their interpreting output may be negatively affected.

These findings have implications for interpreter training, but also for potential speakers. Interpreter training institutions, faced with this new challenge, might wish to adapt their curricula to the developing realities of the markets in order to equip the trainees with the strategies needed to deal with high and very high delivery speeds of written texts. Strategy acquisition for the handling of speed depends on prior acquisition of the fundamental skills of comprehension and analysis and the subskill of recognizing redundancies. Other subskills that could be embedded in training programs include summarizing techniques and the use of omissions as a coping strategy, a memory capacity saver or even a survival strategy. The earlier students are exposed to this increasingly prevalent challenge, the better prepared they will be for coping with speed and applying conscious strategies in the real world. We submit that, through adequate training in strategy use, cognitive resources can be economized or shifted to meet the specific demands of coping with speed.

Even experienced interpreters, who are used to coping with speed, omit information when confronted with challenging and difficult delivery rates. Therefore, we propose that the provision of adequate working conditions for interpreters should be promoted, including adequate speaking time for speakers, so that interpreters can perform to the best of their ability. Despite some organizations having adopted public speaking guidelines, more can be done to make speakers aware of the need to control their delivery rate, especially when reading from written texts. In general, awareness-raising activities for participants at international organizations regarding the potentially negative impact of speed on the interpretation quality should be fostered. Participants need to understand that these high delivery rates impede multilingual communication and that the greatest impact is felt not by the interpreters but by the target audience, receiving the message through the interpreters. If interpreters are not given the conditions to perform to their best, the meeting itself could be compromised.

## Notes

1 Disclaimer: the views expressed herein are those of the authors and do not necessarily reflect the views of the United Nations or the International Labour Organization.
2 The reason why only SI is tested at the LCE is that, since the late 1940s, SI has been the usual interpreting mode in conference settings at the UN (Baigorri Jalón & Travieso Rodríguez 2017). Consecutive interpreting is mainly used in UN field missions.
3 Mr. Anand Grover, Special Rapporteur on the Right of Everyone to the Enjoyment of the Highest Attainable Standard of Physical and Mental Health, and Ms. Joy Ngozi Ezeilo, Special Rapporteur on Trafficking in Persons, Especially Women and Children.

## References

Altman, Janet. 1990. "What Helps Effective Communication? Some Interpreter's Views." *The Interpreter's Newsletter* 3: 23–32.

Baese-Berk, Melissa M., and Tuuli H. Morrill. 2015. "Speaking Rate Consistency in Native and non-Native Speakers of English." *Journal of the Acoustical Society of America* 138 (3): EL223–EL228.

Baigorri Jalón, Jesús. 2004. *Interpreters at the United Nations: A History*. Salamanca: Ediciones Universidad de Salamanca.

Baigorri Jalón, Jesús, and Críspulo Travieso Rodríguez. 2017. "Interpreting at the United Nations: The Impact of External Variables. The Interpreters' View." *CLINA. An Interdisciplinary Journal of Translation, Interpreting and Intercultural Communication* 3 (2): 53–72.

Balzani, Maurizio. 1990. "Le contact visuel en interprétation simultanée: résultats d'une expérience (Français-Italien)." In *Aspects of Applied and Experimental Research on Conference Interpretation*, edited by Laura Gran, and Christopher Taylor, 93–100. Udine: Campanotto Editore.

Barghout, Alma, Lucía Ruiz Rosendo, and Mónica Varela García. 2015. "The Influence of Speed on Omissions in Simultaneous Interpretation: An Experimental Study." *Babel* 61 (3): 305–334.

Barik, Henri C. 1971. "A Description of Various Types of Omissions, Additions, and Errors of Translation Encountered in Simultaneous Interpreting." *Meta* 16 (4): 199–210.

Barik, Henri C. 1973. "Simultaneous Interpretation: Temporal and Quantitative Data." *Language and Speech* 16: 237–270.

Barik, Henri C. 1975/2002. "Simultaneous Interpretation: Qualitative and Linguistic Data." *The Interpreter Studies Reader*, edited by Franz Pöchhacker, and Miriam Shlesinger, 78–91. London/New York: Routledge.

Bühler, Hildegund. 1986. "Linguistic (Semantic) and Extralinguistic (Pragmatic) Criteria for the Evaluation of Conference Interpretation and Interpreters." *Multilingua* 5 (4): 231–235.

Chafe, Wallace. 1982. "Integration and Involvement in Speaking, Writing and Oral Literature." In *Spoken and Written Language: Exploring Orality and Literacy*, edited by Deborah Tannen, 35–53. Norwood, NJ: Ablex.

Chafe, Wallace, and Jane Danielewicz. 1987. "Properties of Spoken and Written Language." In *Comprehending Oral and Written Language*, edited by Rosalind Horowitz, and S. Jay Samuels, 83–113. San Diego: Academic Press.

Changshuan, Li. 2010. "Coping Strategies for Fast Delivery in Simultaneous Interpretation." *JoSTrans* 13: 19–25.

Chernov, Ghelly V. 1994. "Message Redundancy and Message Anticipation in Simultaneous Interpretation." In *Bridging the Gap. Empirical Research in Simultaneous Interpretation*, edited by Sylvie Lambert, and Barbara Moser-Mercer, 139–153. Amsterdam: John Benjamins.

Chiaro, Delia, and Giuseppe Nocella. 2004. "Interpreters Perception of Linguistic and Non-Linguistic Factors Affecting Quality: A Survey through the World Wide Web." *Meta* 49 (2): 278–293.

Cokely, Dennis. 1992. *Interpretation: A Sociolinguistic Model*. Burtonsville: Linstok Press.

Corbin, Juliet, and Anselm Strauss. 2008. *Basics of Qualitative Research*. Thousand Oaks, CA: SAGE Publications.

De Groot, Annette M. B. 1997. "The Cognitive Study of Translation and Interpretation: Three Approaches." In *Cognitive Processes in Translation and Interpreting*, edited by Joseph H. Danks, Gregory M. Shreve, Stephen B. Fountain, and Michael K. McBeath, 25–26. Thousand Oaks, CA: SAGE Publications.

De Manuel Jerez, Jesús. 2014. "L'usage des discours réels dans la formation d'interprètes: pourquoi, comment et quand?" Paper presented at the EVIVA Seminar, Evaluating the Use of Virtual Learning Environments in the Education of Interpreters and their Clients, Brussels, November 28.

Dejean le Féal, Karla. 1978. *Lectures et improvisations: incidences de la forme de l'énonciation sur la traduction simultanée*. PhD diss., Université de la Sorbonne Nouvelle.

Díaz Gálaz, Stephanie, and Constanza López Portuguez. 2016. "La omisión en interpretación simultánea: ¿fallo involuntario o estrategia comunicativa?" *Onomázein* 33. Accessed 15 May 2019. http://www.redalyc.org/articulo.oa?id=134546830021.

Diur, Marie. 2015. *Interpreting at the United Nations: An Empirical Study on the Language Competitive Examination (LCE)*. PhD diss., University Pablo de Olavide.

Gaiba, Francesca. 1998. *The Origins of Simultaneous Interpretation: The Nuremberg Trial*. Ottawa: University of Ottawa Press.

Galli, Cristina. 1990. "Simultaneous Interpretation in Medical Conferences: A Case-Study." In *Aspects of Applied Experimental Research on Conference Interpretation*, edited by Laura Gran, and Christopher Taylor, 61–81. Udine: Campanotto Editore.

Garnham, Alan, Richard Shillock, Gordon Brown, Andrew Mill, and Anne Cutler. 1981. "Slips of the Tongue in the London-Lund Corpus of Spontaneous Conversation." *Linguistics* 19: 805–817.

Gerver, David. 1969/2002. "The Effects of Source Language Presentation Rate on the Performance of Simultaneous Conference Interpreters." In *The Interpreting Studies Reader*, edited by Franz Pöchhacker, and Miriam Shlesinger, 53–66. London: Routledge.

Gerver, David. 1976. "Empirical Studies of Simultaneous Interpretation: A Review and a Model." In *Translation: Applications and Research*, edited by Richard W. Brislin, 165–207. New York: Gardner Press.

Gile, Daniel. 2009. *Basic Concepts and Models for Interpreter and Translator Training*. Amsterdam/Philadelphia: John Benjamins.

Johns, Brendan T., Thomas M. Gruenenfelder, David B. Pisoni, and Michael N. Jones. 2012. "Effects of Word Frequency, Contextual Diversity, and Semantic Distinctiveness on Spoken Word Recognition." *The Journal of the Acoustical Society of America* 132 (2): EL74–EL80.

Kalina, Sylvia. 2000. "Quality in Interpreting and its Prerequisites." In *Interpreting in the 21st Century: Challenges and Opportunities*, edited By Giuliana Garzone, and Maurizio Viezzi, 121–130. Amsterdam/Philadelphia: John Benjamins

Korpal, Pawel. 2012. "Omission in Simultaneous Interpreting as a Deliberate Act." In *Translation Research Projects 4*, edited by Anthony Pym, and David Orrego-Carmona, 103–111. Tarragona: Intercultural Studies Group.

Korpal, Pawel. 2016. "Interpreting as a Stressful Activity: Physiological Measures of Stress in Simultaneous Interpreting." *Poznan Studies in Contemporary Linguistics* 52 (2): 297–316.

Lee, Tae-Hyung. 2002. "Ear Voice Span in English into Korean Simultaneous Interpretation." *Meta* 47 (4): 596–606.

Liu, Minhua. 2009. "How do Experts Interpret? Implications from Research in Interpreting Studies and Cognitive Science." In *Efforts and Models in Interpreting and Translation Research: A Tribute to Daniel Gile*, edited by Gyde Hansen, Andrew Chesterman, and Heidrun Gerzymisch-Arbogast, 159–177. Amsterdam: John Benjamins.

Messina, Alessandro. 1998. "The Reading Aloud of English Language Texts in Simultaneously Interpreted Conferences." *Interpreting* 3 (2): 147–161.

Meuleman, Chris, and Fred Van Besien. 2009. "Coping with Extreme Speech Conditions in Simultaneous Interpreting." *Interpreting* 11 (1): 20–34.

Monti, Christina, Claudio Bendazzoli, Annalisa Sandrelli, and Mariachiara Russo. 2005. "Studying Directionality in Simultaneous Interpreting through an Electronic Corpus: EPIC (European Parliament Interpreting Corpus)." *Meta* 50 (4): n.p.

Moser-Mercer, Barbara, Alexander Künzli, and Marina Korac. 1998. "Prolonged Turns in Interpreting: Effects on Quality, Physiological and Psychological Stress (Pilot study)." *Interpreting* 3 (1): 47–64.

Napier, Jemima. 2004. "Interpreting Omissions. A New Perspective." *Interpreting* 6 (2): 117–142.

Noteboom, Sibout G. 1973. "The Tongue Slips into Patterns." In *Speech Errors as Linguistic Evidence*, edited by Victoria A. Fromkin, 144–156. The Hague: Mouton.

Paltridge, Brian. 2006. *Discourse Analysis: An Introduction*. London: Continuum Discourse Series.

Pio, Sonia. 2003. "The Relation between ST Delivery Rate and Quality in Simultaneous Interpretation." *The Interpreters' Newsletter* 12: 69–100.

Pöchhacker, Franz, and Cornelia Zwischenberger. 2010. "Survey on Quality and Role: Conference Interpreters' Expectations and Self-Perceptions." Accessed 21 May 2019. https://aiic.net/page/3405/survey-on-quality-and-role-conference-interpreters-expectations-and-self-perceptions/lang/1.

Pym, Anthony. 2009. "On Omission in Simultaneous Interpreting: Risk Analysis of a Hidden Effort." In *Efforts and Models in Interpreting and Translation Research: A Tribute to Daniel Gile*, edited by Gyde Hansen, Andrew Chesterman, and Heidrun Gerzymisch-Arbogast, 83–105. Amsterdam: John Benjamins.

Roach, Peter. 1998. "Some Languages are Spoken More Quickly than Others." In *Language Myths*, edited by Laurie Bauer, and Peter Trudgill, 150–158. London: Penguin.

Rodero, Emma. 2012. "A Comparative Analysis of Speech Rate and Perception in Radio Bulletins." *Text and Talk* 32 (3): 391–411.

Ruiz Rosendo, Lucía, and Marie Diur. 2017. "Employability in the United Nations: An Empirical Analysis of Interpreter Training and the LCE." *The Interpreter and Translator Trainer* 11 (2–3): 223–237.

Ruiz Rosendo, Lucía, and Marie Diur. 2018. "Admission Exams at International Organisations: The United Nations' Language Competitive Examination." *CLINA. An Interdisciplinary Journal of Translation, Interpreting and Intercultural Communication* 3 (2): 33–52.

Ruiz Rosendo, Lucía, Mónica Varela García, and Alma Barghout. 2016. "The Omission as a Quality Indicator in Simultaneous Interpreting: An Experimental Study." Paper Presented at the 8th Congress of the EST (European Society for Translation Studies), University of Aarhus, September 15–17.

Ruiz Rosendo, Lucía, and María C. Galván. 2019. Coping with Speed. An Experimental Study on Expert and Novice Interpreter Performance in the Simultaneous Interpreting of Scientific Discourse. *Babel* 65 (1): 1–25.

Seleskovitch, Danica. 1965. *Colloque sur l'enseignement de l'interprétation*. Geneva: AIIC.

Seleskovitch, Danica. 1978. *Interpreting for International Conferences*. Washington, DC: Pen&Booth.

Seleskovitch, Danica, and Marianne Lederer. 1984. *Interpréter pour traduire*. Paris: Didier Érudition.

Setton, Robin. 1999. *Simultaneous Interpretation: A Cognitive-Pragmatic Analysis*. Amsterdam/Philadelphia: John Benjamins.

Setton, Robin, and Andrew Dawrant. 2016. *Conference Interpreting. A Complete Course*. Amsterdam/Philadelphia: John Benjamins.

Shlesinger, Miriam. (2003). "Effects of Presentation Rate on Working Memory in Simultaneous Interpreting." *The Interpreters' Newsletter* 12: 37–49.

Sunnari, Marianna. 1995. "Processing Strategies in Simultaneous Interpreting (SI): 'Saying it All' vs. 'Synthesis'." In *Topics in Interpreting Research*, edited by Jorma Tommola, 109–121. Turku: University of Turku.

# Managing for Quality

## Practical Lessons from Research Insights

*Fernando Prieto Ramos*

Our research-driven journey through multiple national and international institutional settings offers a comprehensive overview of current practices in the pursuit of quality in translation and interpreting. If we review the common underlying threads and themes, and bring further perspective to the prismatic reflections that have been presented, the opening questions of the introduction resonate with renewed significance and nuance – that of the lessons learnt. These lessons emerge from assessing working methods, requirements and results as a condition for confronting deficits and driving toward better practices. In the holistic approach to quality adopted in this volume, one of the first cross-cutting lessons is that ensuring quality requires, above all, *advanced competence* in translation as a decisive catalyst for the assessment of processes and textual products according to institutional needs. Quality translations are the result of expert decisions made under variable workflow conditions, so a holistic lens is needed to (1) identify and foster the talent, resources and procedures that will lead to the best possible outcomes in each situation, and (2) reduce the risks that derive from less-than-optimal solutions.

This process is to a large extent a question of management. As expressed by Vlachopoulos (2009, 17), "the improvement of translation quality is as much a managerial challenge as it is a linguistic and technical one." From a *quality management* angle, the practices assessed in this book can support improvements in the same or other similar settings, by adapting human and material resources to the goals of each institution. It is presumed that, as opposed to profit-driven service providers, for institutional language services, the quality of translation and interpreting is aimed at *effective and reliable communication*. In many cases, as illustrated by most chapters, not only at large international organizations but also in more modestly sized institutions (such as national legislative bodies, the courts and other public departments), translation and interpreting quality is a requirement to ensure legal certainty and protect citizens' rights.

In identifying needs and priorities, international standards such as ISO 17100:2015 for translation services can serve as an aspirational model

DOI: 10.4324/9780429264894

for core aspects of competence and workflow management, even if this instrument is not mandatory for institutional language services. While such needs and priorities can be extremely diverse, the bottom line is comparable in all contexts examined and the lessons can be extrapolated between them. *Well-established institutional language services* at the national and international levels can build on existing strengths and address specific weaknesses by, among other measures: (1) promoting translators' domain specialization, workplace customization and technological competence; (2) ensuring revision and quality checks to the extent possible (especially if outsourcing is necessary); (3) providing and improving resources that can contribute to terminological and phraseological consistency and accuracy, as well as to clear drafting; and (4) raising awareness of the added value of language professionals as assets for quality communication and educating service users about how they can contribute to it (e.g. deadline-setting for translations, consultations on subject matters, reminders on speed for speakers in simultaneous interpreting). Much can also be learnt from ex post quality monitoring processes and from errors formally corrected through corrigenda, especially as increasing automation may have an impact on the inaccuracies and issues that are overlooked.

In the case of institutions with *smaller language services* or even a single professional profile responsible for managing translation or interpreting, the role and impact of this staff in promoting quality will generally be more critical. As also illustrated in the book, entities that have limited or unstable translation or interpreting needs are often fully dependent on outsourcing and might not always secure service provision by qualified translators and interpreters. In those scenarios, the benefits of introducing specialized competence in the process can be particularly dramatic through different *remedial actions*, be it establishing professional screening and monitoring practices, or simply by correcting unprofessional arrangements. As previously noted with regard to international non-governmental organizations (see Pym 2008; Tesseur 2018), budget constraints tend to be the overriding factor in such informal solutions. However, as action research has shown in two institutional environments of this kind, relevant expertise can be more decisive than cost. In light of this research, some institutional decision-makers would be keenly interested in moving from "low cost" approaches to "value for money" by investing in skills (or recognizing in-house talent) in translation and interpreting. The "money" part of the equation demands resources, while the "value" component relies on competence management. Put simply, having a language professional in teams with multilingual communication needs (albeit not necessarily devoted to these functions only) can be both the most quality- and cost-effective, even without accounting for the potential damage to image and reputation that may derive from non-professional ad hoc arrangements.

In fact, the *risks of outsourcing* without sufficient quality control apply to all the settings. Contrary to ISO recommendations on sub-contracting tasks (ISO 2015, 5), and despite the expert capacity of large institutional language services, these cannot not always guarantee full *revision* of all outsourced translations. Quality requirements often vary depending on text purposes and strategic priorities (see, e.g., the DGT fit-for-purpose approach in Strandvik 2018), and may justify simplified quality control mechanisms for non-sensitive documents. However, as also learnt from this volume, *preliminary testing* of individual transla-tors can be equally fruitful to avert risk in outsourcing procedures, by limiting the unpredictability of quality and preventing disproportion-ate post-delivery interventions (see also Prieto Ramos 2017, 71; Sirovec 2020, 205).

For the cases where in-house expert management or quality control is not possible, *certification or other qualification requirements* emerge as a minimum safety net. These requirements, in turn, need to be regularly assessed in order to secure effectiveness, as exemplified by the Finnish examination for authorized translators. In the case of interpreting, ser-vice provision by freelancers tends to be the norm, so for institutions with no in-house expert evaluation procedures (mostly typical of large multilateral and EU institutions), quality evaluation tools for institu-tional users, such as the INTER-Q questionnaire for court interpreting, may offer the only means to spot major quality issues.

In all the organizations examined, regardless of their sizes and struc-tures, *consistency and conformity to institutional conventions* consti-tute, together with accuracy, the most distinctive feature to be preserved in managing translation and interpreting quality. Consistency is perhaps the quintessential component of quality assurance in institutional com-munication in that it requires an overarching insider's vision in accor-dance with the primary aims of *institutional continuity and reliability*. Those who strive for excellence in conveying their message across re-gions or take multilingual rights seriously can only benefit from placing these insights at the center of their strategies. In this endeavor, trainers and researchers have a crucial role to play: building new knowledge and expertise to grapple with persistent and emerging challenges.

## Acknowledgments

I would like to thank all the authors for sharing their expertise in this journey across institutional settings. My gratitude also goes to Diego Guzmán for his technical support, and to Routledge staff for their kind assistance.

## References

ISO. 2015. *ISO 17100. Translation Services – Requirements for Translation Services*. Geneva: ISO.

Prieto Ramos, Fernando. 2017. "The Evolving Role of Institutional Translation Service Managers in Quality Assurance: Profiles and Challenges." In *Quality Aspects in Institutional Translation*, edited by Tomáš Svoboda, Łucja Biel and Krzysztof Łoboda, 59–74. Berlin: Language Science Press. doi:10.5281/zenodo.1048188.

Pym, Anthony. 2008. "Translation vs. Language Learning in International Institutions: Explaining the Diversity Paradox." *Cultus: The Journal of Intercultural Mediation and Communication* 1(1): 70–83.

Sirovec, Saša. 2020. "Achieving Quality in Outsourcing." *Babel* 66(2): 193–207.

Strandvik, Ingemar. 2018. "Towards a More Structured Approach to Quality Assurance: DGT's Quality Journey." In *Institutional Translation for International Governance: Enhancing Quality in Multilingual Legal Communication*, edited by Fernando Prieto Ramos, 51–62. Bloomsbury Advances in Translation. London: Bloomsbury.

Tesseur, Wine 2018. "Researching Translation and Interpreting in Non-Governmental Organisations." *Translation Spaces* 7(1): 1–19. doi:10.1075/ts.00001.tes.

Vlachopoulos, George. 2009. "Translation, Quality and Service at the European Commission." In *CIUTI-Forum 2008 (Enhancing Translation Quality: Ways, Means, Methods)*, edited by Martin Forstner, Hannelore Lee-Jahnke and Peter A. Schmitt, 15–22. Bern, Berlin, Brussels, Frankfurt am Main, New York, Oxford, Vienna: Peter Lang.

# Index

acceptability 181
accessibility to the law 26
accreditation 22, 84, 87, 90, 94, 97, 100
accuracy 1–2, 4–5, 15–16, 94, 128–132, 135, 138–139, 144–146, 191, 195, 210–211; rate (AccuR) 136–139, 141
acquis communautaire 155, 161
action research 5, 174–176, 184, 187–188, 210
adequacy 15, 29, 88–89, 136, 146, 182
Adler, M. 29
administrative language 26
AEQUITAS project 88
Alonso Araguás, I. 91
Alonso Tapia, J. 92
Altman, J. 195
American Bar Association (ABA) 66–67
American Psychological Association (APA) 92
American Translators Association (ATA) 11; certification/exam 64, 66, 72, 74–75, 77–78
Anastasi, A. 92
Angelelli, C. 11, 44, 46, 181
Anthony, L. 31
Antonini, R. 4, 44–46, 52, 57
Antos, G. 29
ApSIC Xbench 121
Aranguena Fanego, C. 88
archaic: and complex word 31, 34, 38; connective 31, 35–38
Assembly Bill 2400 69
assessment: analytic 11; criteria 2, 12, 15, 16; criterion-referenced 11–12; error-based 11; holistic 11; method 12; model 11; practices 10; product-oriented 10; process-oriented 10; setting 10; user-oriented 10, 16
asymmetry 5, 130–131, 138, 145–146
Australian National Accreditation Authority for Translators and Interpreters (NAATI) 4, 10–14, 21
authenticity 11
Authorized Translators' Examination of Finland 3, 9, 12, 14–15, 17, 20
automatic translation services 65

Baigorri Jalón, J. 194–195
Balleto, C. 87
Balzani, M. 194
Baraldi, C. 46
Barik, H. 190–191
Bazerman, C. 132
behavior 45, 86–87, 91–92, 94–100
Behr, M. 90
Bendazzoli, C. 192
Bérczi, A. 153–154
Berruto, G. 28, 29
best practice 1, 27, 38, 124–126
Bhreathnach, Ú. 163–164
Biel, Ł. 151–152, 155
bilingual formatting 66, 68–70
black canvas approach 114
Blasco Mayor, M. 84–87, 91, 93
Bobek, M. 153–154, 157
Borghi, M. 31, 46
borrowing 135, 143–144, 163
Bradbury, H. 175
Brannick, T. 5
Brau, M. 75
Bredel, U. 29
Bühler, H. 195
*bürgenahe Rechts- und Verwaltungsprache* 29

Caciagli, F. 87
calque 143–144, 168

CAT: Integration Client 117, 123; tool 51, 57, 117, 120, 165
certainty 168
certification 1–2, 4, 211, 62–64, 66, 72, 74, 75, 78, 84, 86, 90–91, 100; examination 9, 11–12
Chafe, W. 194
Charter of Fundamental Rights (CFR) 88
Chernov, G. 194, 203
civil law 131
CJEU *see* Court of Justice of the European Union
Clement, A. 86–87
Cloke, F. 163
code: of conduct 86, 91, 98; of ethics 94, 99
Coghlan, D. 5
cognitive resource 204
Collado Aís, A. 89–90
commissioner 178
common law 131
competence 1–2, 21, 130–131; management 174, 209–210; *see also* translation competence/competency
competency 85–86, 90, 94–95; *see also* translation competence/competency
comprehensibility 28, 30, 34, 38, 93
conference interpreting 89
consistency 1–2, 4, 66, 69, 128–132, 134–135, 138–139, 141, 143–146, 162, 167, 168–169, 181, 183, 185, 195, 210–211; consultation 117
Corbin, J. 198, 202
Córdoba Serrano, M. 45
corpus 2–3, 28, 31–34, 38, 131–133, 135–136, 140–143, 146, 155, 176, 180, 197–198
correction rate (CR) 2, 150, 152, 154, 160, 168
corrigendum 2, 5, 150, 153–169, 210
Corsellis, A. 86–87, 93
cost: efficiency 77, 152; effectiveness 1, 66, 77, 188, 210
Council of the European Union 141, 156–157, 159–160, 162
court: Interpretation and Translation Services (CITS) 68, 77; interpreter 64, 66, 72–73, 75–78; Interpreters Act of 1978 63–64, 84; Interpreter Manual and Code of Ethics 72; of Justice of the European Union

(CJEU) 140, 143, 151; proceedings 67; translator 62–63, 76–77
Cravo, A. 176
criminal proceedings 84, 88–89, 91–93, 100
culture-bound term 138
CuriaTerm 140
customer satisfaction rate 152

Danielewicz, J. 194
Dawrant, A. 192, 196
deadline compliance rate 152
deficit language 111–112, 114
De Groot, A. 191
Del Pozo Trivino, M. 84, 86, 93
delivery rate/speed 1, 5, 190–198, 202–205
Delley, J.-D. 38
De Manuel Jerez, J. 192
De Mauro, T. 31
Department of Justice (DOJ) 62, 65, 67, 71
Derlén, M. 151
De Saint Robert, M.-J. 129
dialogic interaction 86
Díaz Cintas, J. 45
dictionary 74, 123, 130
directive 32, 120, 129, 143, 151, 156, 159–160; 2010/64/EU 4, 84, 86–88, 90–91, 93, 97
Directorate-General: for Justice 88, 93, 94; for Translation (DGT) 2, 4, 111–126, 152–153, 156
discrimination index 96
dispute settlement 132, 140, 143
district court 64–65
Diur, M. 195–196
Documents Online 132
Doczekalska, A. 151
domestication 162, 166, 167–169
drafting quality 38
Drugan, J. 152
Dueñas González, R. 69, 71, 73–74, 78
Dunne, K. 122

ear-voice-span (EVS) 191
editing rate 152
Egger, J.-L. 26, 28
Eichhoff-Cyrus, K. 29
*Einfache Sprache* 29
email management 118
EN 15038:2006 standard 152

environmental variable 90
e-Poetry 115
equal authenticity 151
equivalence 9, 16–17, 29, 151
equivalent 35–36, 38, 162–167,
 199, 201
ergonomics 125
error 1, 3, 5, 120, 151–154,
 156–157, 160–162, 168–169, 176,
 180–184, 186–188, 190; analysis
 11, 15; severity 17; type/category
 10, 16–20, 157, 162, 181, 183,
 186, 210
EU law 32, 123, 150–151, 155,
 161, 167
Eurac Research 47
EUR-Lex 123, 132, 155–156,
 159, 162
EURAMIS *see* European advanced
 multilingual information system
Eurofog project 155
Eurolect 155, 161; Observatory
 Project 32
European: advanced multilingual
 information system (EURAMIS)
 115, 123; Commission 2, 4, 51, 88,
 93, 111–112, 129, 140–141, 143,
 152–154, 156, 160; Convention of
 Human Rights 88; Parliament 154,
 156–157, 159–160, 162,
 192–193; Union (EU) 2, 5,
 111–112, 129–130, 132–140–143,
 145–146, 150–156, 158–163,
 166–169, 211
evaluation: criteria 90; procedure
 91–92; tools 84–85, 90, 93, 98
experience 3, 14, 18, 66, 74, 96,
 98–99, 113–114, 185
experimental study 196
expertise 3, 5, 49, 112, 116, 139,
 146,174–175, 178, 186, 188,
 210–211
explicitation 163, 165

false: friend 130, 131, 135, 146;
 testimony 85
Fantuzzi, M. 28
Faraldo Cabana, P. 85
Federal Bureau of Investigation (FBI)
 64, 72, 74, 75, 77
Federal Chancellery 28
federal court: system 63, 65,
 67; Interpreter Certification

Examination (FCICE) 64, 72–73;
 Interpreter Orientation Manual and
 Glossary 63
Fernández Carrón, C. 88
Ferrari, A. 26
Festinger, N. 78
Feuerle, L. 73
field study 96
Finnish National Agency for
 Education (EDUFI) 9, 14, 20
fit-for-purpose 152
Flückiger, A. 29, 38
fraudulent interpretation 85
functional equivalence 10
freelance translation 3, 9, 111–113,
 116, 122, 126, 178, 186, 211

Gaiba, F. 191
Galli, C. 190
Galván, M. 191
García Becerra, O. 89–90
Garside, R. 31
Gavioli, L. 46
Gerver, D. 190, 192
Gialuz, M. 84, 88–89
Giambruno, C. 62, 64, 71, 73, 78, 84,
 86, 90–91
Gile, D. 90, 194
glossary 65, 66, 69–70, 130, 140, 146,
 180, 185, 187
González, R. 84–85
González Núñez, G. 58
González-Hibner, M. 73, 77
Google 123
Grbić, N. 90–91
Grodecki, S. 29
Gruenenfelder, T. 194
guide: to Judiciary Policy 64; to
 Translation of Legal Materials 66
Gulpease Index 30
Gunning Fog Index 30
Guzmán, D. 130

Hale, S. 93
Harris, B. 45
Hemmens, C. 62
Héroguel, A. 11
Hertog, E. 62, 64, 71, 73, 78, 84–88
Hiirikoski, J. 19, 21
Hjort-Pedersen, M. 11
Holz-Mänttäri, J. 178
House, J. 10
Huang, N. 11

Huber, E. 27, 38
Hurtado Albir, A. 181

IATE *see* Interactive Terminology for Europe
inbound: text 63; translation 64, 67–68, 71, 74, 77
independent contractor 62
InfoCuria 124
in-house translation 3, 44, 48–50, 52, 58, 111–112, 122, 126, 175–178, 185
institutional: communication 26, 29; drafting 129; Italian 28–29; monolingualism 46; terminological resources (ITRs) 129–132, 139–146
Interactive Terminology for Europe (IATE) 122–124, 130, 140–143, 162
Interagency Language Roundtable 75
intergovernmental organization 127
interlinguistic concordance 128
international: Association of Conference Interpreters (AIIC) 192; Association of Professional Translators and Interpreters 50; Guidelines on Test Use 92; Labour Conference (ILC) 193; Labour Organization (ILO) 193; legal instruments 129; Network for Terminology (TermNet) 128
international organization 2–4, 128–131, 139, 192–193, 196, 204, 209
interpreter training 204
INTER-Q 4, 91, 93–94, 96–100, 211
interspersing 70
intertextual: inconsistency 169, 181, 184, 186–187; variation rate (InterVar) 135–139, 141
intervention 175–176, 179, 181–186, 188, 211
interview 2, 4, 44–45, 48, 50, 57–58, 87, 97, 114, 125–126; 174, 176–178, 182
IntraComm 124
intralinguistic consistency 128
intratextual inconsistency 136–138
ISO: 13611:2014 94; 17100:2015 10, 21, 55, 128, 175, 178–180, 187, 209; 20228:2019 85, 90
Italian Association of Translators and Interpreters (AITI) 51

Jagmetti, R. 38
Jimeno Bulnes, M. 88
Johns, B. 194
Jones, M. 194

Kalina, S. 195
Kapko, M. 151
Katschinka, L. 90
Kemppanen, H. 22
keylogging data 114
Killman, J. 78
Kinnunen, T. 16
Kivilehto, M. 9–10, 16, 18–19
Kjaer, A. 151
Klein, P. 78
Koby, G. 15
Korpal, P. 191
Korp-Edwards, B. 77
Koskinen, K. 10, 51, 111
Kübler, D. 27

Lai, M. 11
language: competency 12–13; Competitive Examination (LCE) 195–197; proficiency 47–48, 51; Services Translation Test 75; Act of 2007 28; Ordinance of 2010 29
language access: guideline 62; plan 65, 68–70; policy 62; project 71; standard 62
lawyer-linguist 112, 152
Lederer, M. 192
Lee, T.-H. 191
legal: accuracy 151; act 143, 150–153, 155–156, 159–161, 168; certainty 129, 154, 209; drafting 4, 27–28, 31, 38; effect 151; instrument 129, 132, 145
legislative act 2, 5, 26–29, 31–34, 156, 158–160
*Leichte Sprache* 29
Lelieveldt, H. 156
*Lessico di frequenza dell'italiano parlato nella Svizzera italiana* (Frequency Lexicon of Spoken Swiss Italian [LIPSI]) 31–34
LETRINT project 130–131
LEX.CH.IT 31–33, 35
lexical: profile 30, 32, 34, 38; readability 2, 4, 30, 32, 35, 37–38;
lexicometric analysis 130
limited English proficiency (LEP) 68, 70; individual/population 62, 65, 69, 71–72, 76–77

linguistic: accessibility 29; assistance 84, 87–89; clarity 4, 29–30
local court 69
log likelihood ratio significance test 31, 35
Lommel, A. 11, 15, 20

Maaß, C. 29
machine translation 9, 15, 21, 123, 185
Manager's Desk (ManDesk) 116–117, 120
Maslias, R. 112
McCann, W. 62
meaning-changing corrigendum 154, 157, 168
Mellinger, C. 62, 69
Meyer, P. 91, 93, 97
Meylaerts, R. 46, 59
Miettunen, M. 19, 20
Mikkelson, H. 63, 69, 71, 73–74, 78, 84–85
minority language 44, 47
misrepresentation 85
mistranslation 163
mixed-type corrigendum 157, 160, 162
monolingual formatting 66
Monti, C. 192
Mori, L. 26, 32
Moro Ípola, M. 91
Morris, R. 85
Mortara Garavelli, B. 35
Multi-Dimensional Quality Metrics (MQM) 15, 20
multilingual: concordance 151, 169; legislation 26–27
Muñoz Sánchez, P. 45

Napier, J. 194
National Center for State Courts (NCSC) 62, 66–67, 72, 78
National Judiciary Interpreter and Translator Certification Examination (NJITCE) 72–75
natural bilingual 47
Navarro-Hall, E. 86
Network for the Excellence of Institutional Italian (REI) 28
Neves, J. 176
New Mexico Judicial Translation Project Team 71
non-governmental organization 3, 185, 210

non-professional: interpreting and translation (NPIT) 44–46, 59; translation 2–4, 44–45, 48, 50, 52, 58–59, 185, 187; translator 45, 49–52, 57
Nord, C. 178, 188
North Carolina Court Interpreter Certification Examination 72
Nuremberg trials 191

O'Brien, S. 10
objectivity 98
ODS *see* Official Document System
Office for Language Issues 46–47
official language 26, 28, 44, 46–47, 75, 112, 150, 152, 169, 185
Official Document System (ODS) 132
Official Journal of the European Union 150–151, 153, 161–162
off-the-cuff speech 194
omission 5, 190–191, 198–204; with substitution (OmS) 199
ordinary legislative procedure 154, 156, 159–160, 162
Ortega Herráez, J. 62, 64, 71, 73, 78, 85–87
outbound: text 63; translation 64, 66, 68, 70, 76
outsourcing 1, 3, 52, 77, 112, 116, 152, 177, 178, 182, 185, 188, 210–211

Palma, J. 73, 77
Paltridge, B. 194
Pandolfi, E. 31
Penttilä, A. 9, 16
performance 1, 4, 14, 45, 84–86, 92–93, 96–97, 152, 176, 188, 190–192, 194, 196, 198, 204
Pháidín, C. 163
phraseology 11, 33, 117, 124, 150, 162, 167–169
Piemontese, V. 30
Pini, V. 28
Pio, S. 190–191, 199
Pisoni, D. 194
pivot language 112
plain language 26, 29
PM *see* project manager
Pöchhacker, F. 86, 89–90
Polish: Eurolect 5, 150, 155, 157, 160, 169; Law Corpus 162
popular law 27, 38
portfolio manager 152

precedent 139, 145
pre-processing 115
Prieto Ramos, F. 1, 5, 27, 29, 130, 150, 160–161, 174, 176
Princen, S. 156
procedural language 111, 114
process *see* translation process
processing capacity 190, 203
process-oriented approach 152
product *see* translation product
professional: translation company 62; translator 46, 49, 58, 139, 176, 180, 185, 187
project management 5, 116, 118, 125
project manager 112, 174–175, 178–180, 184, 187
ProLexis 119
pseudo-term 33
psychometric principle 84
purely formal corrigendum 154
p-value 96
Pym, A. 64, 191

qualification 113–114
QUALITAS 93
qualitative: analysis/examination 22, 31, 38, 129, 136, 162, 198, 202; data 114, 126; study 100
quality 28–30, 88–90, 93–94, 100, 125–126; assessment 9–10, 86; assurance/control 5, 84–87, 91–92, 94, 100, 151–152, 155, 160, 174, 182–183, 188, 211; criterion 195–196, 198; management 152, 209; manager 152; metric 153–154; *see also* translation quality
quantitative: analysis 19, 31, 34, 38, 96, 100, 129, 156; data 32, 35, 126
QUEST 124
questionnaire 2, 4, 91, 93–96, 97–100, 114

Rayson, P. 31
readability 30, 34–35, 38
Reason, P. 175
recast 120
redundant compound conjunction (RCC) 198–200, 203
register 84, 89–91, 97, 100
regulation 141, 151, 156, 157, 159–162, 168
reliability 92, 97–98, 100, 140
rendition quality 190, 198

replication study 184, 187
requester 64, 115–117
reverse language combination 112
revision 4–5, 12, 21, 48, 51, 55–56, 114, 117–122, 125–126, 162, 176–177, 179–181, 184–188, 210–211
right: to interpretation 4, 88; to translation 4, 88
Rivezzi, G. 87
Roach, P. 193–194
Robertson, C. 151
Ruiz Rosendo, L. 191
Russo, M. 192

Sabatini, F. 34
Saldanha, G. 10
Salmi, L. 9–10, 16, 18–19
Sancho Viamonte, M. 85–87, 91
Sandrelli, A. 192
Šarčević, S. 129, 151
scoring chart 3, 9–10, 16–22
Scott, J. 77
SDL Trados 117–121, 123–125
SEC (2008) 2397 153
second language (L2) 45
Seleskovitch, D. 191–192
self-revision 119, 122, 180, 185
semantic: deviation 128; univocity 4, 128
Serianni, L. 31, 35
Setton, R. 190, 192, 196
Shlesinger, M. 191
short-term memory 190
simultaneous interpreting (SI) 1–2, 190–191, 194, 204
single legal instrument 151
Sirovec, S. 77
Somssich, R. 153–154
Spohn, C. 62
source text corrigendum 157–160
staff translator 62, 76–77
standard 85, 90, 94; for Language Access Services in North Carolina State Courts 67; for Performance and Professional Responsibility for Contract Court Interpreters in the Federal Courts 63; *see also* ISO
state court 4, 65–67, 76
State Department 64, 72, 74, 75
Stefaniak, K. 129, 151, 156–157, 167
Strandvik, I. 112, 152, 156

Strauss, A. 198, 202
stress 191, 203
Sunnari, M. 203
Suojanen, T. 10
superfluous archaism 33
survey 2, 4, 44–45, 48, 50–52, 57–58

TagAnt 31
terminological: consistency 69; consolidation 139; database 129, 144; decision-making 132, 139, 145; dispersion 135; harmonization 136, 146, 187; resource 4–5, 122, 124–126, 128–131, 139; *see also* institutional terminological resources (ITRs)
terminologist 123–124, 145
terminology: consultation 117, 122–123; error 19; management 130, 146
test 91–92, 94–96
text analysis 176
textual fit 155
time constraint 120, 125
Toury, G. 15
TradAm project 47
trade: defense 133, 140–141, 145; policy review 132, 143
translation: best practices 66; brief 188; company 70, 74, 77; competence/competency 1–2, 12–13, 174–175, 186–187; costs 67, 188; expertise 174–175; guidelines 49, 52, 58, 63, 76; management 52, 58, 59, 112, 118, 174–176, 178–180, 187–188; memory (TM) 115, 117, 123; needs 1, 3, 177–179, 185; policy 1–2, 44, 46, 58, 63, 69; practices 44, 46, 48, 50, 53, 58, 67, 76, 176–177, 111, 126; process 4, 44, 48, 50–51, 55, 59, 174, 179, 188; product 1–2, 29, 66, 120, 175–176, 179–180, 187–188, 209; profile 47; protocol 69; quality 48, 54, 58, 65, 128–129, 135, 150–152, 158, 160, 146, 174–176, 178, 180–181, 184–185, 187, 209; regime 46, 49; service 1, 174–177, 179, 185, 187–188; service provider (TSP) 175, 178–180, 182, 188, 209; standard 12, 63, 76 (*see also* ISO); strategy 10–11, 48, 50–51; technology 57; training 78; volume 47–48, 51–53, 181; workflow 114–115, 126, 132, 175, 187
Translation Advisory Committee 69
Translation Quality Guidelines 152
translation-oriented terminology management 128
translator: certification 9, 12; qualifications 71; training 9, 14, 111, 126
Translator's Desktop (TraDesk) 116–117, 120
Travieso Rodríguez, C. 194
TReFLe platform 116
Tuominen, T. 10
Turner, B. 11

Uhlig, D. 155
Uhlmann, F. 29
Unified Court System (UCS) 70
uniform: application 151, 157; interpretation 129, 151, 157
United Nations (UN) 2, 4–5, 74, 75, 77, 129–130, 132–138, 140–146, 160–161, 190, 192–198; Human Rights Council (HRC) 192–193, 197; Office at Geneva (UNOG) 140, 143, 196–197
Universal Periodic Review Working Group 192
University: of Bologna 47; of Geneva 197
univocity 136, 145
UNOGTerm 140, 144
UNTERM 140, 142–145
Urbina, S. 92

validity 92, 96–98, 100, 182
Vanden Bosch, Y. 86–88
Vanden Bulcke, P. 11
variability rate 133
Várnai, J. 153–154
Vásquez, V. 69, 71, 73–74, 78
Vecchione, F. 51, 54, 57
Ventury, G. 32
Viezzi, M. 89
Vigier, F. 78
Vlachopoulos, G. 209
*Vocabolario di base della lingua italiana* (Basic ItalianVocabulary [BIV]) 31–34
Vuorinen, E. 152

Wagner, E. 112
Wallace, M. 84, 92
Whyatt, B. 47
WinLexic 119
WordReference 123
workflow 174, 178, 180, 187, 209–210; assistant 116; manager 117; *see also* translation workflow
working language 177

World Trade Organization (WTO) 4, 129–130, 132–138, 140, 142–143, 145–146; 160–161
WTOTERM 140

XLIFF 116

Zwicky, R. 27
Zwischenberger, C. 90